Trial Courts as Organizations

Trial Courts as Organizations

Brian J. Ostrom, Charles W. Ostrom Jr.,
Roger A. Hanson, Matthew Kleiman

TEMPLE UNIVERSITY PRESS
Philadelphia

Brian J. Ostrom is Principal Research Consultant at the National Center for State Courts.

Charles W. Ostrom, Jr. is Professor of Political Science at Michigan State University.

Roger A. Hanson is Adjunct Professor of Law and Political Science at the University of Colorado.

Matthew Kleiman is Senior Court Research Associate at the National Center for State Courts.

TEMPLE UNIVERSITY PRESS
1601 North Broad Street
Philadelphia PA 19122
www.temple.edu/tempress

Published 2007
Printed in the United States of America

∞ The paper used in this publication meets the requirements of the American National Standard for Information Sciences—Permanence of Paper for Printed Library Materials, ANSI Z39.48-1992

Library of Congress Cataloging-in-Publication Data

Trial courts as organizations / Brian J. Ostrom ... [et al.].
p. cm.
Includes bibliographical references and index.
ISBN-13: 978-1-59213-630-8 (hardcover: alk. paper)
ISBN-10: 1-59213-630-3 (hardcover: alk. paper)
1. Courts–United States. 2. Justice, Administration of–United States. 3. Judicial process–United States. I. Ostrom, Brian J., 1956-
KF8719.T75 2007
347.73′1–dc22

2006037504

2 4 6 8 9 7 5 3 1

Contents

Preface and Acknowledgments

Conversations concerning the quality of public institutions often begin with a twofold question: What are important distinctions in the way organizations operate and do they make a difference in what is accomplished? However, to move beyond the conversational, agreement is necessary on what attributes and characteristics distinguish one culture from another.

In the world of America's state felony criminal trial courts, judges and administrators regularly struggle with developing the kinds of social relations that will help them collaborate and succeed in the provision of justice. The responsibility of judges and administrators is to establish a structure and process that is fair to all participants, operates efficiently, and exhibits concern and sensitivity to the interests and rights of other criminal justice system organizations, such as prosecutors and criminal defense attorneys, as well as individuals, such as defendants, victims, witnesses, jurors, and others. Most individuals involved in the resolution of criminal cases will agree that the courts relatively successful in achieving these goals have a sort of culture that separates them from others. For the last several decades, experts and practitioners alike have accepted the notion that culture affects practitioners' expectations and that those views explain much of what is going on. Yet, no court can say it has a particular type of culture and substantiate the claims with supporting evidence.

The purpose of this book is to take a new approach to understanding the nature and significance of court culture. More specifically, the successful examination of culture and organizational effectiveness in the private sector warrants consideration by observers interested in advancing research on court culture. As a result, in a purposeful and deliberative manner, the ideas, framework, and tools used by business school scholars, such as Robert Quinn and his colleagues, are adapted to assess how judicial bodies operate, perform, and consider operating in the future.

A conceptual framework is developed that identifies four distinct cultures—*communal, networked, autonomous, and hierarchical*—based on clusters of particular values. This analytical structure is then applied to 12 courts in three states, California, Florida, and Minnesota, by surveying the views of judges and court managers on how they get the job done. The varieties of court cultures in the real world are then compared to independent, quantitative measures of performance. Do judicial bodies in some cultures achieve higher performance than courts in other cultures? Finally, current cultures are compared to preferred cultures or ways judges and administrators wish to see their court operate in the future. Do different courts prefer different cultures or is there a common culture courts aspire to reach? Answers to these questions provide a means for exploring the managerial implications of alternative cultural orientations and the impact on court performance.

Many individuals provided assistance, support, and encouragement in preparing this inquiry into court culture. We owe a considerable intellectual debt to the work of Professor Robert Quinn, as well as his multiple collaborators and colleagues in the field of evaluating and changing organizational culture. Quinn's previously published ideas related to diagnosing and changing corporate culture provided critical inspiration for developing our approach to the study of parallel phenomena in the public sector. In addition, we were considerably influenced by the perceptive and provocative insights of Rob Goffee and Gareth Jones in their illuminating work on the character of corporate culture. Thanks to Dr. Candy Kokinakis and Dr. Ingo Keilitz for not only introducing us to the work of these leaders in the study of organizational effectiveness, but for anticipating its relevance to the present study.

In our effort to discern the meaning of culture, we thank the many judges, administrators, attorneys and researchers who generously gave of their time in helping determine what values define distinct court cultures. Their participation in a demanding pair-wise comparison exercise enabled us to formulate an empirically based fourfold typology of cultures by analyzing quantitatively the responses of the "volunteers."

It is also important to acknowledge that, without the cooperation of judges, attorneys, and administrators in selected court systems in California, Florida, and Minnesota, the concept of court culture would have never confronted reality. We thank all the participants in the California Superior Courts of Contra Costa County, Napa County, and Ventura County; the Florida Circuit Courts of Duval County and Pinellas County; and the Minnesota District Courts of Dakota County, Hennepin County, Kandiyohi County, Olmsted County, Ramsey County, St. Louis County, and Virginia County. We salute these individuals who took our requests and related questions seriously. The clarity and importance of our results reflect the purposeful and insightful perspectives with which they carry out their ongoing work.

We must also acknowledge the institutional and collegial support that enabled us to complete the inquiry, keep it on track, and gain the benefits of informed advice in responding to emerging and sometimes perplexing issues of interpretation. The authors are grateful for the generous support of the National Institute of Justice at the US Department of Justice [2000-NIJ-CX-0030] and the encouragement of Andrew Goldberg, our project monitor. All opinions and conclusions are those of the authors and do not necessarily reflect the policies or positions of the National Institute of Justice.

The National Center for State Courts also warrants our thanks for serving as a "home" to the investigators and for our many colleagues who regularly and diligently provided constructive comments and oversight as our work progressed. In particular, Neil LaFountain, Bill Hewitt, Richard Schauffler, and Shauna Strickland made many suggestions on earlier drafts that we all found most helpful. Shannon Roth, Sherry Keesee-Buchanan, and Pam Petrakis provided important administrative support and assisted in maintaining the research on schedule and within budget. Wes Poole and Neal Kauder, of Visual Research, guided us in the design and visual presentation of our results.

As part of its grant award, the National Institute of Justice permitted us to form a knowledgeable advisory committee of researchers and practitioners. The committee worked especially intensively at the outset of the project to help point the research in the right direction. For their role on the advisory committee, we would like to acknowledge the following individuals: Honorable Kevin Burke, John Clarke, Honorable B. Michael Dann, James Eisenstein, Honorable Nancy Farmer, James Gregart, Daniel Hall, Ingo Keilitz, Kathy Mays, Honorable Jonathan Silbert, and Thomas Turbeville.

Finally, we would like to thank our families who have both supported this research and had to deal with our many absences—both physical and mental. Thank you Maureen, Zach, Candy, Quinn, Leah, Liz, and Kristina.

This project proves, once again, that social research is a social activity. We drew on many others throughout the critical stages of the inquiry. In the end, though, we are accountable for all of the decisions, inferences, and interpretations contained herein.

Brian J. Ostrom
Charles W. Ostrom, Jr.
Roger A. Hanson
Matthew Kleiman

1 Organizational Culture in American Trial Courts

Introduction

Courts rightly proclaim the virtues of institutional independence as a necessary condition for the achievement and maintenance of civil society's fundamental precepts, such as the rule of law, individual rights, and impartial resolution of disputes. Without questioning the critical nature of judicial independence, the American system of checks and balances imposes some restraint on each branch of government. The Conference of State Court Administrators has expressed, in a forceful and clear statement, what the check on courts entails:

> The administration of justice should reside with the courts, both as a constitutional matter—judicial administration is inherent in the courts' adjudicative role—and as good governance. [However] with judicial governance come the rights and interests of the other branches of government and the public to hold the judiciary accountable *for effective management of court business*. [Emphasis added]

In this regard, some court experts have expressed doubts about the courts' abilities to discharge their institutional obligations effectively.

The reason for the skepticism is the absence of an appropriate management culture. For example, Tobin (1997, p. 8–9) writes:

> The executive and legislative branches ... have been reluctant to accord broad management latitude to a branch that has been historically uncomfortable with a management culture and inclined to diffuse power among individual judges.... *Courts must either create an effective and credible management system* or lose control over their internal management, and ultimately, the independence of the judiciary. [Emphasis added]

These two pronouncements imply a critical role for the *management culture* of courts in shaping the future of the American court system, which can be stated in the form of a basic syllogism. Courts are independent bodies only if they administer justice effectively. They administer justice effectively only if they have a sound management culture. Therefore, courts will be independent and effective only if they operate with a sound management culture.

Developing and molding an appropriate court culture is an enterprise with consequences, one that judges and administrators should attend to as purposefully and deliberatively as they do when making legal decisions, issuing orders, and distributing institutional resources. In many ways culture shapes and defines what is possible in the work environment.

As an introduction to the importance of organizational culture in the trial courts, consider the following vignette:

At a recent national state court conference, two trial court administrators from different areas of the country sat comparing notes on how things were going back in their home courts. They discovered they had a lot in common. Both manage mid-sized courts with about twenty-five judges and cope with court-wide perceptions that workload levels are on the rise. During the last few years, both have been deeply involved in the design and construction of new courthouses and both oversaw the implementation of new case management systems. Finally, each court used a master calendar for resolving criminal cases.

However, when conversation turned to day-to-day processing of criminal caseloads, they found less to agree about. The first administrator noted that time to disposition in her court had steadily improved over the last three years. The last two presiding judges had made effective criminal case management a priority, and it remained a topic covered at every monthly judges' meeting. Data from the new automated system on time to disposition, age of pending caseload, and average number of continuances focused the discussion of potential strategies for additional improvements in case flow. Judges were setting and enforcing rules of criminal case management. Issues raised by the police, prosecutors, and public defenders related to case scheduling practices were addressed at quarterly meetings convened by the presiding judge and court administrator. By no means did all of the meetings' participants always agree, but the conversation was taking place and all were learning to improve the overall operation of the criminal justice system. In fact, many members of the bench, enthusiastic about improvements in case processing, were openly recommending the creation and use of additional performance measures related to access and fairness.

The second administrator noted how work was a bit different in his court. He wasn't really sure what the average time to disposition was because the judges had limited interest in knowing. In addition, the new automated system was proving difficult to use. One thing he did know was that continuances were readily available and trial calendars typically had more than thirty cases set per judge. The administrator had a number of ideas to improve the situation, but felt he had essentially no support from the judges. Meetings of the bench were infrequent and unstructured, and it was widely known that the head prosecutor and head public defender were reluctant to be in the same room with each other. "Given all our similarities in size and structure," said the first administrator, "I wonder why everything else is so different?" "I don't know," said the second, "but our culture has always been kind of dysfunctional."

"Yeah, I guess it's just two different cultures."

"We do seem to have a different culture—but how do you get a grip on something like culture and, if you do, what can you do to change it?"

If the scenario laid out in the preceding text were unique, then it would merely present a frustration for the people involved. But this scenario is not unique. It has long been recognized by court administrators and judges that culture plays an important role in how courts function.

Some management cultures are thought to inhibit modernization, reform, and performance. Others are seen as more conducive to the development and adoption of better ways of doing things. For at least the last thirty years there has even been a term for how courts conduct business: *local legal culture*. In essence, this notion has emerged as a shorthand phrase to refer to a host of norms and resulting behaviors not otherwise easily explained. Unfortunately, simply naming a phenomenon is not the same as measuring it and using it to both explain and improve court performance. Without a vocabulary and set of tools to distinguish fundamental types of cultures, courts will continue to struggle in building a management culture that supports and expects to achieve high-quality case resolution.

This book provides a comprehensive framework along with a set of steps and tools to assess the prevailing culture guiding the management and performance of trial courts—an essential and often overlooked public institution. The material explains how *culture assessment* furthers observation and measurement of the abstract concept of court culture, thereby making it an explicit part of court management and reform efforts. Assessing court culture yields systematic information compatible with and useful to understanding court performance and the allocation of court resources. To substantiate that claim, a practical approach is developed to clarify the role and import of culture. This book helps explain the core dimensions of court culture and is designed to assist students of public policy and court managers learn how to work through a systematic culture analysis.

Nature and Relevance of Culture to Courts

Culture is often described as the *glue* that operates at many different levels in an organization. Schein (1999) argues that to comprehend what matters in culture, one must strive to understand the espoused values (i.e., the values that shape why an organization acts in a particular way) and basic assumptions (i.e., jointly learned values, beliefs, and assumptions that become shared and taken for granted in an organization) that shape the way work gets done in the organization. Therefore, culture is the mental representation of the work environment that members of the organization carry in their heads. Schein's advice, when applied to the study of courts, is to focus on the shared mental models that judges, administrators, and staff hold and take for granted. A court's management culture is reflected in what is valued, the norms and expectations, the leadership style, the communication patterns, the procedures and routines, and the definition of success that makes the court unique. More simply: "The way things are done around here."

Culture evidences itself in the "accumulated shared learning of a given group" (Schein 2004, p. 17). For courts, shared learning comes from shared experience in meeting the aims of the judicial branch. If a court's culture is the result of that court's accumulated learning, how does one describe and catalog the content of that learning? Schein says the shared elements of learning in the work environment eventually coalesce into patterns; culture is the manifestation of those patterns.

Kotter and Heskett (1992) offer an approach to further clarify the relevant patterns within an organization by distinguishing both shared values and observed behaviors. At the deeper and less visible level are the basic values and assumptions held by the group that tend to persist over time. At a more observable level are the behavior patterns or work style that new employees are automatically encouraged to follow by their fellow employees. Both values and behaviors blend together to create an organizational culture. Kotter and Heskett go on to conclude that culture can have powerful consequences in that the specific character of an organization's culture can either help or hinder a firm's performance. "All firm's have cultures . . . these cultures can exert a powerful effect on individuals and on performance . . . this influence may even be greater than all those factors that have been discussed most often in the organizational and business literature—strategy, organizational structure, management systems, financial analysis tools, leadership, etc." (Kotter and Heskett 1992, p. 9).

For at least three reasons, the time is right for courts to take seriously the role of culture. First, relative to ten years ago, few courts today boast about maintaining the status quo. Court leaders and managers now speak more freely and expansively about their administrative responsibilities and efforts to create a "high performance workplace." Experimenting with new kinds of problem-solving courts (e.g., drug courts), adopting explicit outcome-based performance measures, meeting higher customer expectations, and using more sophisticated technology are a few signs of how courts are changing. Effective management is seen as integral to promoting institutional goals of meaningful judicial governance and meeting public expectations of fairness and quality service delivery.

However, change is difficult. A great deal of investment in past practices makes leaders reluctant to take on the challenge of changing embedded processes, structures, and tasks. But, as Schein observes, "If we want to make organizations more efficient and effective, then we must understand the role that culture plays in organizational life" (1999, p. 14).

Second, strategic planning initiatives have swept through the courts much as they have in other organizations, but, as elsewhere, the failure rate of planned organizational change in courts is dramatic. Cameron and Quinn (1999, p. 1) report:

> It is well known that about 3/4 of reengineering, TQM, and strategic planning efforts have failed. Most interesting about these failures is the reported reasons for why they didn't work. The most cited reason was neglect of the organization's culture. In other words, failure to change the culture doomed other kinds of organizational change initiated.

In fact, it is increasingly being realized that it is the nature of relationships within the organization that matters; the way people act toward each other, the *social capital* of the organization. This view is confirmed by research conducted by the Gallup organization (Buckingham and Coffman 1999). The most important variable in employee productivity and satisfaction is not pay or benefits or office space. Rather, the quality of the relationships between employees and supervisors and managers accounts for the variance in the degree of workers' satisfaction. Effectively managing organizational relationships places a premium on the development by court administrators and presiding judges of appropriate and flexible organizational skills for leading, directing, and encouraging people.

Third, following Roscoe Pound's 1906 speech to the American Bar Association (ABA) on "the causes of popular dissatisfaction with the administration of justice," the "conventional wisdom"[1] has held that the problems of courts are best addressed by improving structure and process (Gallas 1976). The causal link between structures, resources, and processes (inputs) and court effectiveness and the well-being of those served by the courts (outcomes) is simply assumed. Quite often court assessment and improvement projects are prescriptive in nature. However, as the history of court reform shows, the identification and transfer of *best practices* among courts has been particularly spotty.[2] What works in one court just does not take hold in most others, and the failure is often attributed, albeit after the fact, to differences in culture.

Note that these three reasons for the timeliness of focus by courts on the role of culture concentrate on the changing nature of the organizational environment and how work is accomplished in courts, not on the purposes of courts. The 16,000 state trial courts have the same fundamental purposes: guarantee justice and liberty, enhance social order, resolve disputes, maintain rule of law, provide equal protection, and ensure due process. What differs is how courts organize and manage themselves to achieve these goals. The principal value of studying court culture is the belief that it offers the opportunity to better understand and improve the provision of justice in our society.

Courts are the most understudied major public institution in terms of organizational culture and performance. Executive agencies or departments are much more likely to be objects of such study. Courts have been on the periphery of organizational research—especially culture and performance assessment—largely because the conventional wisdom cites intractable obstacles to the enterprise (e.g., Gallas 1987). Common perceptions include the following:

- Courts are viewed as so decentralized, fragmented, and autonomous that they defy comparison and contrast along common dimensions.
- Courts are seen as lacking measurable performance goals due to their pursuit of justice, quality, and other intangible objectives.

As a result, in relevant literature in the public sector (e.g., DiIulio 1989; Rainey 2003; Wilson 1989), courts are omitted from the discussion and, as such, reside outside the framework of modern public organizational studies.

It is not surprising, therefore, that there is a modest body of work viewing trial courts as organizations (e.g., Blumberg 1967; Eisenstein and Jacob 1977; Feeley 1992; Heumann 1976; Mohr, 1976).[3] More specifically, a review of the literature identifies only three focused inquiries on trial court culture and performance. Because the aim of the current research is to advance knowledge and its policy implications concerning the role of trial court culture, a critical examination is necessary to determine what previous studies have established and what questions remain unanswered.

Previous Research

Pertinent inquiries conducted by other scholars focus on criminal courts and how cultural orientations shape the timeliness of case resolution. The studies share a comparative approach, examining courts in several states to determine what accounts for why case resolution in some courts is more timely than in others.

Local Legal Culture

The term *local legal culture* arose in studies of delay reduction in criminal courts during the 1970s. In 1976, Nimmer observed that the "local discretionary system" is a major obstacle to criminal court reform efforts. Nimmer (1978, p. 87) went on to claim that lengthy case processing times are "most directly associated with prevailing informal norms of the judicial process and with the personal motivations of participating attorneys and judges." Following a comprehensive study in state trial courts, Church et al. (1978, p. 54) concluded:

> The speed of disposition of civil and criminal litigation in a court cannot be ascribed in any simple sense to the length of its backlog, any more than court size, caseload, or trial rate can explain it. Rather, both quantitative and qualitative data generated in this research strongly suggest both speed *and* backlog are determined in large part by established expectations, practices, and informal rules of behavior of judges and attorneys. For want of a better term, we have called this cluster of related factors the "local legal culture."

Church et al. (1978a) define local legal culture as the "established expectations, practices, and informal rules of behavior of judges and attorneys." According to Church et al., the speed of disposition is attributable more to the views of judges and attorneys than to structural, resource, or procedural distinctions among courts. The authors suggest that these expectations are "stable," implying that efforts to reduce court delay likely will be met by strong resistance unless the expectations themselves are the subject of planned change. The concept of local legal culture has come to imply that court performance is *primarily* governed by shared beliefs, expectations, and attitudes within the local court community about how fast criminal cases *should* move.

There are limitations of the concept put forth by Church et al. (1978a) of culture that surface when considering what the concept implies for the reduction of delay. Simply stated, very little in the nature of his concept suggests what *levers* might be manipulated to speed up litigation. What aspects of expectations, practices, or informal rules should be adjusted to curb delay? Thus, local legal culture is a needed and a welcome starting point to examine how things are done in trial courts, but a fuller understanding of its nature and significance calls for more extensive conceptualization and measurement making it possible to connect different norms to differences in performance in a coherent analytical framework.

Work Orientations

Church et al.'s (1978a) notion of local legal culture is the subject of considerable attention and conceptual enrichment in several interrelated studies by a subsequent group of three collaborators: Eisenstein, Fleming, and Nardulli (Eisenstein et al. 1987; Fleming et al. 1992; Nardulli et al. 1988). These scholars studied three criminal courts in each of three states.

Basically, Nardulli et al. (1988) claim that "norms" exist within every community concerning how the courts should "operate" and that differences in these norms contribute greatly to the varieties of ways that business is conducted. They accept and agree with the essential premise of the earlier discovery of Church et al. (1978a), but they advance their insight by suggesting what the norms are all about. The norms are called "work orientations," signaling that norms are complex and have multiple consequences.

Work orientations "are rationalizing principles" that court leaders "use to explain why particular tasks or functions" are structured the way they are in their respective courts. These powerful forces are not the same from court to court, but they also are not unique to each court community. Indeed, the scholars see three types of distinctive work orientations in the courts they studied: (1) *structural* or *formal*, (2) *efficiency*, and (3) *pragmatic* orientations.

The first orientation emphasizes the compliance with *professional norms* including close adherence to rules and the rejection of expediency. The second orientation places a premium on the efficient use of resources and promotes the expeditious handling of cases, even if the achievement of *smooth* handling occasionally calls for deviation from rules. Finally, a pragmatic orientation is the most flexible approach to how work is to be done because it is whatever the consensus is at a specific point in time. No long-term commitment is made to a particular manner of conducting business. The prevailing norm is deemed satisfactory until a problem emerges calling the existing paradigm into serious question. Then, new agreements on ways of resolving cases are necessary and appropriate and the emerging consensus guides the court until it, too, ultimately proves problematic.

The concept of *work orientations* is a unique and important contribution, although this idea came to Nardulli et al. (1988) after fieldwork completion and during the distillation of their research results. They are, thereby, constrained in indicating precisely and rigorously the orientation or combination of orientations fitting any of the nine courts under study. Hence, the actual content of practitioners' work orientations remains relatively unmeasured and undocumented.

Attitudes of Legal Practitioners

Ostrom and Hanson (1999) demonstrated in a subsequent inquiry the nature and utility of focusing on a combination of attitudes among legal practitioners. These researchers conducted an examination of the patterns of views held by prosecutors and criminal defense attorneys in each of nine mid-sized communities: Albuquerque, Austin, Birmingham, Cincinnati, Grand Rapids, Hackensack, Oakland, Portland, and Sacramento. Ostrom and Hanson divided the nine courts into three equal-sized subgroups according to degrees of timeliness: very expeditious, moderately expeditious, and least expeditious. They then surveyed front-line attorneys for their views on the workings of the state trial court where they practiced and how they assessed the opposing side. Specific findings from the investigation revealed that attorneys have distinctive attitudes toward the leadership role played by a court, a court's ability to communicate its expectations clearly, the degree to which the opposing side is well trained and prepared for trial, and the extent to which the opposing side operates in an adversarial manner. Simply stated, if attorneys see a court exercising firm leadership, a court stating its policies clearly, and the opposing side is equipped for trial, the court is among the most expeditious subgroup. Conversely, if the attorneys see a court as a foggy communicator, a source of weak leadership, and the opposing side is seen as ill trained and ill prepared, the court is of lesser expeditiousness. Hence, Ostrom and Hanson provide strong evidence that culture is a combination of norms reflected in different behavior patterns among courts. Interestingly, in all three subgroups, attorneys view the opposing side as a strong adversary, suggesting the timely resolution of cases does not require counsel to abandon the goals of protecting society (prosecutor) or to defend a criminal defendant's constitutional rights (defense attorney).

However, Ostrom and Hanson (1999) did not address the nature and effects of parallel judicial and court administrators' views. Are there discernible distinctions in their attitudes and do those distinctions make a difference in timeliness and other aspects of court performance? If so, what are the dimensions on which judicial and court administrators' attitudes rest? For example, why are some judges more oriented to expect that attorneys are prepared? Or why are some judges more inclined to see communication with the bar as an essential responsibility?

An Unfinished Research Agenda

Church et al. provided the initial impetus by popularizing the concept of local legal culture. However, no indication of how to conceptualize or measure the concept was provided. Nardulli, Eisenstein, and Fleming extended the notion of culture by elaborating three distinct work orientations made up of different constellations of norms. Although this is a significant development, there is little guidance on how to identify, measure, and interpret the particular norms associated with each work orientation. Ostrom and Hanson provide evidence that culture is reflected in different behavior patterns among courts as well as in different attitudes on the part of prosecutors and defense attorneys.

The consensus among the three bodies of previous research related to court culture is the important influence norms, beliefs, and attitudes held by judges, attorneys, and court administrators have in shaping how courts operate. These investigators stress the importance of practitioners' views in accounting for why courts perform differently. Consequently, previous research provides solid justification for inquiry into the specific norms and values associated with different culture types, a methodology for measuring culture, and an investigation into the consequences of cultural variation.

The Setting for Cultural Assessment

The conceptual framework and methodology developed in this book demonstrate the specific power of culture in one setting: inside the courthouse. Therefore, fully evaluating the current conception of court culture and investigating the linkage to court performance require active participation by a sample of state trial courts. Following in the tradition of previous researchers, the dynamics of culture is investigated in the context of the criminal trial process. The selection of state criminal courts (not federal, appellate, or civil courts) as the focus of analysis reflects the complexities involved in this sort of research and the need to clearly focus the study.

Four criteria were used to select research sites from state trial court systems. The first criterion is an adequate number of state systems to gain a sense of whether distinctive cultures are aligned with particular geographical areas of the country or whether individual courts have counterparts in states located a considerable distance from them. A second criterion is choosing multiple courts within each state to determine if cultural identity is similar or different within a given state. In other words, do statewide structure, organization, doctrine, and rules promote a homogenous culture in a state? A third criterion is variation in the size of the participating courts in order to determine if institutions in smaller-sized communities consistently hold to a distinctive culture, different from those in metropolitan areas. Finally, because the judges and court administrators must complete a cultural survey and cooperate in extensive interviews, court leaders must be willing to participate in the research effort.

Using these several criteria, twelve general jurisdiction courts were selected from three geographically diverse states: California, Florida, and Minnesota. These twelve courts are felony criminal state trial courts where defendants face penalties of more than one year in jail or prison and judges can resolve cases by taking a guilty plea, conducting a trial, or through some other method (e.g., dismissal, participation in treatment program, or diversion). These are courts where serious crimes ranging from burglary to robbery to rape are prosecuted and adjudicated.

The jurisdiction of the courts varies minimally, but there some important distinctions. In California, where the Superior Court is unified, the test courts are located in Contra Costa, Napa, and Ventura Counties. Unification means there is a single-tier trial court in each of California's 58 counties handling all felony and lesser offenses, usually called misdemeanors, at all stages of the criminal process.

Florida's criminal trial system is somewhat different with the state divided into twenty regional Judicial Circuits. Many of the Circuits include more than one county. The Circuit Court for Duval County (in the 4th Circuit) and the Circuit Court for Pinellas County participated in the study. Florida maintains a two-tiered system: a County Court where judges handle felonies only through first appearance, and a Circuit Court where judges resolve felonies, in every Circuit. Clay and Nassau Counties are also part of the 4th Circuit, but they are not part of the current research.

Minnesota's state trial court shares attributes with both California and Florida. The State is divided into ten Judicial Districts, with two districts composed of only one county. The 2nd District is Ramsey County and the 4th District is Hennepin County. Both Ramsey and Hennepin Counties are in the current study. A particular countywide jurisdiction trial court is selected from other Districts. They include District Courts for Dakota (1st), Olmsted (3rd), and Kandiyohi (8th) Counties. In the 6th District, two District trial courts with citywide jurisdiction are chosen from St. Louis County. They are District Courts for Duluth and Virginia. In Minnesota, the trial court is unified, which means that all phases of the felony process, including both felonies and misdemeanors, are handled in a single-tier court.

To gain an understanding of what the counties, courts, and their accompanying criminal justice system look like, a survey of basic elements is presented and summarized in Table 1-1. The counties are a blend of urban and rural communities, ranging in population from 1.1 million in Hennepin County, Minnesota (Minneapolis), to 41,000 in Kandiyohi, Minnesota. Population density varies substantially, from 32 people per square mile in St. Louis County, Minnesota (Duluth) to nearly 3,300 per square mile in Pinellas County, Florida (St. Petersburg). Contra Costa County, California (Martinez); Napa County, California; and Duval County, Florida (Jacksonville) exhibit

TABLE 1-1. COURTS UNDER STUDY

	County Characteristics								Court Characteristics					
	Population, 2000		Race, 2000			Crime, 2000			Judges		Prosecutor		Public Defender	
	Persons	Persons per sq. mile	% White	% Black	% Hispanic/ Latino origin	Violent crime per 100,000 population	Felony calendar type	Judicial Assignment to Felony Cases	Total	Handling Felony	Total	Handling Felony	Total	Handling Felony
California														
Contra Costa	948,816	1,318	65.5	9.4	17.7	471	H	Chief Judge	40.5	11.2	93	65	80	40
Napa	124,279	165	80.0	1.3	23.7	256	M	Master Calendar Judge	8	2	20	15	13	6
Ventura	753,197	408	69.9	1.9	33.4	276	H	Chief Judge	33	6	102	57	49	23
Florida														
Duval	778,879	1,007	65.8	27.8	4.1	1,092	I	Random	61	11	86	60	65	40.2
Pinellas	921,482	3,292	85.9	9.0	4.6	809	I	Random	44	9	152	80	89	52
Minnesota														
Dakota	355,904	625	91.4	2.3	2.9	132	M	Random	18	4.5	35	14	11	7
Hennepin	1,116,200	2,005	80.5	9.0	4.1	534	H	Chief Judge Crim Division	75	17	148	56	91	56
Kandiyohi	41,203	52	93.6	.5	8.0	240	H	Random	6	1	4	3	3	3
Olmsted	124,277	190	90.3	2.7	2.4	233	M	Court Administrator	6.5	1.5	14	7	6	5
Ramsey	511,035	3,281	77.4	7.6	5.3	539	M	Weekly block system	46	8	66	40	30	10
St. Louis	200,528	32	94.9	.8	.8	235	I	Random	13	3	28	10	7	7

Source: US Census Bureau, *State and County QuickFacts.*
Source for Violent Crime per 100,000:
California: Office of the Attorney General, http://caag.state.cs.us/cjsc/statisticsdatatabs/CrimeCo.htm;
Florida: Florida Department of Law Enforcement Total Index Crime by County, 1989–2001;
Minnesota: Minnesota Planning, http://www.mnplan.state.mn.us/mm/indicator.html.
Note: M = Master calendar; H = Hybrid calendar; I = Individual calendar.

the greatest racial diversity, whereas several smaller communities in Minnesota are the least diverse, with Caucasians comprising more than 90 percent of the population. Violent crime rates also vary remarkably, ranging from a low of 132 per 100,000 population in Dakota County, Minnesota (Hastings) to 1,092 per 100,000 population in Duval County, Florida.

With respect to court structure, judges preside over an adversarial process in which prosecutors confront public defenders representing criminal defendants, as shown in Table 1-1.[4] This commonality, although important, does not mean the court systems are identical in all ways.

As desired, the size of the twelve felony courts (as measured by the number of full-time equivalent judicial positions) exhibits considerable variation. Similarities appear in the size of Contra Costa and Ventura Counties in California and a pair of counterparts in Florida (Duval and Pinellas) and Minnesota (Hennepin and Ramsey). There are four courts—spread over three states—that have a similar number of judges handling strictly felony cases (Contra Costa, Duval, Pinellas, and Ramsey).

Conversely, there is considerable range across the courts in Minnesota, with Hennepin having many more judges and attorneys than Kandiyohi at the opposite end of the spectrum. A considerable gap exists also between the size of Contra Costa and Napa Counties in California. (In Table 1-1, information is presented on St. Louis County as a whole, and not the two cities of Duluth and Virginia, to facilitate comparisons with the other sites).

Other sources of differences among courts will help determine if particular cultural configurations occur under certain conditions. By knowing the institutional characteristics of the courts, the sites are examined to see if particular cultural patterns arise only with courts operating with a particular structure, organization, or particular procedures. In this regard, three differences seem especially important.

First, the method of financing the courts varies among the three states, at least during the time-period covered by the current research. Florida operates with a local funding arrangement in which counties are the source of court resources, whereas California is in the process of moving from local to state funding and Minnesota already operates with a state-funding mechanism. To the extent that different financing schemes shape the degree of uniformity with which policies and procedures are put into practice, these differences were noted: Florida's reliance on local units of government to support court operations affirms in an overall manner the local autonomy of the judiciary more than the state-funded situations in California and Minnesota.

A second dimension of institutional variation concerns the method of selecting the professional participants. Judges, the chief prosecutor, the chief public defender, and the clerk of court in Florida are elected to fill and to retain their positions at regularly scheduled competitive elections. In contrast, in California and Minnesota, only prosecutors and judges are elected in competitive elections to fill full terms. Public defenders are appointed as are court administrators and clerks of court. In fact, in California, the positions of court administrator and clerk of court are combined into one position, chief executive officer, and appointed by the court. The widespread use of elections likely leads to a stronger sense of independence among the professional participants in Florida than those in the other two states.[5]

A third dimension of variation concerns the basic ways of assigning cases to judges and in designating what aspects of the legal process a judge presides over in handling cases. Courts often structure their case assignment and calendar systems with an eye toward improving case management efficiency. In an individual calendar system, a court manager or presiding judge typically assigns felony cases (in some random fashion) to an individual judge soon after "bind over" or indictment. The assigned judge handles all motions or other proceedings until the case is concluded. Conversely, in a master calendar system, different judges may handle arraignments, motions, and trial, depending on who is assigned to handle those duties and who is available on the scheduled date.

The independence grounded in the electoral process in Florida parallels the random assignment of cases to judges and the use of individual calendars in both courts under study and in the rest of the State. Hence, in Florida a judge has the responsibility of handling a case from arraignment to resolution. A judge's caseload—the basic work unit in all courts—is defined without external guidance or input, and the handling of a case from beginning to end reinforces the Florida judges' sense of exclusive control in how they discharge their responsibilities.

In contrast, in California and Minnesota, the presiding judge of a court is likely to play a dominant role in deciding what cases are assigned to judges based on considerations of balancing workloads, judicial expertise, and skills with case complexities, and so on. Alternative schemes exist among the different courts in California and Minnesota. Judges in some courts in both states operate under a hybrid calendar,[6] whereas judges in other courts operate under a master calendar. The difference between the individual calendar system used in Florida and the master calendar used in California and Minnesota is that judges preside over all key procedural events in the life of the cases assigned to them in Florida, whereas a master calendar judge in California or Minnesota specializes in conducting a particular event (e.g., arraignment), but does not necessarily preside over the trials in the same set of cases.

Thus, the institutional aegis under which the judges work in the three states is different in terms of source of funding, method of selection of court professionals, and the assignment and handling of cases, although the type and amount of work they face is strikingly similar. In contrast, an important similarity likely affects how courts go about changing their cultures. Cultural change depends on suggestion by a court's leadership team of the value of cultural assessment and how to implement desired modifications. However, the role and authority of presiding judges and court administrators is a work in progress when compared to leadership positions within many other public and private organizations. In the twelve courts, and likely in many others, the position of presiding judge is one of limited tenure. In Florida, a term is one year, whereas in California and Minnesota, it is two years, although successive terms are permitted in all three states. The possibility of renewable or successive terms is important to facilitating continuity in the leadership of the court, as well as to institutionalizing effective management practices. The issue of continuity is not simply an issue of term length; if the court develops a culture change plan, then the job of the leadership team is to implement that plan, rather than impose individual agendas that may vary highly from one presiding judge to the next.

Culture and Performance

In addition to developing a means to conceptualize and measure court culture, actual work practices in the twelve courts provide a direct means to investigate the relationship between alternative cultural orientations and variations in court performance. Court performance is assessed with reference to the time-honored indicator of timeliness as well as *nontraditional* areas such as public access and procedural fairness.

Timeliness

Within the span of the last four decades, the court management field has taken appreciable strides in pursuing improvements in court operations. Specific initiatives are quite familiar and readily recalled. Timeliness was an initial focal point of attention, with case management techniques and standard time frames as key ideas. William Gladstone's maxim that "justice delayed is justice denied" provided the vision statement, the rallying cry for why court management mattered. In the last four decades, research has been conducted on all levels and types of courts in different-sized communities located in various regions. Some areas have received more attention than others, and not all of the findings have been clear, consistent, and well integrated into a cumulative knowledge base. Yet, despite these limitations, two fundamentally important patterns have been uncovered through systematic inquiry, and these act as guideposts in directing needed study.

The first proposition concerns caseload composition. Similarities in cases coming to courts are more striking than their differences.[7] For example, if felony criminal cases are grouped by the seriousness of the offense (e.g., homicide, other crimes against the person, property crimes, drug crimes, and other types of felonies), the rank ordering of the categories is the same in most communities, regardless of population size or geographic location. Property crimes, including burglary, theft, and fraud, are generally the most frequent cases, followed by drug sale and possession-violation cases. Other crimes against the person, including rape, assault and robbery, usually constitute the third largest category. Homicide cases and other types of felonies (e.g., kidnapping) are each small fractions of the caseload compared to the other three categories (see, e.g., Hanson et al. 1992; Hanson et al. 2002; Ostrom and Hanson 1999).

The second proposition is that similar caseloads are resolved differently. The manner of resolution can be measured in alternative ways, but a simple and observable indicator is timeliness. What is striking from the literature and experience is the wide variety of case-processing times. Some courts take five or more times as long as the more expeditious courts to resolve cases, despite little difference in caseload composition.[8] Hence, an intriguing question arises: how and why do some courts get the same basic work done in noticeably different time-frames than do other courts?

Previous research has addressed this question, but with limited success. In fact, the last wave of academically oriented research (e.g., Fleming et al. 1987; Luskin and Luskin 1986, 1987) found case characteristics (e.g., severity of offense) and court procedures (e.g., types of calendars) accounted for only a minimal amount of intercourt variation in the processing time of felony criminal cases. Moreover, the best predictors of the pace at which individual cases are resolved are found to be different across courts.

It is likely that the answer to the question of why courts take different amounts of time to resolve similar workloads lies in organizational culture. There can be little doubt that this concept is fundamental to understanding how and why courts go about resolving cases in particular ways. And, more importantly, the concept of culture has significance for court management well beyond reducing delay.

Court Performance Standards

Delay reduction as the primary focus of court management is shifting slowly to a more expansive notion of what constitutes a well-performing court. The *Trial Court Performance Standards* (TCPS), begun in 1987, represents a milestone in the development of concepts, techniques, and strategies to examine the performance of courts and the justice system (Commission on Trial Court Performance Standards 1990). With the TCPS, timeliness has been supplemented by other values, such as access and fairness, and a generally broader notion of accountability than implied by timeliness alone.

The choice of performance indicators selected to gauge the impact of culture on performance in the twelve courts highlights the management challenges facing judicial branch leaders. For courts (and nonprofit, public organizations), there is no dominant indicator of success like *profitability*. Management experts have long called for the development and use of multiple criteria to gauge effectiveness. Therefore, the unsettled issue is not with the current conception of court performance goals, but, rather, with the development of a management culture conducive to achievement of performance in a complex setting. Meeting performance targets based on multiple criteria puts a premium on finding ways to help court leaders develop a better understanding of their organizations and themselves.

In addition, although court management has made significant progress in articulating what it means to be an effective court, the goals seem competing. Courts should be timely, but also judges should devote sufficient time and attention to ensure justice is done. Courts should be more accommodating and less intimidating to the public, but they also should give priority to caring for the people in the organization. Efficient documented procedures are desired, but flexibility in adapting to particular circumstances also is valued. Clearly, high performance requires a means to resolve the dilemmas and apparent conflicts inherent in today's court environment by gaining a manageable perspective on dealing with competing values. Greater clarity on court organizational culture is essential to this task.

Organizational Roadmap

The remainder of this book is organized to provide a means to diagnose court culture and to discover whether a relationship exists between court culture and court performance. Chapter 2 begins with a review of the efforts of private sector specialists to understand and explain organizational culture in corporations and other for-profit organizations. The methods used by these scholars to develop conceptual categories of culture are examined and extended to the world of courts. Cultural orientations are found to show their influence in the types of beliefs held by judges and practitioners on specific work dimensions. Within the setting of courts and the larger justice system, the work areas include case management, judicial–staff relations, change management, courthouse leadership, and internal organization.

In Chapter 3, the contributions of previous research and the insights and observations of court scholars are integrated with the structure, tools, and measures described in Chapters 1 and 2. What emerges from integrating these two areas of inquiry is a framework tailored to the study of court culture and its consequences. Specifically, a Court Culture Assessment Instrument (CCAI) is developed. In addition, numerical and graphical ways to examine the responses and hence display cultural archetypes are presented. The direction, strength, and congruency of culture are examined in each of the sites.

Next, to make the adaptation of the framework to courts convincing and warranting consideration, Chapter 4 provides an elaboration of the four court cultures. On a conceptual level, the ways that each culture shapes—in both positive and negative ways—how work is done across the five different work areas is examined. Site visit observations as well as literature drawn from earlier court studies are cited to clarify and enhance the understanding of alternative court cultures.

A test of the court culture typology is the basis for Chapter 5, with specific reference to the performance consequences of each of the four cultural archetypes. This issue is addressed by analyzing the impact of culture on multiple performance criteria including timeliness, access, fairness, and managerial effectiveness. The association between culture and these values is examined from case level data on timeliness as well as the perspectives of practicing attorneys, including prosecutors and public defenders in all twelve courts. The analysis finds a provocative relationship between the attorneys' views on court performance and the type of culture guiding the court where they practice.

In Chapter 6, the extent to which judges and court administrators seek to move away from their court's current culture is examined. Do courts want more of the same? Does every court tend to want to move to a different culture in the future? Or is there some common theme? The answers to these questions are noteworthy because a commonly preferred cultural mosaic emerges for the future. Despite the wide range of existing cultures, the commonly desired culture is one where particular culture types are preferred for different areas of work.

Chapter 7 summarizes the key findings from the current research in the form of six propositions that help to explain how and why courts with strikingly similar caseload sizes and composition perform strikingly differently. Taking off from the six propositions, Chapter 7 explores the management implications of the cultural mosaic in some detail. In particular, challenges to the governance of courts surfaced by the data are discussed. Recommendations are offered on how performance might be enhanced.

2 A Framework for Court Culture

Introduction

Court culture is conceived as the beliefs and behaviors shaping "the way things get done" by the individuals—judges and court administrators—who have the responsibility to ensure cases are resolved fairly and expeditiously. Quinn (1988, p. 66), a leader in the study of organizational culture, offers a concise definition:

> When we think of the manifestation of values in organizations, it is their cultures we are thinking of. Simply put, culture is the set of values and assumptions that underlie the statement, "*This is how we do things around here.*" Culture at the organizational level, like information processing at the individual level, tends to take on moral overtones. While cultures tend to vary dramatically, they share the common characteristic of providing integration of effort in one direction while often sealing off the possibility of moving in another direction. [Emphasis added]

Following the development of a multidimensional model of organizational culture (Quinn and Rohrbaugh 1983), Quinn and his colleagues embarked on nearly two decades of subsequent studies exploring the cultural implications of competing values for a wide variety of companies. Cameron and Quinn (1999, pp. 3–4) make clear the relevance of culture as they summarize the traits of successful private sector businesses:

> The major distinguishing feature in these companies, their most important competitive advantage, the most powerful factor they all highlight as a key ingredient in their success, is their organizational culture.
>
> The sustained success of these firms has had less to do with market forces than company values; less to do with competitive positioning than personal beliefs; less to do with resource advantages than vision. In fact, it is difficult to name even a single highly successful company . . . that does not have a distinctive, readily identifiable, organizational culture.

Growing awareness that culture matters to performance and long-term success in the world of business triggered the emergence of culture analysis as a definable area in the field of management and organizational studies largely beginning in the 1980s (e.g., Ouchi 1981; Deal and Kennedy 1982; Pascale and Athos 1981; Peters and Waterman 1982). In fact, Ouichi and Wilkins (1985, p. 458) believe that "the study of organizational culture has become one of the major domains of organizational research, and some might even argue that it has become the single most active arena, eclipsing studies of formal structure, or organization-environment research and bureaucracy."

As organizational culture became a presence in private sector research, Wilson (1989) made the case for including organizational culture in the study of public sector organizations. In doing so, Wilson opened the door for integrating work on private sector organizational culture into the study of the public sector with the following claim: "Organizations matter, even in government agencies" (p. 23). He offers a provocative means to bridging the private–public dichotomy when he says "[e]very organization has a culture, that is, a persistent, patterned way of thinking about the central tasks of and human relationships within an organization" (p. 91). As such, Wilson believes culture is a core topic for public sector organizational analysis, because organizations have a culture just as an individual has a personality

(p. 93). Building upon the analogy of organizational personality, he goes on to provide his own definition of culture: "Organizational culture consists of those patterned and enduring differences among systems of coordinated action that lead those systems to respond in different ways to the same stimuli" (p. 93). Organizational culture is a relevant and important facet of all bureaucracies—public and private.

When shifting the focus to public institutions, Wilson (1989, p. 91) anticipates some difficulties in diagnosing a public organization's culture. Specifically, public organizations do not necessarily have a single culture:

> *Many government agencies have multiple, competing cultures.* Some manage the competition well, some do not. A major responsibility of an executive is not only. . . to infuse the organizations with value, it is also to discover a way by which different values (and the different cultures that espouse those values) can productively coexist. (Wilson 1989, p. 101) [Emphasis added]

If multiple—and competing—cultures are a hallmark of government agencies, the specter of managing the multiple cultures within an organization is raised. If Wilson is right, the expectation is that public organizations will manifest a *mosaic* of complementary and competing cultures. Identifying and understanding the resulting mosaic and the relationship to performance becomes vital to public sector management.[1]

The idea that culture is germane to understanding how public sector organizations go about their business is compelling. It is not surprising, therefore, to find DiIulio (1993) suggesting that the measurement of organizational culture is an important part of any public administration improvement strategy. DiIulio (1989) proposes the following agenda for doing so:

> (1) To observe how members at every level of an organization "really behave," (2) to relate systematically these observations to the formal character of the organization in order to see what (if any) connections exist, and (3) to search systematically for the connections (if any) between organizational activities and real world outcomes.

The key research focus is to discover the relationship between organizational behavior and the ability of the organization to reach its stated ends. If the "public management variable" is present *and* important, it remains for researchers to demonstrate the connection. DiIulio goes on to say:

> The immediate future of public management studies ought to lie largely in exploratory efforts at "recovering" this variable, which means defining it, measuring it, and specifying the conditions under which it matters to the actual quality of citizens' lives, either in conjunction with or independent of variables that are not directly related to how public organizations are led, structured, and coordinated. (1989, p. 127)

DiIulio's inclinations, if on target, can be effectively implemented by taking a page from work done in management and organization studies in the private sector.

Following the direction of Wilson and DiIulio's arguments, three reasons persuasively suggest private sector studies can inform the specific topic of court culture. First, the concept of court culture and the parallel private sector investigations both revolve around the idea that "the way things get done" (i.e., work orientations) defines the character of the organizations. To the extent that judges and administrators in one court have particular views on how cases should be resolved, they will organize themselves differently than individuals in another court with different views. The centrality of work orientations as a basis for understanding courts is consistent with commonly heard conversations among practitioners. When judges get together and talk about their courts they almost always begin by saying, "Well, this is the way that we do it in my court." These statements are symptomatic of each court's culture. Second, work orientations shape the degree of a court's effectiveness. This linkage has been demonstrated in the private sector, and a parallel relationship is worth exploring in public institutions, including courts. Third, business school scholars have shown that private organizational culture is susceptible to measurement and that the results yield a typology of cultures.

Of course, some scholars argue that what is known about private organizations cannot be a basis for understanding public bodies. This viewpoint is exemplified in the oft-cited claim by Wallace Sayre that public and private organizations are "fundamentally alike in all unimportant respects." More specific assumptions underlying this argument are public agencies, which in contrast to private bodies, lack a clear bottom line (e.g., profit and market performance), have a diverse set of goals and performance criteria, are more *open* and with greater exposure to public scrutiny; in addition, managers of public organizations have shorter time horizons (Allison 1988, pp. 287–288). Yet, when looking at the "temperaments, skills, and techniques" of judges, court managers, and court employees, the differences between public sector and private sector organizations and management are minimal. This point of view is expressed in the observation of Lynn that

> [T]he two sectors are constituted to serve different kinds of societal interests, and distinctive kinds of skills and values are appropriate to serving these different interests. The distinctions may be blurred or absent, however, when analyzing particular managerial responsibilities, functions, and tasks in a particular organization. The implication of this argument is that lesson drawing and knowledge transfer across sectors is likely to be useful and should never be rejected on ideological grounds. (2003, p. 3)

Therefore, a useful starting point for the study of court culture is with the private management literature examining culture in a wide range of organizations.

Two Leading Theories of Organizational Culture

Two sets of experts in the study of private organizations have developed complementary perspectives on how work orientations shape the performance of companies. Because they both provide conceptual frameworks to classify organizations and to measure how closely entities in the real world correspond to conceptual categories, they indicate testable propositions about the linkage between culture and performance. For this reason, these perspectives are a promising base from which to construct a framework for the study of court culture. Hence, a review of these established theories illuminate the foundation for the current investigation of the nature and significance of court culture and institutional performance.

Robert Quinn and Colleagues

Since the early 1980s, Quinn and his colleagues have sought to define and explain organizational culture. Recognizing the complexities of culture as a theoretical construct, they chose to ground their characterization of culture in the language of organizational effectiveness. This focus was based on the fact that most organizations only pay attention to a subset of many possible indicators of effectiveness. Quinn and his colleagues reasoned that the selective use of indicators likely is accounted for by cultural differences. Different cultures have different conceptions and priorities on what constitutes effectiveness. As a result, a way to conceptualize and measure organizational culture can be gleaned from a thorough and quantitative analysis of attitudes toward organizational effectiveness.

In a groundbreaking article, Quinn and Rohrbaugh (1983) identified seventeen key indicators of organizational effectiveness: conflict/cohesion, morale, value of human resources, training and development, quality, flexibility/adaptation, readiness, growth, evaluation by external entities, utilization of environment, profit, productivity, planning goals, efficiency, information management and communication, stability, and control.[2] These values represent what people potentially value about an organization's behavior.

To determine whether particular values cluster together, Quinn and Rohrbaugh asked a number of organization theorists to engage in a paired comparison exercise and to indicate how closely each of the seventeen general effectiveness criteria is related to each of the other criteria. Their hypothesis is that cultures are formed by different clusters of values, which, in turn, are the basis for different conceptions of organizational effectiveness.

In testing this hypothesis, Quinn and Rohrbaugh (1983) turned to authorities in the study of organizations and used their judgments to see whether distinct organizational archetypes might emerge. The payoff of this approach is that it paved the way to combine a rigorous methodology with the insights of organization specialists. Using survey data from the experts',[3] Quinn and Rohrbaugh's analysis uncovered two dimensions by which to define and configure the measurement of organizational effectiveness.[4] The first dimension is related to organization structure and contrasts effectiveness criteria emphasizing flexibility, discretion, and dynamism from criteria emphasizing stability, order, and control. At one end of the continuum an organization is viewed as effective if it is changing and adaptable. At the other end, an effective organization is stable and predictable.

The second dimension is related to organizational focus and contrasts an internal, employee-oriented focus with an external, community-oriented focus. At one end of the second dimension, an organization is viewed as effective if it stresses cohesion, morale, and internal communication. At the other end, an effective organization pays close attention to how it is viewed by external groups and individuals and its ability to manage the environment.

Taken together, these two dimensions define four quadrants, each representing a distinct culture type. Somewhat unexpectedly, Quinn and Rohrbaugh were able to connect these cultural types to the traditional literature, thereby providing a strong sense of plausibility to the experts' paired comparisons. The four types of organizational culture, along with key characteristics are presented in Figure 2-1 (Cameron and Quinn, 1999). Cameron and Quinn have used their method—often referred to as the *competing values framework*—to assess a wide range of business-oriented organizations. In doing so, they find that over 80 percent of organizations fall into one of the four cultural types (p. 40).

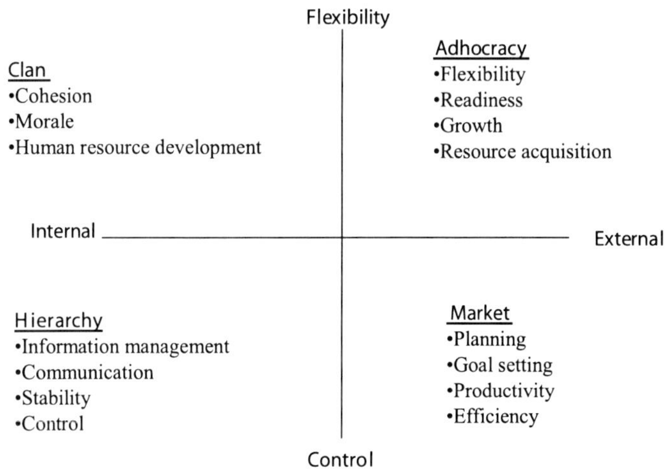

Fig 2.1 Competing Values Model

In subsequent research, Cameron and Quinn (1999, p. 19) developed the concept of six key "aspects" of organizational life, which they refer to as the content dimensions of organizational culture. They are: dominant characteristics, organizational leadership, management of employees, organizational glue, strategic emphases, and criteria for success. Cameron and Quinn contend that every organization has these aspects, but each aspect operates in accordance with a particular type of culture. For example, underlying differences between cultures likely show up in the different ways employees are managed, the level of communication, or willingness to take risks. The use of organizational aspects as a way to demonstrate cultural differences also raises the possibility of combinations of cultures. In fact, a specific focus of attention was to see if the presence or absence of a single culture over all six dimensions is related to the degree of effectiveness.

We condense and summarize the model of Cameron and Quinn graphically in a "value" matrix for the competing values framework, as shown in Table 2-1. The value matrix provides a synopsis of the four culture archetypes as well as an indication of how they differ across six content dimensions. Thus, culture is characterized with reference to these six distinct vantage points and summarizes how a culture is manifested in specific areas of organizational concern.

Rob Goffee and Gareth Jones

Goffee and Jones (1998) provide a somewhat different approach to measuring and identifying culture. As a starting point, they focus their attention on culture as the social architecture of the organization and display this idea through the use of a two-dimensional diagram. The vertical axis is the dimension of *sociability*, whereas the horizontal axis is *solidarity*. Each dimension runs from low to high. The key to understanding their conception of organizational character lies in the definition of its two dimensions.[5]

Sociability is the degree of friendliness among the people working in an organization (1998, p. 23). For Goffee and Jones, this dimension is an essential element of culture. They identify several benefits associated with organizations having a high degree of sociability:

> Working in such an environment is a pleasure, which promotes high morale and esprit de corps. Sociability is also often a boon to creativity because it fosters teamwork, the sharing of

TABLE 2-1. COMPETING VALUES VALUE MATRIX

	Cultural Archetypes			
Content Dimensions	Clan	Adhocracy	Market	Hierarchy
Dominant Characteristics	The organization is a very personal place. It is like an extended family. People seem to share a lot of themselves	The organization is a very dynamic and entrepreneurial place. People are willing to stick their necks out and take risks.	The organization is very results oriented. A major concern is with getting the job done. People are very competitive and achievement oriented.	The organization is a very controlled and structured place. Formal procedures generally govern what people do.
Organizational Leadership	The leadership in the organization is generally considered to exemplify mentoring, facilitating, or nurturing.	The leadership in the organization is generally considered to exemplify entrepreneurship, innovating, or risk taking.	The leadership in the organization is generally considered to exemplify a no-nonsense, aggressive, results-oriented focus.	The leadership in the organization is generally considered to exemplify coordinating, organizing, or smooth-running efficiency.
Management of Employees	The management style in the organization is characterized by teamwork, consensus, and participation.	The management style in the organization of characterized by individual risk taking, innovation, freedom, and uniqueness.	The management style in the organization is characterized by hard-driving competitiveness, high demands, and achievement.	The management style in the organization is characterized by security of employment, conformity, predictability, and stability in relationships.
Organizational Glue	The glue that holds the organization together is loyalty and mutual trust. Commitment to this organization runs high.	The glue that holds the organization together is commitment to innovation and development. There is an emphasis on being on the cutting edge.	The glue that holds the organization together is the emphasis on achievement and goal accomplishment. Aggressiveness and winning are common themes.	The glue that holds the organization together is formal rules and policies. Maintaining a smooth running organization is important.
Strategic Emphases	The organization emphasizes human development. High trust, openness, and participation persist.	The organization emphasizes acquiring new resources and creating new challenges. Trying new things and prospecting for opportunities are valued.	The organization emphasizes competitive actions and achievement. Hitting stretch targets and winning in the marketplace are dominant.	The organization emphasizes performance and stability. Efficiency, control, and smooth operations are important.
Criteria for Success	The organization defines success on the basis of the development of human resources, teamwork, employee commitment, and concern for people.	The organization defines success on the basis of having the most unique or newest products. It is a product leader and innovator.	The organization defines success on the basis of winning in the marketplace and outpacing the competition. Competitive market leadership is the key.	The organization defines success on the basis of efficiency. Dependable delivery, smooth scheduling, and low-cost production are critical.

> information, and an openness to new ideas. . . . [it also] creates an environment in which people are more likely to go beyond the formal requirements of their jobs. They work harder than technically necessary to help their colleagues—that is, their community—look good and succeed. (1998, p. 25)

Goffee and Jones readily acknowledge sociability can have a negative side in some organizations. They note: "The prevalence of friendships may allow poor performance of members to be tolerated. . . . In addition, high sociability environments are often characterized by an exaggerated concern for consensus. The result: the best *compromise* gets applied to problems, not the best *solution*" (1998, p. 28). As Goffee and Jones indicate, sociability is neither good nor bad, it just is. Sociability is important because it brings into focus ways individuals relate to one another in the organization.

Solidarity addresses the degree to which members of an organization have clearly understood goals, shared commitments, and common tasks geared to getting the job done, regardless of "whether they personally like each other or not" (Goffee and Jones 1998, p. 28). A professional football team is an example of an organization seeking high solidarity. In the current era of free agency, player loyalties go to the highest bidder. No requirement mandates that teammates like each other. Instead, the primary consideration is the team's winning percentage. Players may have little to do with each other off the field. Success means producing a "well-oiled machine" on the field. Each team member has a role and set of tasks clearly articulated and aligned with the ultimate goal of winning. An organization with solidarity has clear goals, agreed upon procedures for reaching the goals, and an understanding of which behaviors will be rewarded.

Solidarity also has its potential downside. "Too much focus on the group's goals and requirements can be oppressive or hurtful to those individuals who get in the way" (Goffee and Jones 1998, p. 31). Professional football provides a clear example of how a high solidarity culture will terminate individuals as soon as they no longer satisfy the needs of the organization. Although less extreme, court culture can exhibit some of the same attitude. Courts seeking to make the workplace more structured, rule driven, and technology reliant will allocate training monies, make promotions, and generally reward judges and administrators who are in harmony with the controlled pursuit of performance. Individuals who value a more sociability-oriented

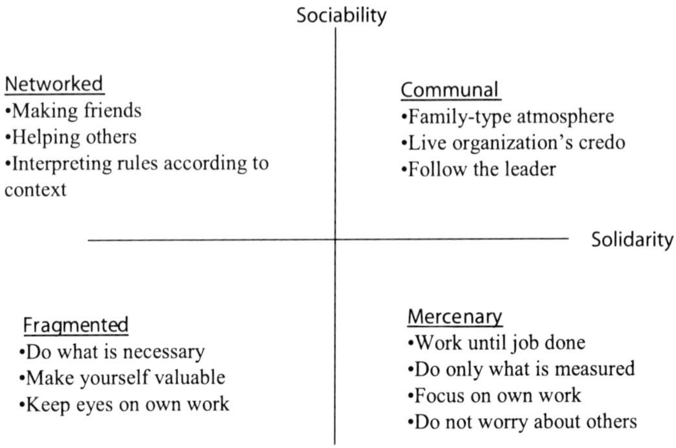

Fig 2.2 Goffee and Jones

environment will object to the more solidarity-driven values and behaviors.

Based upon the two dimensions, Goffee and Jones posit that four cultures occur at the intersection of *sociability* and *solidarity*. Figure 2-2 provides a visual depiction of the dimensions, along with the associated characteristics of each cultural archetype.

Goffee and Jones also use "content dimensions" to describe more specific and detailed differences between various culture types. Using the four dimensions of *physical space*, *communication*, *time*, and *identity*, they indicate how each culture affects an organization in particular ways. We summarize and graphically portray Goffee and Jones' perspective on organizational culture through the value matrix shown in Table 2-2.

Lessons Learned

In sum, five important lessons emerge from these two sets of scholarly studies. First, organizations are classifiable and comparable using an appropriately developed conceptual framework. Second, frameworks are built upon some type of values clarification, meaning cultures are distinguished based upon the types of values they emphasize. Third, a cultural framework builds upon the views of experts in the field as to what values are related to each other and which are potentially

TABLE 2-2. GOFFEE AND JONES VALUE MATRIX

	Cultural Archetypes			
Content Dimensions	Networked	Mercenary	Communal	Fragmented
Physical Space	Offices doors are open or unlocked; people move freely into and out of each other's rooms. Large allocations of space are for social acitivities.	Space is allocated functionally—in ways to get the job done. An open plan or flexible desk use is possible—but in order to assist with simple, efficient, and cost-effective methods or means of task achievement, not "chatting".	Much space is shared either formally or informally. It may sometimes be difficult to determine whose office you are in, and there are few barriers between departments or functions. There are unlikely to be big differences in space allocation between people.	Space is designed to help individuals work without interruption. Office doors are closed and offices are well equipped so that employees are effectively self-contained.
Communication	There is a lot of talk. Although there are formal hierarchies and processes, much communication takes place around the formal systems in face-to-face conversation, on the phone, in "meetings before meetings."	Communication is swift, direct, and work-focused. Terse memos and data laden reports leave little room for "idle" conversation.	There is communication in every channel, but oral, face-to-face methods are likely to dominate. Nonverbal communication is important; dress, color, and symbolism may all help individuals to feel close to others. Communication flows easily inside between all levels.	Talk is limited to brief one-to-one exchanges in the corridor or on the phone. Meetings are resisted (What's the point? Difficult to arrange; hard to manage). Individuals will talk only to those who are worth talking to; otherwise the deal is "I leave you alone if you leave me alone."

(Continued on following page)

TABLE 2-2. GOFFEE AND JONES VALUE MATRIX (Continued from previous page)

Content Dimensions	Cultural Archetypes: Networked	Mercenary	Communal	Fragmented
Time	People use work time to socialize—and they are not penalized for doing so. In addition, social activities are often extensions to the working day. People get to know each other quickly.	Long hours are the norm, although it is acceptable to leave once the job is done. This is clearly signaled, since time and performance measures are explicit. Private time is precious and, where possible, protected.	People live at work; professional life is so engaging that "conventional" time is ignored. Work and non-work life dissolve into one; even when at home work can be a preoccupation. Work becomes a way of life.	People go to the office only when they need to; absence is the norm. Achievement, not time, is the measure. Most time is devoted to the pursuit of individual professional and technical excellence; anything that interferes with this can be considered a waste of time.
Identity	People identify with each other; close ties of sociability heighten feelings of similarity as individuals. Differences are understated and, if expressed at all, are seen in subtle variations of dress code and speech patterns. Excessive displays of personal difference are resisted.	People identify with winning. Although norms of behavior emerge here as anywhere, differences between individuals are acceptable and encouraged if they assist in achieving the result. What draws people together are shared experiences, goals, and interests rather than shared sentiments or feelings.	People identify with the values and mission of their company. The credo is lived; the words are played out, enacted, debated, applied, developed. Work becomes a way of life. Logos, symbols, war cries abound. The company attracts fierce loyalty.	People identify with values of individualism and freedom; with personal technical excellence; with organizations that minimize interference. There are significant personal differences between individuals, but these are unlikely to impede achievement, and they confirm values of freedom.

competing. Fourth, the process of defining and differentiating among values will also benefit from the opinions and insights of those who live and breathe the culture. Fifth, different theorists have produced different conceptions of organizational culture, but important similarities in the classification schemes suggest the lessons learned are transferable to the study of court culture types. One early decision is selecting the sociological terms of *sociability* and *solidarity* as the dimensions by which to conceptualize court culture.

These two dimensions, which underlie the nature of culture types, are compatible with the two fundamental challenges and responsibilities confronting courts as organizations. One challenge revolves around the central mission of courts to handle certain types of conflicts and disputes in their communities. Solidarity is an idea harmonious with the goals of courts to structure the job so as to resolve all cases timely and fairly. The second challenge, managing personnel—including judges, court administrators, and line staff—is a critical and difficult task facing courts, especially when they grow in size and complexity. Court employees have a wide range of educational and experience backgrounds. Therefore, sociability bears on the kind and manner of attention given to judges and court staff by their colleagues.

Conceptualizing Court Culture

To transfer the theoretical and measurement approaches of private organizational culture to the court setting, an effective strategy proves to be the methodology laid out by Quinn and Rohrbaugh (1983). When specifically tailored to courts, the steps include the following:

- Locate a small set of core values that trial courts identify as important by reviewing literature and consulting with disciplinary experts.
- Ask *knowledgeable* experts—judges and court administrators—to assess the degree of similarity and dissimilarity between the various values using a carefully formulated questionnaire.
- Employ the statistical analysis technique of multidimensional scaling to extract and name the two most important dimensions.
- Identify culture types based upon the values that cluster together in each quadrant.
- Determine primary work areas for court organizational assessment.

- Align the particular value that best describes each culture's approach in a given work area. Continue until all cultural values for each combination of work area and culture type are completed. The result is a Court Cultural Value matrix.

By following this methodology, it is possible to define, measure, and specify a court's organizational culture(s). Beyond the direct relevance to court management, the approach provides a means to address DiIulio's (1989) call for defining and measuring the public management variable.

The first step is identifying a comprehensive set of values. A list of more than fifty court-related cultural norms and values were identified in a thorough review of the relevant literature (e.g., Boyum 1979; Church 1982; Eisenstein et al. 1987; Eisenstein and Jacob 1977; Fleming et al. 1992; Henderson and Kerwin 1982; Hewitt et al. 1990; Mohr, 1976; Nardulli et al. 1988; Ostrom and Hanson 1999; Stott 1982; Trial Court Performance Standards Commission, 1990; and Warren 1998). Minimizing overlap and eliminating redundancy produced a set of sixteen distinct cultural values and norms: case differentiation, chain of command, collaborative problem solving, collegiality, constrained change, continuity with the past, decentralization, discretion, efficiency, flexibility, innovation, judicial consensus, rule oriented, self managing, sovereignty, and teamwork (see Appendix 2-1 for complete descriptions).

Second, to determine whether these values are the grounds for different culture types and which values are interrelated and which ones are at odds with one another, a set of experts was asked to complete a series of paired comparisons between each of the sixteen cultural values.[6] Using a questionnaire consisting of 120 paired comparisons with the sixteen values presented in a randomized order, approximately 70 individuals from around the country with considerable court experience were targeted as possible respondents (see Appendix 2-2 for a more complete description of the paired-comparisons exercise). Fifty-three individuals returned completed questionnaires.[7] On the basis of responses from each of these individuals, the resulting proximity matrices served as the primary data input into the analysis. Each element of the matrix is an ordinal measure of how similar (or dissimilar) two cultural values are viewed by a particular respondent.

Third, the responses held by the seasoned practitioners were analyzed to determine exactly how they saw values relating to or diverging from one another. The values clustering together constitute the basis for distinct cultures. Specifically, a multidimensional scaling analysis was conducted and found the respondents' proximities to be represented in two dimensions (see Appendix 2-3 for an overview of the analysis technique and results).

The first dimension is the extent to which a court has clearly understood and shared goals, common tasks, and agreed-upon procedures for reaching the goals. At one end, a court pursues shared goals and tasks, has agreed upon procedures for reaching the goals, and values communication within the court. At the other end, a court stresses independence, autonomy, and individuality among the judges and court staff in how they carry out their work. Because this dimension is consistent with the implications and nuances of the characterization by Goffee and Jones (1998), it will be referred to as the *solidarity* dimension.

The second dimension captures the ways in which the individuals within the courthouse community relate to one another. At one end of the dimension, the court is closely connected in a communal or clan-like way, whereas at the other end little need for social interaction occurs as rules and structure determine what is to be done. This is interpreted as the *sociability* dimension.

The aforecited substantive interpretations of the two dimensions fit with the following observation from Goffee and Jones:

> Culture—It is an organization's common values, symbols, beliefs, and behaviors. Culture comes down to a common way of thinking, which drives a common way of acting.... Usually these shared assumptions, beliefs, and values are unspoken—or implicit. And yet in their silence they can make a difference between a company that wins and loses, and for the individual, they can make the difference between commitment and disaffection.... Culture, then, is about sustainability. *Culture is the underlying social architecture.* (1998, p. 15) [Emphasis added]

Therefore, the Solidarity and Sociability dimensions in tandem provide a blueprint of the social architecture and a basis to define and distinguish alternative court cultures.

The dimensions of *sociability* and *solidarity* describe two distinct continuums, and individual courts occupy positions at different points along the spectrum of each continuum. Taken together, the two dimensions form the following four quadrants, each representing a distinct court culture: (1) *communal*—low *solidarity*, high *sociability*; (2) *networked*—high *solidarity*, high *sociability*; (3) *hierarchical*—high *solidarity*, low *sociability*; and (4) *autonomous*—low *solidarity*, low *sociability*.

Although the dimension names chosen by Goffee and Jones (*solidarity* and *sociability*) are used, somewhat different names for the four culture types were selected, due to the particular set of norms and values extant in courts. To elaborate the four culture types more fully, a set of five content dimensions (or hereafter work areas) were developed in order to compare the four culture types. The selected areas are as follows:

Case Management Style. Scheduling, arranging, and conducting case events is the essence of case management. Courts vary in how they schedule, arrange, and conduct events, but the activities must happen. Otherwise cases are unresolved and fail to move forward toward resolution. What prompts and guides case management varies considerably across courts and reflects a court's perspective on service delivery.

Judge–Staff Relations. The design and maintenance of relationships of authority as well as the development and training of the entire workforce is the essence of judge–staff relations. As such, the focus is on the procedures and criteria used for directing, monitoring, evaluating, and motivating court staff, as well as career development.

Change management. Addressing change in a planned and orderly fashion is change management. The aim is to more effectively implement new methods and systems that will help a court improve the way it does business. Some changes to be managed may lie within and be controlled by the court. Other changes will be triggered by events outside the court and over which the court exercises little or no control (e.g., new legislation).

Courthouse leadership. Directing judges and court staff in the exercise of key procedural events is courthouse leadership. In every court, a judge or leadership team decides priorities governing the completion of events, but the agenda-setting and the manner of selecting priorities varies from court to court.

Internal organization. Deciding how to organize the courthouse workforce to accomplish the necessary tasks is the essence of internal organization. The focus is on the division of labor and responsibilities among judges and court staff in enabling the case events to occur. As such, this area focuses on the deployment of staff, the structuring of the work environment, and training that affect and shape the delivery of key services.

The four culture types are expected to vary across each of these areas of work. The court culture framework and the variety of culture types is expressed through a *value matrix*, constructed in a manner consistent with those used to characterize the *competing values framework* and Goffee and Jones.

It should be noted that the development of the value matrix for court culture moved beyond the sixteen values displayed in Appendix 2-1. Given four culture types and five content dimensions, it is necessary to have twenty values to *populate* the resulting value matrix. Like Quinn (1988),[8] not only have some additional values been introduced, some definitions were altered compared to those in the original analysis. These changes reflect a growing understanding of court culture as this research has moved forward.

Table 2-3 displays the value matrix and provides a succinct description of the four court culture types as well as an indication of how they differ across five areas of work. Each of the twenty values contained in the matrix describes a specific attribute, an interpretation or approach associated with each work area, and how the attribute is typically manifested in a particular court culture. This classification scheme assumes all courts have the same work to do in guaranteeing justice and liberty, but they organize themselves differently to accomplish these goals depending on their culture. Stated positively, every court proceeds in a deliberative and purposive manner to resolve cases. However, the meanings of *deliberativeness* and *purposefulness* ultimately are defined by the culture of a particular court.

This typology with associated values is a theoretical construct that can be brought to bear on the world. The degree to which specific values are emphasized in an individual court defines that court's cultural approach to primary areas of work. For example, when it

TABLE 2-3. COURT CULTURE VALUE MATRIX

Content Dimensions	Cultural Archetypes			
	Communal	Networked	Autonomous	Hierachical
Case Management Style	**Flexibility** — General agreement on performance goals exists, but centralized judicial and administrative staff leadership is downplayed and creativity is encouraged. As a result, individual judges apply court rules, policies, and procedures in alternative, acceptable ways.	**Judicial Consensus** — Judicial expectations concerning the timing of key procedural events come from a working policy built on the deliberate involvement and planning of the entire bench. Follow through on established goals is championed and encouraged by a presiding (administrative) judge.	**Self-managing** — Limited discussion and agreement on the importance of court-wide performance goals exist. Individuals judges are relatively free to make their own determinations on when key procedural events are to be completed.	**Rule-oriented** — Judges are committed to the use of case flow management (e.g., early case control, case coordination, and firm trial dates) with the support of administrative and courtroom staff. Written court rules and procedures are applied uniformly by judges.
Judge–Staff Relations	**Egalitarian** — An effort is made by judges to limit the psychological distance between them and administrative courtroom staff. Hierarchy and formal processes exist, but court staff members go outside normal channels when it seems appropriate to "do the right thing."	**People Development** — Judges value and promote a diverse workforce and diversity of ideas; act to enhance professional administrative and courtroom staff development; and seek to treat all staff with fairness and respect.	**Personal Loyalty** — Individual judges uses their own criteria to monitor, evaluate, and motivate courtroom and other staff. Judges have wide discretion in how they recruit, manage, and organize their courtroom support staff.	**Merit** — Administrative and courtroom staff members are closely monitored and evaluated through regular and structured performance appraisals. Work related feedback, merit recruitment, and promotion are emphasized.

Change Management	**Negotiation** — Changes in court policies and procedures occur incrementally through judicial negotiation and agreement. In practice, procedures are seldom rigid, with actual application open to interpretation by semi-autonomous work teams of individual judges and corresponding court staff.	**Innovation** — Judges and court managers seek input from a varied set of individuals (e.g., judges, court staff, attorneys, and public) and measure court-user preferences concerning policy changes. Individual judges and administrative staff are encouraged to monitor court performance and to recommand necessary adjustment.	**Continuity** — Judges resist a rule and process-bound organizational setting. Centralized changes initiatives may be considered unfeasible because each judge exercises a wide scope of latitude in the choice of case-processing practices and judges are perceived to resist court wide monitoring.	**Modern Administration** — Judges and administrative staff seek cutting edge technology and modern administrative methods to support administrative procedures that reduce errors and enhance the timeliness of case processing and the accuracy of record keeping.
Courthouse Leadership	**Trust** — Judicial and administrative staff leaders seek to build personal relationships and confidence among all judges and court staff members; emphasize mutually agreed upon goals with staff members; and attempt to help all obtain satisfaction from work.	**Visionary** — Judicial and administrative staff leaders seek to build an integrated justice system community. All judges and court staff are asked to meet organizational performance goals that focus on results that matter to those served by the courts rather than simply those who run them.	**Independence** — Centralized court leadership is inhibited because judges prefer to work with few external controls. Each judge and corresponding courtroom staff members are concerned primarily with their own daily responsibilities and exhibit little interest in efforts aimed at improving court or system-wide performance.	**Standard Operating Procedures** — Judicial and administrative leaders rely on clearly established rules and directives—preferably in writing—to guide court operations. The system may appear impersonal given the emphasis on knowing and using the proper channels to get things done.
Internal Organization	**Collegiality** — Information on a wide variety of topics (e.g., caseflow, resources, personnel) is shared through informal channels reflecting personal relations among judges, administrative, and courtroom staff. Judges and court staff strive for consensus and to reconcile differences.	**Teamwork** — Judges and administors seek a shared court-wide view of what needs to be accomplished. This knowledge facilitates judges and court staff, drawing from different departments and divisions if necessary, to work collaboratively to perform case processing and administrative tasks.	**Sovereignty** — Courtroom practices reflect the policies and practices employed by individual and autonomous judges. Therefore, accepted practices are slow to change, stability and predictability are emphasized, and confrontation minimized.	**Chain of Command** — Explicit lines of authority among judges, administrative staff, and courtroom staff create a clear division of labor, and formalize expectations that judges and court staff will do the jobs that they are assigned.

comes to case *management style*, the matrix in Table 2-3 makes clear four approaches based on alternative values extant in the real world of court management: *Communal* courts emphasize *flexibility; networked* courts emphasize *judicial consensus; autonomous* courts emphasize *self-management; hierarchical* courts emphasize *clear rules*.

Archetypal court cultures are identified by reading down a single column of the matrix. For example, consider the values hypothesized to be espoused in the *networked culture*:

- Case Management Style: Judicial Consensus
- Judge–Staff Relations: People Development
- Change Management: Innovation
- Courthouse Leadership: Visionary
- Internal Organization: Teamwork

There is no expectation that any particular court will be characterized exclusively by the values of a single culture type. Rather, most courts will embrace, to a greater or lesser extent, all values comprising each culture across each of the five work areas. In the real world, court culture is a matter of emphasis and degree rather than perfect alignment.

The court culture value matrix represents a step on the path toward a stronger evidence-based and conceptually clearer understanding of the "way work gets done" in a trial court. Figure 2-3 provides a graphic summary of the key characteristics of each culture type.

A short overview of each culture type is provided to illustrate how the current conception of court culture conceives and distinguishes among alternative ways courts conduct and manage their business.

Communal: Judges and administrators emphasize the importance of getting along and acting collectively. Rather than established rules and firm lines of authority, communal courts emphasize the importance of group involvement and mutually agreed-upon goals. Flexibility is a key to management. Procedures are open to interpretation and creativity is encouraged when it seems important to "do the right thing." The court environment is best managed through teamwork and developing a humane work environment. Court customers are often viewed as partners when designing court policies and procedures.

Networked: Judges and administrators emphasize creativity and innovation. Efforts to build consensus on court policies and practices extend to involving other justice system partners, groups in the

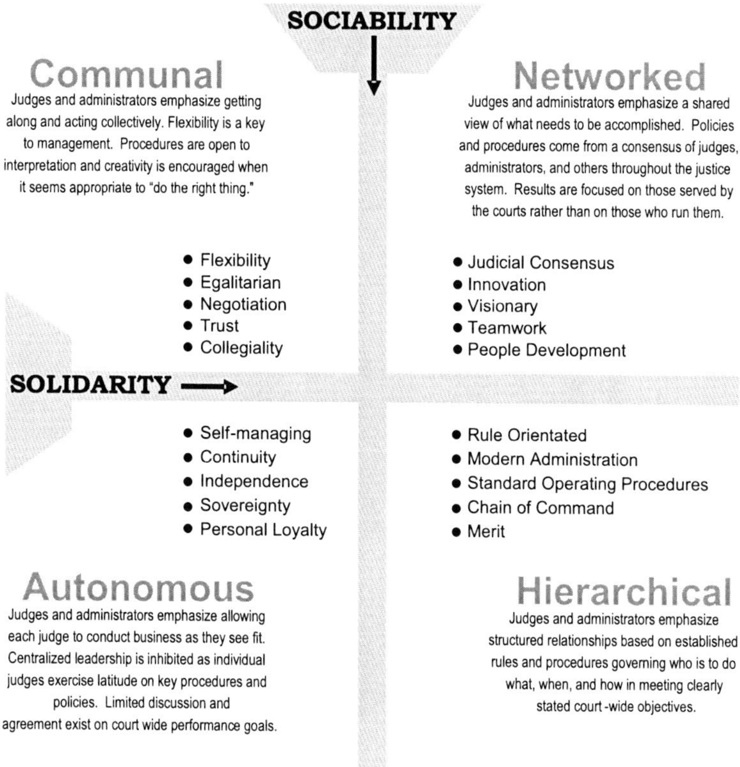

Fig 2.3 Narrative Summary of Four Court Cultures

community, and ideas emerging in society. As innovators, these courts will be drawn to incorporate the latest thinking in specialty courts, problem-solving courts, and therapeutic justice. Court leaders speak of courts being accountable for their performance, for the outcomes they achieve, not just the ways and means they use to achieve them. The networked court seeks a challenging and complex organizational structure that endeavors to achieve both high solidarity and high sociability in the choice and implementation of management practices.

Autonomous: Judges and administrators emphasize the importance of allowing each judge to conduct business as he or she sees fit. Many judges in this type of court are most comfortable with the traditional adversarial model of dispute resolution. Under this traditional approach, the judge is a relatively passive party who essentially referees investigations carried out by attorneys. Centralized leadership is inhibited as individual judges exercise latitude on key procedures and policies. Limited discussion and agreement exist on court-wide performance criteria and goals. It is not surprising that "judicial activism," or case management, has trouble catching hold in these courts.

Hierarchical: Judges and administrators emphasize the importance of established rules and procedures to meet clearly stated court-wide objectives. These courts seek to achieve the advantages of order and efficiency, which are deemed essential goals in a world of limited resources and calls for increased accountability. Effective leaders are good coordinators and organizers. The approach is to create a structured decision-making environment through the creation of rules, adoption of court technology, and a monitoring system to assess compliance. Recognized routines and timely information are viewed as mechanisms for reducing uncertainty, confusion, and conflict in how judges and court staff make decisions.

Summary

As practitioners and researchers know, courts are different from one another, and culture is thought to contribute to those differences. Yet culture's constituent parts have not been pinpointed. One likely reason is most notions of culture refer to (Cameron and Quinn 1999, p. 14):

> Taken-for-granted values, underlying assumptions, expectations, collective memories, and definitions present in an organization.... Unfortunately, people are unaware of their culture until it is challenged, until they experience a new culture, or until it is made overt and explicit through, for example, a framework or a model.

Quinn and his colleagues have made a considerable effort trying to establish the overall validity of their scheme. From their perspective, a framework must (1) resonate among the members of an organization, (2) be supported by an empirical literature, and (3) have a verified foundation.

To ensure that court culture makes sense to practitioners in the court world, the construction of a typology of cultural values begins with the judgments of seasoned judges, court administrators, attorneys, and scholars on how a comprehensive battery of values hang together. The purpose of the exercise was to determine what combinations of values tend to be held in common and what values tend to be contending. The values clustering together constitute the basis for distinct cultures. Because there are four separate sets of interrelated values, a fourfold court culture typology is proposed, including *communal*, *networked*, *autonomous*, and *hierarchical* cultures.

In addition, the court culture framework is similar to previous research. For example, the classification of cultures into four types resembles the effort of Nardulli et al. (1988) to distinguish three types of "work orientations." The examination of court culture across five areas of work, such as case management style and judge–staff relations, also resembles Ostrom and Hanson's (1999) effort to measure attorneys' views toward resources, performance, management, and practices and procedures.

Hence, the four culture types and five work areas of the current research build on previous studies. What is new and different is the effort made to identify the substantive meaning of culture. The values making up the *norms, beliefs, and attitudes* associated with each type of culture are specified. In addition, the identification of five work areas clarifies how each culture is manifested. Each type of cultural orientation is conceptualized as shaping case management, judicial-staff relations, change management, courthouse leadership, and internal organization. Developing a means to measure where courts in the real world fall within this framework is the subject of Chapter 3.

3 Measuring Court Culture

Introduction

Culture, a complex multifaceted concept, has achieved a position of prominence as a leading explanation for how organizations perform. Yet, despite the importance attached to culture, previous research in the area of trial courts has not developed a method for describing the similarities and differences in cultural orientations. As a result, discussions about the complexities and multiple facets of court culture are more descriptive than analytic. Practitioners and researchers alike might assert that a court's culture is manifested in particular ways and accounts for its performance in specific ways, but those assertions rest more on acute observations than on systematic measurement and empirical testing.

A methodology for identifying a court's culture requires a set of measures and tools to capture the multiple and complex configurations of views held by judges and administrators within and among several different jurisdictions and then map these views in an orderly manner into distinct conceptual categories. However, development of a set of quantitative yardsticks is likely to be controversial. Quinn and Spreitzer (1991, p. 116) offer the following observation on the need for a rigorous framework to examine organizational cultures comparatively:

> Studies of organizational culture have traditionally relied on qualitative methods such as in-depth, open-ended interviewing and ethnographic observation. The goal has been "thick description." However, the advantages of the qualitative approaches have been bought at a cost. In using qualitative approaches it is exceedingly difficult to make analytic comparisons across organizations. As a result, there are many important theoretical questions that cannot be answered until culture can be measured with a reliable, easily administered instrument that permits the systematic observation of organizational culture.

In concurrence with these sentiments, systematic quantitative measurement of culture is the path taken to address the questions guiding current research.

Court Culture Assessment Instrument

To measure culture, an instrument called the Organization Culture Assessment Instrument (OCAI), fully described in Cameron and Quinn (1999), is relied on.[1] Building upon the structure of the OCAI, we develop a Court Culture Assessment Instrument (CCAI) consisting of a five-part questionnaire. Each part of the questionnaire incorporates a particular row of the Court Culture Value Matrix, as shown in Appendix 3-1.

An underlying assumption behind the questionnaire is that each type of culture shapes work done in different areas. Consequently, each part of the questionnaire focuses on a specific work area (e.g., case management style) with four alternative statements describing how work gets done in a particular cultural orientation.

Respondents are asked to divide 100 points among the four statements, depending on how closely they think each proposition describes the situation in their court. In addition, individuals are asked to describe the relative correspondence between the four cultures and each work area "as of today" and "how they would like the court to be in five years." The former descriptions are referred to as a court's *current* culture type and the latter as the *preferred* culture type.

As an illustration, the *case management style* portion of the instrument is shown with hypothetical responses in Table 3-1. If assuming

TABLE 3-1. CASE MANAGEMENT STYLE

		Current	Preferred
I	There is general agreement on performance goals, but centralized judicial and administrative staff leadership is downplayed and creativity is encouraged. As a result, there are alternative acceptable ways for individual judges to apply court rules, policies, and procedures.	20	40
II	Judicial expectations concerning the timing of key procedural events come from a working policy built on the deliberate involvement and planning of the entire bench. Follow through on established goals is championed and encouraged by a presiding (or administrative) judge.	5	10
III	There is limited discussion and agreement on the importance of court-wide performance goals. Individual judges are relatively free to make their own determinations on when key procedural events are to be completed.	70	10
IV	Judges are committed to the use of case-flow management (e.g., early case control, case coordination, and firm trial dates) with the support of administrative and courtroom staff. Written court rules and procedures are applied uniformly by judges.	5	40
	Total	100	100

a respondent thinks alternative III is most similar to the current emphasis in their court, alternative I is somewhat similar, and alternatives II and IV are hardly similar at all, 70 points might be given to III, 20 points to I, and five each to II and IV.[2] No matter how the points are distributed, it is essential that the total is 100 points.[3]

Turning to the preferred emphasis, a respondent might feel that alternatives I and IV both should be emphasized highly in their court, whereas alternatives II and III should receive much less emphasis. To reflect these preferences, a respondent might give 40 points each to I and IV and 10 points each to II and III.

All judges with a criminal docket as well as the senior court administrators in each of the twelve courts were asked to complete the questionnaire.[4] The results are presented in the form of the average (mean) number of points each culture received on a particular work area across all respondents, as shown in Table 3-2. These mean values represent an important central tendency for each court on each culture type, with the standard deviation, median, and coefficient of variation for each of the means presented in Appendix 3-2.

TABLE 3-2. RELATIVE EMPHASIS ON CURRENT COURT CULTURE ON WORK AREAS

		California			Florida		Minnesota						
Content Dimension	**Culture Type**	Contra Costa	Napa	Ventura	Duval	Pinellas	Dakota	Hennepin	Kandiyohi	Olmsted	Ramsey	Duluth	Virginia
Case Management Style	*Communal*	14	14	17	28	29	28	20	29	30	20	32	31
	Networked	21	31	26	23	15	15	25	24	20	26	11	14
	Autonomous	32	19	25	34	37	35	27	21	20	20	36	23
	Hierarchical	33	36	31	16	19	22	28	25	30	35	22	33
Judge–Staff Relations	*Communal*	25	22	11	27	18	30	19	14	24	21	18	21
	Networked	26	33	40	31	35	27	20	36	34	32	35	26
	Autonomous	23	11	18	26	33	23	47	19	16	31	23	19
	Hierarchical	26	35	31	16	14	20	15	31	27	17	25	34
Change Management	*Communal*	25	25	18	27	33	37	25	26	35	28	31	32
	Networked	22	25	26	16	18	15	24	32	37	29	23	24
	Autonomous	32	11	10	30	23	28	31	16	10	17	34	15
	Hierarchical	22	39	46	27	28	20	20	25	18	27	13	29
Courthouse Leadership	*Communal*	24	39	40	33	18	32	21	38	37	29	31	39
	Networked	17	19	29	20	18	18	22	26	36	28	17	19
	Autonomous	35	16	17	26	49	32	36	24	11	29	43	17
	Hierarchical	24	26	14	21	15	18	21	11	17	14	10	24
Internal Organization	*Communal*	19	26	24	24	24	25	22	31	26	25	20	26
	Networked	22	31	36	22	18	19	23	34	32	25	30	26
	Autonomous	26	19	20	29	33	31	34	16	24	25	38	24
	Hierarchical	33	24	20	24	24	25	20	20	18	26	13	24
N = Judges		11	5	24	24	6	7	42	6	7	10	6	5
N = Senior Administrators		11	7	4	4	2	6	26	1	3	4	4	3
N = Total		22	12	28	28	8	13	68	7	10	14	10	8

Documenting Current Court Culture

CCAI Results

When comparing the relative cultural emphases across the courts, it is evident that considerable variation exists both within and between the courts. All courts show a nonnegligible presence of each of the four types of cultures, as seen by the fact no culture type receives less than 10 points. Conversely, no cultural category exceeds the 50-point threshold. In short, every court finds some resonance with each culture type. Given that no court has a single cultural orientation, the relative emphasis toward one or more of the quadrants is important to examine. As an example, consider Ramsey County where the average combined scores for judges and senior administrators on *case management style* reveal that the current cultural emphasis is high on the *solidarity* dimension. Out of a total of 100 points, Ramsey County has average scores of 20 for *autonomous* and 20 for *communal* (low *solidarity*), whereas they have average scores of 35 for *hierarchical* and 26 for *networked* (high *solidarity*). Turning to Ramsey County's scores for *judge–staff relations*, one finds a different picture. Out of a total of 100 points, Ramsey County has average scores of 31 for *autonomous* and 21 for *communal*, whereas they have average scores of 17 for *hierarchical* and 32 for *networked*. For this work area, there is a clear indication of "competing values"[5] in that judges want to be on their own yet be part of a well-functioning network. As a final example, Ramsey County's scores for *courthouse leadership* yields a different picture. In this work area, of a total of 100 points, Ramsey County has average scores of 29 for *autonomous* and 29 for *communal*, whereas they have average scores of 14 for *hierarchical* and 28 for *networked*. When it comes to *courthouse leadership*, the court clearly does not want a hierarchical chain of command. An examination of Table 3-2 shows that similar patterns can be found in many of the other courts.

Court Culture Kites

The complexity of the multiple combinations of points given to alternative cultural orientations makes it difficult to interpret relationships within and between courts. Given this problem in inferring patterns, Tufte argues for the graphic display of data. He writes "often the most effective way to describe, explore, and summarize a set of numbers—even a very large set—is to look at pictures of those numbers" (Tufte 1983, p. 1).

Cameron and Quinn (1999, p. 55), drawing upon the work of John Tukey (1977), also note that "insight and understanding is best created, not by submitting data to statistical tests, but by creating pictures of the data . . . It is possible to see more relationships, do more comparisons, and identify more interesting patterns by analyzing images and representations than by simply looking at the results of numerical analyses." Following their lead, visible representations of the average scores for each of the work areas are transformed into "culture kites." To construct a culture kite, it is first necessary to develop the appropriate type of culture "graph paper." Cameron and Quinn (1999, p. 59) suggest the format in Figure 3-1. The point values for each of the four culture types for a given work area are plotted on the axis. The axes—although

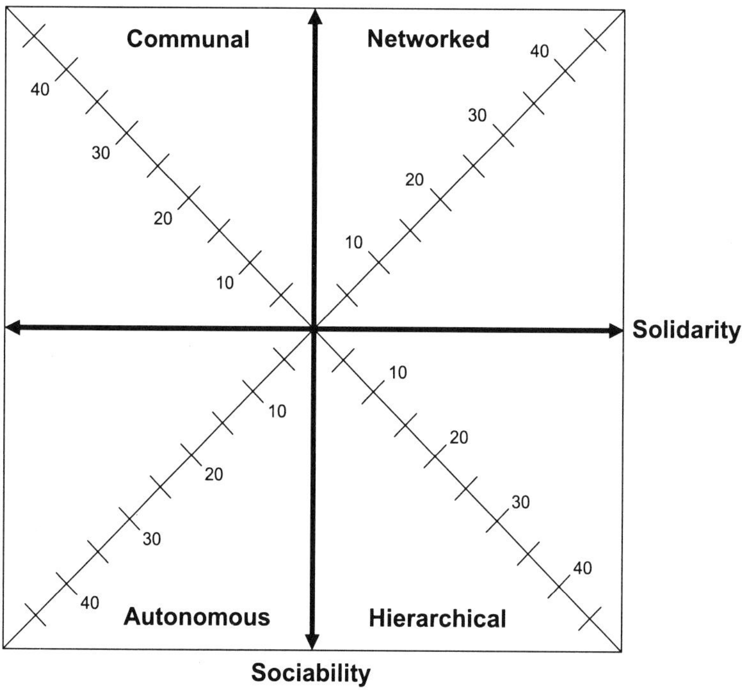

Fig 3.1 Court Culture Kite

perpendicular—run diagonally and are calibrated from 0 to 50 points. Once the points are determined, what remains is to connect the dots.[6]

To see more clearly the way in which a culture kite is built as well as to assess its efficacy in demonstrating the general cultural orientation of a court, a culture kite for *case management style* in Ramsey County is displayed in Figure 3-2. For Ramsey, the *case management style* culture kite takes its shape from average scores of 20 in *communal*, 26 in *networked*, 20 in *autonomous*, and 35 in *hierarchical*. The resultant figure provides a visual representation of a court's cultural profile. The filled-in shape bears a strong resemblance to a traditional child's kite (with the *hierarchical* quadrant serving as the kite's tail).

Examination of the basic shape of a *kite* makes sense of a court's culture. The primary cultural emphasis for *case management style* in Ramsey County falls in the *networked* and *hierarchical* culture types

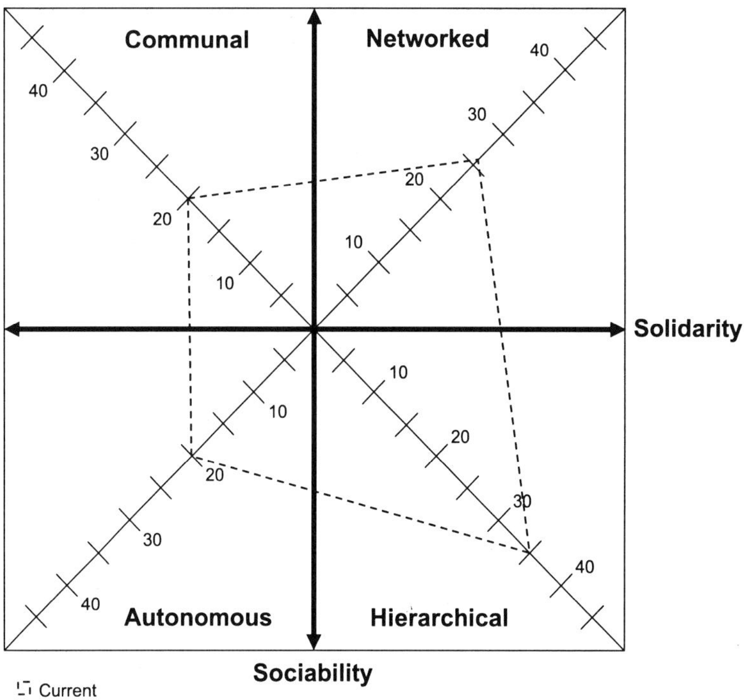

Fig 3.2 Case Management Style in Ramsey

because the corners of the kite that extend the farthest reflect the higher scores on the *networked* and *hierarchical* cultures, both high on the *solidarity* dimension. The *center of gravity* is clearly toward high *solidarity* and slightly toward low *sociability*.[7] In this way, the court culture kite diagrams provide a visualization of the court culture that goes beyond attaching a single label to a court's culture. Based on the kite diagram, Ramsey County court favors *solidarity* in general and a *hierarchical* culture in particular when it comes to *case management style*.

To gain some insight into the variation within a single court, it is instructive to look closely at two additional work areas. Figures 3-3 and 3-4 present the Ramsey culture kites for *judge–staff relations* and *courthouse leadership*, respectively. The figures indicate that there are multiple cultures at work in the Ramsey County courthouse.

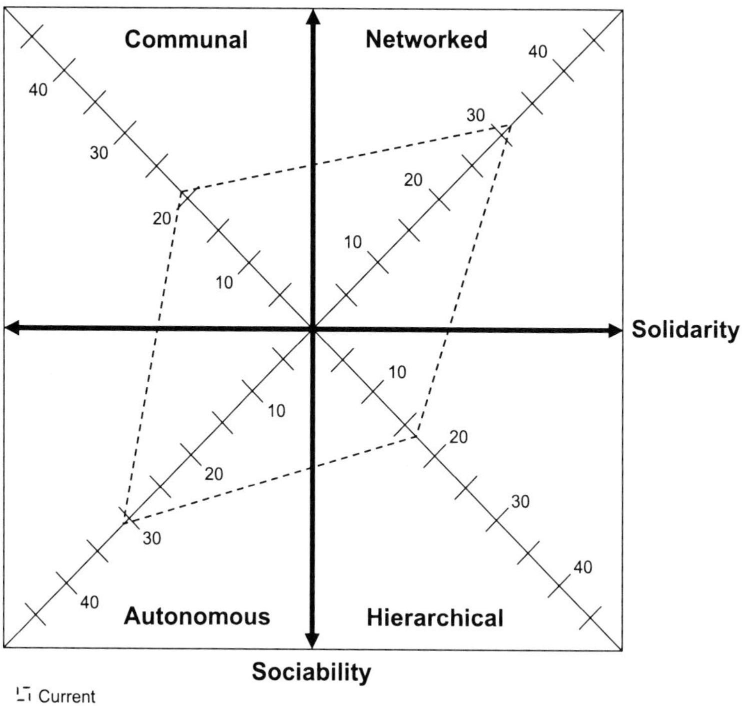

Fig 3.3 Judge-Staff Relations in Ramsey

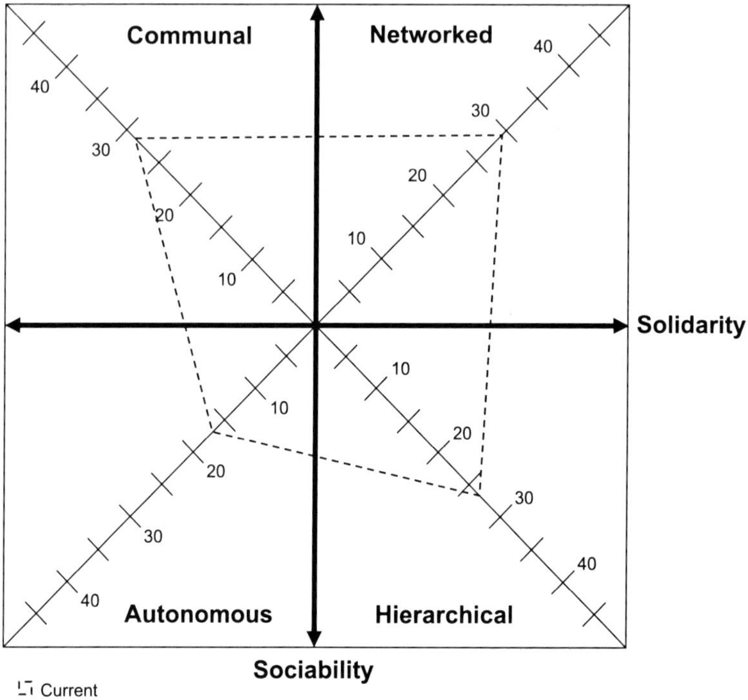

Fig 3.4 Courthouse Leadership in Ramsey

The culture kite for *judge–staff relations* (Figure 3-3) is different from that for *case management style* (Figure 3-2). Unlike the case management style figure, little emphasis is given to a *hierarchical* culture. Instead, there is a slight preference for an *autonomous* culture. Surprisingly, the polar opposite of *autonomous*—*networked*—has the second highest point value. This is an example of *competing values*. From a visual point of view, Cameron and Quinn (1999, p. 71) refer to this paradoxical shape as a "cigar."[8]

The culture kite for *courthouse leadership* in Ramsey County has a shape more like a trapezoid than a kite.[9] This shape is a result of the fact that the court gives almost equal weight to three of the four possible types of culture, as shown in Figure 3-4. The center of gravity is decidedly toward low *solidarity* and high *sociability*. In short, the *communal* category is the best description of the culture in this work area.

From examination of three of the five culture kites for Ramsey County, a metaphorical description is introduced to characterize variation among work areas. When one considers each of the filled-in kites as a *tile*, the combination of tiles across the five work areas creates a *mosaic*. When the five work areas are considered together, the resulting cultural mosaic provides a telling and readily understood means for viewing a court's cultural orientation.

Having examined Ramsey County's current culture in multiple work areas (and thereby obtaining the cultural mosaic), a fuller perspective is gained by looking at more courts across a common work area. To this end, culture kites for three additional courts—Olmsted, Ventura, and Pinellas Counties—are presented Figures 3-5, 3-6, and 3-7, respectively. (The entire set of culture kites for the twelve courts and five content dimensions is displayed on the National

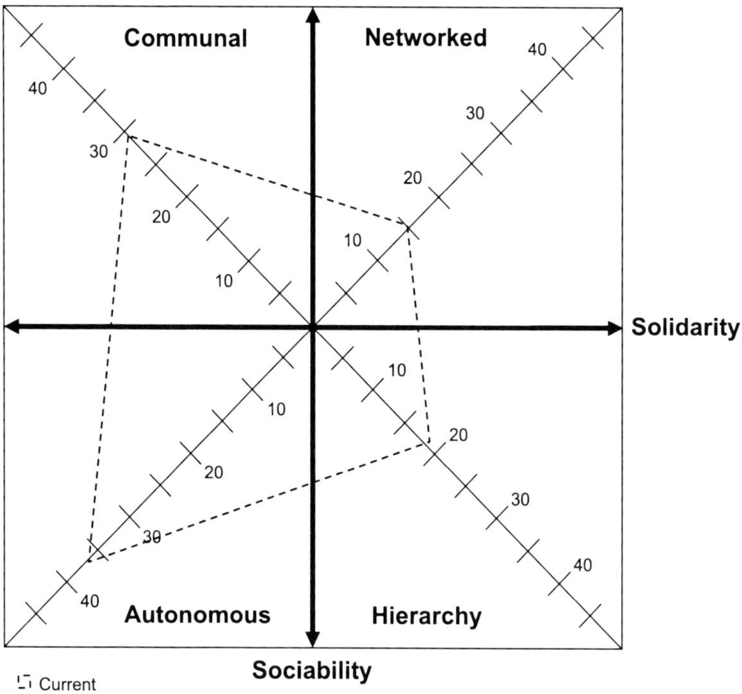

Fig 3.5 Case Management Style Pinellas (FL)

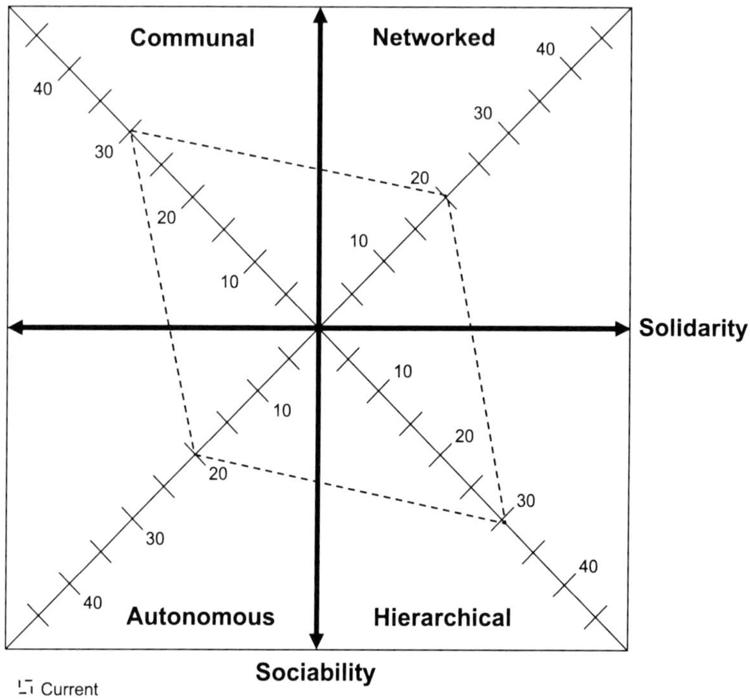

Fig 3.6 Case Management Style Olmsted (MN)

Center for State Courts web site: www.ncsconline.org/court culture.)

The *case management style* kite for the Pinellas County court in Figure 3-5. is shaped by average scores of 29 in *communal* and 37 in *autonomous* (both low on *solidarity*) as well as 15 in *networked* and 19 in *hierarchical* (both high on *solidarity*). When comparing Ramsey with Pinellas, note that the basic *kite* shapes are similar, although the *tail* is in the *autonomous* quadrant for Pinellas compared to the *hierarchical* quadrant for Ramsey. The Pinellas kite's center of gravity is in the low *solidarity* area and stands in stark contrast to that found in Ramsey.

Plotting the *case management style* scores from Table 3-2 for Olmsted (MN) yields the kite diagram in Figure 3-6. An examination of this kite shows that there is no clear center of gravity and hence no tendency toward high/low *solidarity/sociability*. This court emphasizes

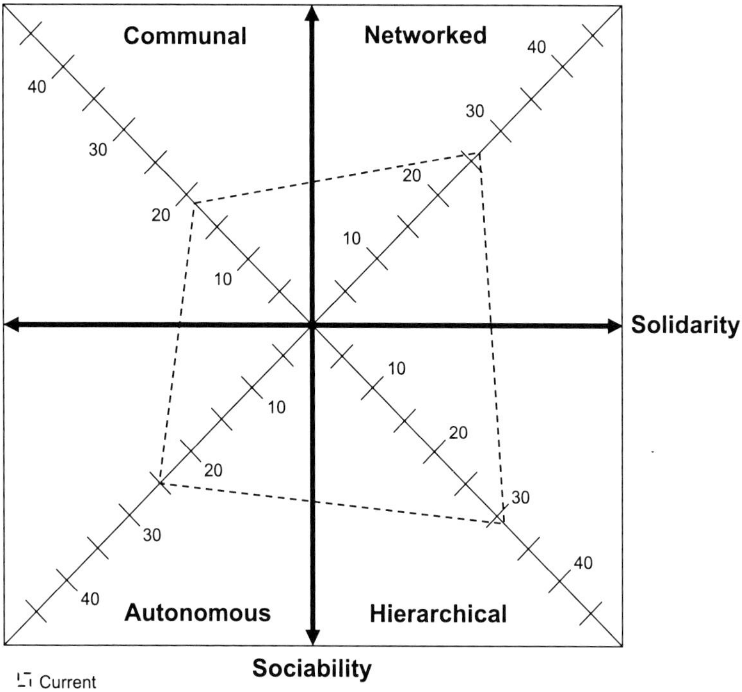

Fig 3.7 Case Management Style in Ventura (CA)

both *communal* and *hierarchical* values, reflected in the previously mentioned *cigar* shape.

Finally, in Figure 3-7, another picture emerges for the *case management style* kite in the Ventura (CA) court. Although there is faint suggestion of a *kite shape,* Ventura's kite looks more like a trapezoid because the judges and court administrators report that *autonomous*, *networked*, and *hierarchical* are approximately equal in emphasis, whereas *communal* is relatively low. The center of gravity is clearly toward the bottom right of the diagram. Culture kites illustrate how the complexities of numerical results are made more apparent and discernible through visual display.

Interpreting Culture Kites

Interpreting and making sense of the culture kites relies on a three-step approach: (1) determine the court's primary culture type as well as its overall strength, (2) inspect the *center of gravity* of the kite relative to the two dimensions of *solidarity* and *sociability*, and (3) assess cultural congruence.

Strength of Primary Culture

A court's primary culture type refers to the culture type that receives the highest average score. The primary culture types include examples of all of the four culture types, as seen in Table 3-3. Sixty primary cultural identifications exist for the twelve courts across the five dimensions: 19 are *autonomous*, 12 are *hierarchical*, 11 are *communal*, 14 are *networked*, and there are three ties. *Case management style* is predominantly *hierarchical* and *autonomous*, *judge–staff relations* is primarily *networked* and *hierarchical*, *courthouse leadership* is evenly divided between *autonomous* and *communal*, and *internal organization* is primarily *autonomous* and *networked*.

The strength of the primary culture is determined by the extent to which one culture dominates. Strength is important, as Cameron and Quinn (1999, p. 63) note: "Strong cultures are associated with homogeneity of effort, clear focus, and higher performance in environments where unity and common vision are required." The opposite of a strong culture profile is one that is diverse or eclectic. Although it is widely believed in the business world that strong cultures produce excellent performance, Kotter and Heskett (1992 p. 142) argue that strong, well-coordinated cultures must first be appropriately aligned with business needs to create high performance. "[A]lignment, motivation, organization, and control can help performance, but only if the resulting actions fit an intelligent business strategy for the specific environment in which a firm operates." Their research shows that "strong cultures with practices that do not fit a company's context can actually lead intelligent people to behave in ways that are destructive." Therefore, strength can have both positive and negative attributes. This insight is particularly relevant for courts for which achieving multiple goals, including timely case processing, access to the courts, and procedural fairness, may not be best accomplished through a single, strong cultural orientation. High performance within the different work areas will likely require different behaviors and methods of doing business.

In terms of current culture, the evidence suggests that the primary cultures in each of the twelve courts are not particularly well defined or strong. Almost all of the courts show at least 30 percent of the

TABLE 3-3. PRIMARY TYPE AND STRENGTH OF COURT CULTURE BY WORK AREAS

		Case Management Style		Judge–Staff Relations		Change Management		Courthouse Leadership		Internal Organization	
		Primary Culture	Strength	Primary Culture	Strength	Primary Culture	Strength	Primary Culture	Strength	Primary Culture	Strength
California	**Contra Costa**	H	33	N/H	26	A	32	A	35	H	33
	Napa	H	36	H	35	H	39	C	39	N	31
	Ventura	H	31	N	40	H	46	C	40	N	36
Florida	**Duval**	A	34	N	31	A	30	C	33	A	29
	Pinellas	A	37	N	35	C	33	A	49	A	33
Minnesota	**Dakota**	A	35	C	30	C	37	A	32	A	31
	Hennepin	H	28	A	47	A	31	A	36	A	34
	Kandiyohi	C	29	N	36	N	32	C	38	N	34
	Olmsted	H	31	N	34	N	37	C	37	N	32
	Ramsey	H	35	N	32	N	29	C/A	29	*	26
	Duluth	A	36	N	35	A	34	A	43	A	38
	Virginia	H	33	H	34	C	32	C	39	C/N	26

Note: C = Communal; N = Networked; A = Autonomous; H = Hierarchical.
* No primary culture.

total cultural emphasis in the principal culture category, yet seldom is there overriding dominance. For example, in Duval County, the strength of the *autonomous* culture in *case management style* is 34, the strength of the *networked* culture in *judge–staff relations* is 31, and the strength of the *communal* culture in *courthouse leadership* is 33. Duval has three different cultures, although none is particularly strong. Consequently, individual courts are an amalgam of cultural emphases, both within and across specific work areas. A fertile area for subsequent research is determining whether cultural diversity is the result of conscious choice or rather is due to the fact that courts have historically paid little attention to overall goals and direction.

The Center of Gravity

If there are two cultures of approximately equal weights, the kite shows whether the underlying values are complementary (e.g., high *solidarity*) or represent competing values. The more pronounced the cigar shape, the more the court is pursuing competing values. The center of cultural gravity provides insight into the nature of the management task in a given work area. The stronger a court's primary culture, the greater the likelihood that all court personnel are on the same page. As the culture becomes more diffuse, the extent to which the center of gravity moves away from the *origin* provides an indication of whether there is a tendency toward either high or low *solidarity/sociability*.

A comparison of the shapes of the kites in Figures 3-4 and 3-7 shows trapezoid-type shapes—without a strong primary culture—that are the mirror image of one another. *Courthouse leadership* in Ramsey leans toward low *solidarity*, whereas *case management style* in Ventura leans toward high *solidarity*. In contrast, the competing values of *communal* and *hierarchical* cultures exist in Olmsted and place the center of gravity between both *solidarity* and *sociability* dimensions (Figure 3-6).

Cultural Congruence

Congruence is the extent to which the same culture type is emphasized in all parts of the organization (i.e., across all work areas). None of the twelve courts has the same primary culture type across the five work areas, as shown in Table 3-3. Hennepin, and Duluth are the only courts that have the same dominant culture type in four of the five work areas, with Contra Costa and Hennepin being the only two courts to be consistently on the low end of the *sociability* dimension. Ramsey has traces of all four culture types in its five dimensions. The remaining courts have a mixture of at least two different culture types. For example, the judges and administrators in Kandiyohi emphasize the two culture types high on *sociability—communal* and *networked*. Dakota, on the other hand, is consistently on the low *solidarity* end of the spectrum, with its emphasis shifting between *autonomous* and *communal* culture types. Hence, limited consistent cultural congruence exists in the courts under study. Some courts, in fact, emphasize *competing values* indicating that their cultures may be working at cross purposes with themselves.

The degree of congruence is also an important variable. Duluth shows its cultures to be very congruent, whereas those in Ventura tend toward incongruence. In Duluth, the *autonomous* culture type is clearly in evidence across the five work areas. For the areas of *case management style*, *change management*, *courthouse leadership*, and *internal organization*, the emphasis placed on the *autonomous* culture is stronger than the other dimensions. It is only in the area of *judge–staff relations* that a different emphasis emerges. The dominance of the *autonomous* culture in Duluth indicates a strong culture, but one that may not be perfectly aligned with achieving the larger institutional goals of the court.

In Ventura, incongruence suggests this court has different goals and strategies that vary across the work areas. For example, judges and administrators stress *networked* for *judge–staff relations* (score of 40), *hierarchical* for *change management* (score of 46), and *communal* for *courthouse leadership* (score of 40). For some work areas they prefer values high on *solidarity* and for others values high on *sociability*. Ventura appears to be strongly incongruent.

The incongruence in current court cultures has two striking characteristics. One is the lack of uniformity. Incongruent cultures can still be similar if incongruent patterns are shared among courts. However, it is not the case that the courts have the same combination of orientations (e.g. *hierarchical*) in *case management style* and a contrasting culture (e.g., *communal*) in *courthouse leadership*. Second, and perhaps more importantly, is the absence of overwhelming dominance of any particular culture on any work area. For a work area, one culture may dominate, but the presence of other orientations indicates court cultures are an amalgam.

In private sector research on organizational culture, congruence is vital. Cameron and Quinn (1999, p. 64) suggest that:

> Congruent cultures, although not a prerequisite for success, are more typical of high performing organizations than incongruent cultures. Having all aspects of the organization clear about and focused on the same values and sharing the same assumptions simply eliminates many of the complications, disconnects, and obstacles that can get in the way of effective performance.

Although cultural incongruence may lead to "complications, disconnects, and obstacles" in the private sector, there is a suggestion that public sector organizations may not be able to choose congruence. In fact, James Q. Wilson (1989, p. 101), offers as a general hypothesis that "[m]any government agencies have multiple, competing cultures." If multiple cultures—in the form of the previously described cultural mosaic—are the hallmark of government agencies, it is important to characterize the range of differences within a single organization in an analytic and structured way. The CCAI provides a powerful foundation for characterizing the cultural incongruities in trial courts.

The amalgamation of different cultures in a single work area may threaten the ability of a court to articulate clear and comprehensible criteria on how work should be done, to obtain necessary agreement on policies, and to gain sufficient cooperation in applying policies and procedures. As Wilson (1989, p. 101) notes, "A major responsibility of an executive is not only... To infuse the organizations with value, it is also to discover a way by which different values (and the different cultures that espouse those values) can productively coexist." It is this fuzziness and lack of cultural coexistence that inhibits high performance. Hence, a question addressed in subsequent chapters is whether courts seek to minimize fuzziness when asked to reflect upon the cultures they would like to see in the future.

Overall Culture Type

An overall categorization of culture is necessary to compare and contrast courts in terms of their performance. As students of public organizations know, to relate culture to outcomes is no easy task. DiIulio (1989, p. 131) makes the following observation:

> Any serious effort to analyze the conditions under which public management matters to the actual quality of citizens' lives will be fraught with methodological, practical, and moral shortcomings. But unless the future of public management studies involves a deep and abiding concern with what ends particular public organizations ought to achieve and how to manage these organizations accordingly, the field will crumble into academic irrelevance.

In the remainder of this chapter, attention is focused on the formulation of a single characterization of each court. The overall culture type is a composite measure serving as a proxy for the "public management variable" suggested by DiIulio.

Although there are several possible strategies for assessing the similarity of cultural patterns across the twelve courts, the most promising uses the correlations between the twelve courts across the five work areas, as shown in Table 3-4. Once calculated, the correlations are used to locate each court in an overall *culture space* and determine similarity groupings among the twelve courts.[10]

Cultural similarities as well as dissimilarities exist within each of the three states. For example, in California, the Ventura and Napa courts have a correlation of 0.79 suggesting relative cultural similarity. The two courts from Florida have a statistically significant correlation of 0.56 suggesting a moderate degree of similarity. In Minnesota, the only statistically significant correlations are between the three smallest Minnesota courts: Kandiyohi, Olmsted, and Virginia. It is worth noting that Hennepin—the state's largest court—has a significant negative correlation with Virginia, the smallest court.

Turning to an examination of cross-state patterns, Napa and Ventura in California are positively correlated with Kandiyohi and Virginia in Minnesota. Pinellas in Florida is positively correlated with Hennepin and Duluth in Minnesota. Duval in Florida is positively correlated with Dakota in Minnesota. Finally, Ramsey in Minnesota is correlated with Ventura. On the other hand, Contra Costa has a significant negative correlation with Olmsted, whereas Napa has significant negative correlations with both Hennepin and Pinellas.

To provide a quantitative picture of the cultural relationships among courts, multidimensional scaling is employed to analyze the correlation matrix.[11] This approach has the advantage of using all of the data from the cultural assessment instrument by placing every court

TABLE 3-4. CORRELATION COEFFICIENTS BETWEEN THE AVERAGE CULTURAL SCORES

	California			Florida		Minnesota						
	Contra Costa	Napa	Ventura	Duval	Pinellas	Dakota	Hennepin	Kandiyohi	Olmsted	Ramsey	Duluth	Virginia
Contra Costa	1.000											
Napa	–0.067	1.000										
Ventura	–0.186	**0.790**	1.000									
Duval	0.134	–0.274	–0.076	1.000								
Pinellas	0.360	**–0.445**	–0.137	**0.560**	1.000							
Dakota	0.357	–0.327	–0.293	**0.771**	**0.634**	1.000						
Hennepin	0.326	**–0.582**	–0.359	0.192	**0.541**	0.184	1.000					
Kandiyohi	–0.314	**0.517**	**0.711**	–0.071	–0.046	–0.093	–0.362	1.000				
Olmsted	**–0.466**	0.420	**0.467**	–0.226	–0.310	–0.065	–0.435	**0.697**	1.000			
Ramsey	0.071	0.263	**0.450**	–0.081	0.254	–0.039	0.315	0.439	0.394	1.000		
Duluth	0.334	–0.330	–0.074	**0.505**	**0.680**	0.681	0.358	0.237	0.050	0.081	1.000	
Virginia	–0.158	**0.611**	**0.499**	–0.039	–0.183	0.178	**–0.489**	**0.522**	**0.579**	0.116	0.082	1.000

Correlation coefficients $p < .05$ (2-tailed) in bold.

into a common and complete culture space. Each court is observable as to where it is relative to other courts in terms of its similarities and differences across all of the five work areas of trial court culture, as shown in Figure 3-8.

There are two or more courts in each of the four quadrants, as shown in Figure 3-8. To maintain consistency, the four quadrants are identified using the four existing cultural orientations. Three courts, Kandiyohi, Olmsted, and Virginia, are in the upper left hand corner and labeled as having a *communal* culture. Three courts, Napa, Ventura, and Ramsey, are high on both dimensions and these courts are labeled *networked*. Four courts, Dakota, Duluth, Duval, and Pinellas, are labeled as *autonomous* because they are low on both dimensions. Finally, there are two *hierarchical* courts, Contra Costa and Hennepin, high on *solidarity* and low on *sociability*.

When comparing the relative position of the courts in culture space it is evident that *location* is consistent for the most part with the average culture type scores in Table 3-2. The four courts labeled *autonomous* are indeed autonomous. This is largely true for the *communal* and *networked* courts. Contra Costa tends to be *hierarchical*. Conversely, Hennepin is not a clear case of a *hierarchical* culture. However, when

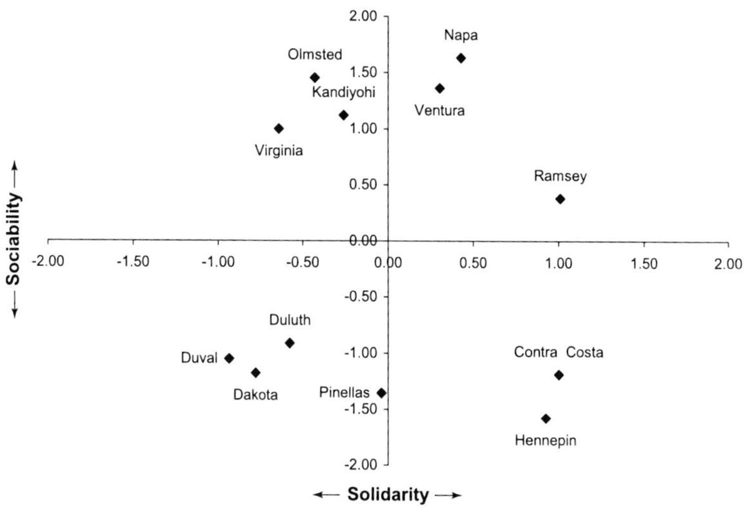

Fig 3.8 Culture Types for the Twelve Courts

taking all aspects of its culture profile into account, it is more accurate to say Hennepin is relatively more *hierarchical* than the other courts, with the exception of Contra Costa. Hence, there are four groupings of courts based upon the similarity/dissimilarity of their cultural profiles across the five work areas.

Although size has not explicitly been introduced into the characterization of court culture, size of the trial court appears to affect the position of trial courts on the *sociability* dimension. For example, all of the courts in the *communal* quadrant are small. Furthermore, it appears that larger courts tend to be lower on the *sociability* dimension. The relationship between size and *sociability* is not ironclad, however, as Duluth is a small court with low *sociability* and Ventura is a relatively large court that is high on *sociability*. Future research might investigate further the relationship between court culture and court size on the dimension of *sociability*.

These results demonstrate that American trial courts are not all of one type, contrary to the received tradition that courts are *autonomous*. Courts are often characterized as decentralized, fragmented, and populated by judges who chafe under administrative control. Although there is a considerable degree of autonomy in some areas of every court, the conventional wisdom fails to be supported by systematic data.[12]

Summary

To bring greater precision and evidence to the discussion of court culture, instruments have been adapted from private sector organizational studies. The result, the CCAI, captures the views of judges and administrators on how they see their court operating in five key work areas: (1) *case management style*, (2) *judge–staff relations*, (3) *change management*, (4) *courthouse leadership*, and (5) *internal organization*. Results obtained from administrating the CCAI in the twelve courts are presented graphically in the form of culture kites. These diagrams show the strength, center of gravity, and congruence of court culture across the five work areas.

The significance of these findings is twofold. First, the conventional wisdom and scholarly literature asserting that American trial courts possess primarily *autonomous* cultures are not supported by the data from the twelve courts. All of the courts have an *autonomous* culture in some respect, but none of the courts fall completely and uniformly into that camp. Consequently, the information gathered through structured, rather than descriptive, cultural assessments is likely to be a valid and reliable basis for court improvement, since it enables one to move beyond the traditional notions of courts as strictly autonomous bodies.

Second, the fact that in most courts different cultures are strong on different areas of work is striking, unexpected, and divergent with the theory and reality of private sector cultures, where congruency is found to be essential for organizational effectiveness. In the well-managed business, one culture tends to dominate all areas of work, although the predominant culture might vary from organization to organization. Building upon insights from James Q. Wilson, public organizations may not have the luxury of a single culture and instead face multiple and often competing cultures. If incongruence is a fact of life in public organizations such as trial courts, it underscores the challenging nature of leadership facing presiding judges and court administrators and helps to explain why court reforms are difficult to put into place.

In addition to documenting the multifaceted nature of the cultural mosaic in courts, an overall culture type is developed in response to DiIulio's search for the public management variable. This variable separates the twelve courts into similarity groups with respect to the complexities and nuances found in the cultural mosaic. As such, the overall culture type designation provides a firm foundation to test the hypothesis that patterns of culture across the five work areas affects performance.

In anticipation of assessing the effect of culture on performance, the four culture types are first described and illustrated in greater detail in Chapter 4.

4 Elaborating the Four Cultures

Introduction

In the previous and subsequent chapters, *quantitative* data are used to measure and diagnose culture in the former and assess the impact of culture on performance in the latter. This chapter takes a *qualitative* approach through extensive and structured conversations with judges, senior court administrators, and attorneys during twenty-three on-site visits to the twelve courts. Each site was visited by at least two members of the research team. A detailed list of over 150 judges, administrators, prosecutors, and defense attorneys who participated in the interview process is found in Appendix 4-1.

A battery of questions was used in interviews of judicial and administrative leaders as well as key officials in the prosecution and public defender offices to gain an understanding of the felony adjudication process in each location.[1] The general protocol for the in-person interviews is presented in Appendix 4-2. The specific interview questions solicited information on the basic steps in the criminal trial court process from arrest to case resolution. Because the felony process was clarified in each court, each interviewee was encouraged to discuss their views on why business was conducted in a particular fashion and their thoughts on the strengths and weaknesses of current practice.

At the end, the interview probed interagency communication and cooperation.

An important finding from the interviews is that judges, administrators, and attorneys are aware of distinctive patterns to "the ways things are done" in their court—whether or not they use the term *culture*. The respondents were eager to tell the story of how the culture in their court came to be as well as to offer insights into why it exists. A second important finding is that the *stories* and *perspectives* reflected—to a great degree—the basic principles of the underlying four culture types. When viewed through the lens of respondents' particular culture type, their responses made "cultural sense." In fact, the four culture types underscore different conceptions of management in courts. What should judges be engaged in to promote the resolution of cases? Should the judiciary keep to its traditional role as impartial decision makers on questions of fact and law? To what degree should court administrators bear the responsibilities of managing court caseloads? The four cultures reflect different answers to these essential questions about the adjudicative tasks of judges and administrative management of the work setting. Hence, the qualitative data help to amplify the conceptual framework.

With use of the information gathered during the interview process as well as citing literature from earlier court studies, the aim of this chapter is to make the four cultural archetypes vivid, convincing, and familiar by detailing the ways—both positive and negative—that culture shapes the way the work of the court is done. To achieve these ends, the nature of *communal, networked, autonomous, and hierarchical* courts is discussed in terms of the roles of court administrator and judge along with the ways in which culture plays out in dominant *case management style, judge–staff relations, change management, courthouse leadership*, and *internal organization*. Emphasis is given to the attributes most closely associated with each culture type as if a court were to operate exclusively and coherently in one of the four archetypes.

Communal Courts

In a *communal* court, collegial decision-making is highly valued. Egalitarian principles lead the participants to seek the resolution of complex problems (e.g., rehabilitation of youthful offenders) through communication, cooperation, and compromise. What is striking in a *communal* court is the value placed on teamwork. In addition, as an empirical observation, these courts tend to be relatively small. Therefore, the typical *communal* court is relatively small, exhibits a strong sense of community, and builds trust based upon familiarity. The goal of local consensus leads to the avoidance of strict adherence to externally imposed standards or criteria.

Primary Roles

Court Administrator. The court administrator in a *communal* court is seen as part of the management team, in that judges want to use the advantages of the administrator's tools (e.g., expertise in technology) where appropriate. Yet, limited interest among the judges in the tools of case management or establishment of clear staff routines may frustrate a court administrator who is interested in reform. As a result, the court administrator is tied closely to the judges in terms of working relationships, but expectations for the administrator's position do not revolve around the successful implementation of structure and rules.

Judge. The emphasis is on collegial decision making. Judges expect their colleagues to work together to achieve reforms, although the ultimate result might only be a proximate solution (Caldeira 1977, pp. 168–170). The *communal* court's culture is based on a commitment to common goals and the extension of that commitment to the idea of teamwork. Each judge has his or her own position, but judges are members of an organization, whose goals they hold jointly and believe they can achieve only by acting in concert. What is striking is the emphasis on teamwork, not just the goal of resolving legal policy problems.

Case Management Style

In the arena of *case management style* there is a common desire to meet a somewhat looser version of national time standards. For example, all judges might seek to resolve at least 75 percent of their criminal cases within 180 days after arrest (rather than the American Bar Association [ABA] standard of 98 percent in 180 days). As one *communal* court judge put it, "the mechanical idea of efficiency doesn't work here. We want cases resolved, but also give them the time they need."

One powerful and fundamental norm surfaced during interviews in *communal* courts is that the primary job of a judge is to ensure that attorneys are prepared. Judges interviewed agreed that attorneys are to be ready and able to negotiate at successive pretrial conferences and to go to trial only when negotiations have reached the point of diminishing returns. Yet, judges in these courts tend to remain relatively hands-off in the settlement process. They trust the attorneys to cooperate appropriately and "get it right." In fact, an attorney from a *communal* court observed "if there are issues during pretrial conference, the judge sends the lawyers into the hall to resolve them." The relatively small size of *communal* courts allows judges to use more informal methods to communicate and promote attorney preparation.

The *communal* court commitment to timeliness is counterbalanced by the recognition—given the relative low attachment to *solidarity*—that each judge is in the position to design and execute the way timeliness is achieved. However, judges are not completely autonomous, as a sense of trust exists among the judges that their colleagues are likewise pursuing timeliness. This theme was concisely expressed by one communal court judge who said, "Everyone knows they have a job to do," and "the only way to get it done is through teamwork."

Given the low level of *solidarity*, *communal* courts do not make the measurement of case-processing time a high priority; consequently, judges may overestimate their actual level of performance. If judges tell each other they are working to achieve timeliness, these claims have credibility based upon trust. Every judge is assumed to be a diligent, well prepared team player. As a result, verbal assertions that cases are being resolved expeditiously might mask serious deficiencies in the points of view of other participants. This concern was summarized succinctly by one public defender who noted that in his *communal* court, "no one takes the schedule seriously," "continuances are inevitable," and trial date certainty is "historically unlikely."

Judge–Staff Relations

The design and maintenance of relationships of authority as well as the development and training of the entire workforce is the essence of *judge–staff relations*. As such, the focus is on the procedures and criteria used for directing, monitoring, evaluating, and motivating court staff, as well as career development. The hallmark of the *communal* culture is egalitarianism, where there is an effort to limit the psychological distance between judges, administrators, and staff. Although there are rules and procedures in the *communal* court, staff are encouraged to do what it takes to get the job done, even if it means improvising.

Communal court cultures often lack monitoring mechanisms and may overlook problems for an unnecessarily long period of time. This type of court culture depends on each judge and staff member fulfilling his or her commitment to court-wide goals. The approach to improvement emphasizes informal persuasion and personal relationships by persons committed to the reform goals and willing to be active. Because limited centralized leadership exists, performance assessments are episodic. And the failure to regularly assess performance will lead some to view this type of court as too self-satisfied for contemporary times. On the downside, the emphasis on *sociability* makes it difficult to reign in personnel problems. Friendship is valued and formal authority is eschewed. Consequently, it is often hard to change nonproductive behaviors.

Change Management

A *communal* court does not search continuously for new modes of case resolution or ways to expand traditional court services. Before changes are made, consensus on the bench is required. Mobilization of agreement takes time, but once new ideas are accepted, they become well integrated into the ongoing system with an increased likelihood of success. As an illustration, in one *communal* court both judges and court administrators remarked on the length of time from when the idea of creating a drug court first arose until its adoption seven to eight years later. Neither group viewed this time-frame in any negative sense. Rather, they seemed to accept it as the natural consequence of all of the participants having to agree on exactly what set of drug offense cases are suitable for specialized handling (defendants needing treatment) and which ones warrant traditional felony prosecution (sellers of drugs).

Communal courts make only a modest investment in research and development capacity to refine policies or to look to the outside for new ideas on how to better render court services. A *communal* court might become overly content with its methods because judges and staff are presumed to be getting the job done and done well. Therefore, a *communal* court may ignore problems and resist self-improvement on a continuing basis. For example, differentiating calendars according to the seriousness of the offenses might be superior to placing all cases on the same track even without a crisis of rising caseloads and shrinking resources. Yet, a *communal* culture will likely be slow to realize the intrinsic benefits of special calendars as well as other opportunities for efficiency.

Courthouse Leadership

In *communal* courts, the formal positions of the presiding judge and court administrator have limited authority. However, judges are likely to be friends and graduates of the same law school in many instances. Because of the personal nature of the bonds, considerable trust exists among the members of the court. When individuals join the court, active mentoring is the policy. Hence, whereas *communal* courts might aspire to the highest performance goals, formal criteria may not be elaborated. As one judge remarked concerning his court's light touch on continuance policies, "Judges are active but not overbearing."

The limited amount of formal authority and the limited extent of standardized criteria constrain the presiding judge and court administrator and may lead to problems. Judges are not trouble-shooters and certainly not overseers exercising supervisory control. Because administrative management tends to be an unwanted chore, it is handled as little as possible or simply ignored. As a result, when judges or court staff encounter difficulties, they must take initiative to surface the problem themselves. Until they do, the difficulties and problems might remain relatively unnoticed.

Internal Organization

The team approach in the *case management* sector has its parallel in the arena of *internal organization*. Judges and staff are allies in a partnership designed to make the court run smoothly. Senior staff are regarded as essential aids in all phases of court operations, although a court administrator's charge is judicially determined. Court managers in a *communal* court enjoy an environment in which they are treated as equals with judges, at least when they are on assignment to help complete a task in line with judicial goals and guidelines (e.g., determining the costs and benefits of closed-circuit television to conduct arraignments). In those situations, senior staff are not concerned about being second-guessed.

A potential disadvantage of the *communal* culture type is the minimal independence of the court administrator. Many court management experts stress that the effective manager is one who demands to be held accountable and responsible on terms he or she defines (Gallas 1987; Saari 1982). In contrast, administrators in *communal* courts serve the judiciary in a constrained fashion and might not be expected to provide input and advice. Consequently, a considerable lag might exist before problems are brought to the attention of the bench (e.g., an increasing backlog).

Networked Courts

A *networked* court emphasizes creativity and innovation. It places value on its external relations with other organizations in the justice system, groups in the community, and ideas emerging in society.[2] As innovators, *networked* courts incorporate the latest thinking in specialty courts, problem-solving courts, and therapeutic justice. Coupled with an interest in other reform efforts such as case management and alternative dispute resolution, these courts perceive a benefit in creating a menu of procedural alternatives that allow the parties and the court to customize dispute resolution to fit each case. Consequently, the *networked* court creates a challenging and complex organizational structure that endeavors to achieve both high *solidarity* and high *sociability* in the choice and implementation of management practices.

The *networked* court is engaged in the simultaneous pursuit of multiple short- and long-range objectives to meet its goal of greater effectiveness. One court, for example, was seeking to build external support for a drug court, developing better management reports in an effort to reduce continuances, actively participating on a statewide committee to improve the court budget process, and implementing a more comprehensive employee evaluation program, among other initiatives.

Primary Roles

Court Administrator. In a *networked* court, the administrator is viewed as a middleman between the judges and the court's environment, with a wide breadth of outreach responsibilities (Butler 1977, p. 190; Stott 1982, p. 158). With this strategy, the court administrator is actively engaged in finding the right level of planning, control, and feedback to optimize relations both within the court and between the court and the larger justice system community. Because relations with the outside world often require skills, training, and knowledge unrelated to the duties of adjudicating cases, an administrator in a *networked* court might rise to statewide or national prominence without posing a challenge to the judiciary's sense of pride, professionalism, or power.

Judge. Judicial leaders in a *networked* court monitor the outside environment, identify important trends, and are not reluctant to try new ways of doing business. Therefore, these courts are among the first to experiment with specialized dockets, such as a drug court, family court, or domestic violence court, where sanction options include treatment as well as incarceration. Here a judge is looking beyond the legal issues in a case and focusing on the social conditions out of which controversies arise. This socially involved role can take judges well beyond their customary responsibilities. Tobin (1999, p. 224) notes that although judges are traditionally seen as neutral arbiters, "many people now appearing before a judge are seeking a protector, healer or advocate not a detached referee." The therapeutic justice movement leads judges to play a much different role than played by the traditional adjudicator.

Case Management Style

The *case management style* in the *networked* court is negotiated through give and take discussions involving all judges (e.g., setting of time deadlines for guilty pleas to be accepted prior to trial). In addition, the views of justice system partners are sought. As one judge in a *networked* court said:

> Because our caseflow management plan was reached by consensus with our DA and PD, we overcame many predictable

> obstacles before they surfaced. We explained the logic of case management and convinced the DA and PD that efficiency would reduce caseload; they came to realize their caseloads corresponded to the life of their cases.

Once a policy is promulgated, the responsibility for implementation shifts to the presiding judge and court administrator.

Judges interviewed in the *networked* courts under study understand the importance of timeliness. In collaboration with the court administrator, all spoke of efforts to improve the efficiency of case processing. Many acknowledged the need to revamp current practice in their own courts, with many judges conversant in the latest thinking on case-flow management. A central theme in the *networked* courts was control of continuances. One court uses a mandatory readiness conference scheduled one week before the trial date to facilitate and encourage pleas. A judge in this *networked* court observed that this conference is viewed by the prosecution and defense as the "last, best chance to resolve the case without trial," with the judge tough on continuances after the conference concludes. The management team in this court has worked hard to build cooperation between the civil and criminal divisions so that sufficient judges are available to conduct all criminal trials scheduled. As the court administrator puts it, "There is always an open port for every ship—trials will go as scheduled."

A potential stumbling block of the *networked* court is follow-through. Some judges whose views are not similar to those of the majority might continue their past practices (e.g., automatically granting all stipulated requests for extensions of time), with the result that case-flow management plans fail. Another test for case management in the *networked* court comes from the acknowledged interest in decreasing the role and importance of formal decision making (adversarial model) and increasing the use of more discretionary, problem-solving approaches to decisions. The therapeutic model puts greater emphasis on individualized outcomes, making attention to established timeframes secondary. As a result, case management plans might not live up to their potential.

Judge–Staff Relations

In the area of *judge–staff relations*, there is a strong human relations focus. The court promotes a diverse workforce and works to increase the professionalism of its staff. The *networked* court seeks clear procedures as well as close and professional supervision of all staff. With an emphasis on staff development, court personnel will move into positions of increasing responsibility as they gain experience. A culture of regular performance evaluations as well as training opportunities will be supported.

Given the professionalism of the relations, the *networked* court may experience relatively high turnover rates at the entry level positions as the skilled employees move into other court positions of increasing responsibility. In addition, the staff will not view themselves as working directly for the judge but rather for the supervisor. This may lead to situations where judges and their courtroom staff are not particularly synchronized.

Change Management

The manner in which a *networked* culture effects case management has its parallel in the *change management* arena. Ongoing concern for good working relationships with other justice agencies, receptivity to ideas and groups in the local community, and attention to initiatives coming from the state's administrative office are prominent values. Judges have the responsibility of serving their customers. For example, the presiding judge and court administrator may direct outreach efforts toward groups believed to warrant special and dedicated attention, such as abused children and drunk-driving victims and their families. They are more likely to have elder abuse and criminal mediation centers. As another example, two *networked* courts studied are located in California, a state that has just recently unified its court structure and adopted state funding of the trial courts. Both courts moved early to embrace consolidation and have actively participated in state policy committees that are working through the details of state funding. The rationale for this active involvement was neatly summed up by one court administrator who noted, "the second rule of revolution is to exploit the inevitable."

A potential pitfall arises because the *networked* court might be too willing to try new ideas. The court may be overly optimistic with the ease innovations can be introduced and maintained. Success in this endeavor requires a change in court policy actually being accompanied by a direct, consistent change in the policies and practices of the other justice agencies. As a result, the *networked* court might have a spotty history of reform with several instances of planned changes not taking hold because of a lack of prepared and adequate responsiveness to problems that should have been anticipated.

Courthouse Leadership

The *networked* court is active in building effective internal relations among the judges as a means to better connect with the major institutional offices, the bar, and the public. In the *networked* courts examined, judge meetings are held at least monthly, if not weekly. Once issues are identified, the court can take the lead on their resolution. For example, the presiding judge in one *networked* court discussed the benefits of sustained coordination between the court, prosecution, public defense, sheriff, and probation on criminal-case scheduling practices. "The pay-off for the court is that the judges are far less frustrated; schedules are now coordinated, dockets run more smoothly making court hours more productive with a lot less waiting around."

A possible pitfall for a *networked* court is that the broad spectrum of interests being served might steer the presiding judge and court administrator to focus excessively on particular segments of the caseload and fail to monitor overall court performance. They might lose interest, energy, or both in devoting the considerable effort necessary to support a coherent set of overall criteria, if consumed by the intricacies of special problem areas. Another leadership issue relates to the ability of judges to effectively implement a full menu of procedural alternatives to best meet the individual needs of defendants coming before the court. Critics may question whether courts have "the manpower, the talent, the tools or the authority" to be not just "dispute resolvers" but "problem solvers—the handymen of our society" (Dubois 1982, p. 4).

Internal Organization

Networked courts combine the advantages of democratic decision making with focused leadership on implementation of agreed-upon policies. Underlying values are mutual respect and an inclusive approach to decision making, with a goal of building a stronger and a more just court system. During the planning phase of any specific initiative, the required communication process creates extensive time commitments. Of utmost importance to success in a *networked* court is a strong and highly personal alignment between the presiding judge and the court administrator.

It is easy for the *networked* court to become overextended and lose focus. A court trying to excel in so many ways may fail to achieve excellence in any single area. Another potential pitfall arises with a change in presiding judge. Even an experienced court administrator might find it difficult to adapt to the style and expectations of the new court leader. Consequently, changes in judicial leadership sometimes create transitional challenges. In addition, a *networked* court often ascribes to ambitious goals in the workplace involving teamwork, clear paths of professional development, and commitment to treating all staff with courtesy and respect. Making these aspirations a reality requires a very effective leadership team and good relations between management and staff. High staff expectations place steep demands on management for consistent follow-through and problem solving.

Autonomous Courts

The *autonomous* court is characterized by the judicial preference for limited administrative controls. The judges in the *autonomous* court are comfortable with the traditional adversarial model of dispute resolution where the judge referees investigations carried out by attorneys. Prosecutors and defense attorneys have broad leeway in setting the pace of proceedings, with ample pretrial time to investigate and prepare arguments. It is not surprising that *judicial activism*, or case management, has trouble catching hold in these courts.

Primary Roles

Court Administrator. Responsibilities of the court administrator in this type of court are likely to be circumscribed to more operational areas such as finance, space, equipment, and technology (Butler 1977, p. 189). Assisting judges with case management is likely a minimal part of the administrator's portfolio. Resnick (1982) argues strongly against the advent of "managerial judges" and the accompanying loss of judicial restraint. Opponents of case management fear that active participation by the judge in a proceeding increases the likelihood of partiality. Further, judicial management is said to produce decisions less visible and more difficult to review. Finally, they believe that such an approach "may teach judges to value statistics, such as quantity of pretrial dispositions more than quality" (Bohlman and Bohlman, 1994, p. 238).

Judge. The *autonomous* culture aspires to be a model of individual justice. In *autonomous* courts, judges are in the position of bringing their skills, knowledge, and experience to bear in deciding substantive issues, free of outside pressures. Law is a tradition-bound profession, and evidence compiled by scholars indicates the *autonomous* role is substantial. Reviews of judicial attitudes find that many judges see their primary responsibilities as making decisions in adherence with precedent, exercising considerable restraint in interpreting the law, balancing contending legal principles, and pursuing truth and seeking justice in individual cases. In pursuit of these fundamental goals, some judges will see administrative controls as usurping their prerogatives and threatening the independence of substantive judicial decision-making. A defining characteristic of the *autonomous* court is that there is little agreement among judges on the relative merit of many procedural alternatives. In this type of court, judges who are interested in exerting firmer control over the process will likely confront colleagues who view many pretrial decisions as having "large doses of the uncontrolled discretion that marks 'management'" (Yeazell 1994, p. 673). Reformers face a daunting task to the extent change is seen as part of a movement to trade justice for speed and efficiency.

Case Management Style

Case management does exist; however, each judge is free to choose the best application of procedural rules governing the litigation process (e.g., when discovery should be completed, how many continuances should be granted). Choice is shaped by each judge's individual perspective on the correct steps to take in each case rather than established court-wide rules. Because each judge controls his or her own courtroom, it is possible for an *autonomous* court to be expeditious if each judge learns how to handle cases efficiently. Talented judges can devise their own best practices.

Contextual factors are influential in how well this type of court performs. In the *autonomous* courts examined, individual judicial calendars are the norm and both prosecutors and public defenders use vertical representation.[3] Attorneys, moreover, handle their cases generally before the same judge where the same attorney opposes them. Because a public defender's office handles criminal defense work in all the courts, the number of criminal defense attorneys is smaller and these attorneys are more experienced, on average, than if criminal defense work was handled on an assigned basis. The presence of the same opposing attorneys in their respective courtrooms is what prompted one judge from an *autonomous* court to say, "We have a cohesive bar. Everyone knows everyone." Judges and attorneys are not all friends, but the repeat appearance of the same professional participants produces a mutual understanding and trust. For example, a prosecutor in one *autonomous* court commented, "You see the same attorneys over and over again so everyone knows the rules of the game." A public defender in the same *autonomous* court echoed these sentiments by noting of the prosecutors "their word is their bond." Continuing relationships are a key source of credibility in an *autonomous* culture.

An *autonomous* court might be a conglomerate of decision-making styles ranging from orderly and expeditious to disorganized and slow. Because the judges have no tradition of regular meetings or other systematic communication on matters of court policy, there is no machinery, occasion, or opportunity for the court to agree on and enforce policies that might improve matters. One judge in an *autonomous* court remarked the "we never see each other" and "each judge operates like a separate court." "Statistics are the last thing on my mind—I'm treading water" was another comment. As a result, timeliness in the pace of litigation across different *autonomous* courts varies, although the distribution of processing times is likely skewed toward the slower end.

The *autonomous* court culture can be wracked with multiple problems. Trial calendars frequently are overbooked, with no coordinated effort among judges to provide meaningful trial dates. Attorneys are frequently unprepared and continuously seek continuances. The impetus for the original development of case management is regularly on display in many *autonomous* courts. One founder of the managerial movement argues that the criteria essential for effective court operations "are change, communication, decision making, and leadership" (Saari 1982, p. 42). Such characteristics are all scarce in the court with an *autonomous* culture.

Judge–Staff Relations

In an *autonomous* court, a close relationship exists between a judge and the court staff who work directly for him or her. Court staff members know what is expected of them and how to enhance the work of the judge to whom they are assigned. For the court administrator, the scope of authority is limited to operational areas such as budgets and facilities. As long as the court manager does not seek to impose administrative policies, relations with the judges should be positive.

A possible problem with intra-courtroom personal loyalty is that with it competition and conflict may abound. Each individual courtroom has collegial relations, but inter-courtroom relations might exhibit virtually no cooperation. One of the few areas of court-wide agreement will be unified resistance to overtures from the presiding judge or court administrator to introduce court-wide personnel policies.

Change Management

Change management in an *autonomous* court also is constrained in scope. Judges appreciate the traditional process of dispute resolution and do not see it as cumbersome or unnecessarily time and resource consuming for attorneys, litigants, and the public. No resistance arises automatically to proposals for making improvements in how the court prepares a budget, updates technology, or increases space availability. However, new programs or procedures are difficult to introduce, but not impossible. Innovations are likely to be voluntary, limited in number, and not encouraged to grow.

Change management is subject to blocking coalitions of judges opposed to new ideas. As an example, one of the *autonomous* courts explored the possibility of having a child care area for those clients with small children. The court administrator found a room and got local businesses to donate furniture and toys. When the administrator presented the complete idea to the judges, it was summarily dismissed as a bad idea. Despite all of the hard work and the minimal cost, it represented change.

A presiding judge or court administrator interested in transforming an *autonomous* court must answer a simple question: Why should a judge change behavior in response to reform? Current practice is neither random nor arbitrary. Rather, it reflects long-standing accommodations of various interests likely viewed as desirable by the practitioners. Because some judges will have a stake in the status quo, claims of undue *judicial activism* can undermine change initiatives. A new management plan is not sufficient; reforms must supply adequate incentives or impact will be negligible.

Courthouse Leadership

Courthouse leadership is most prevalent in each individual courtroom, where the judge exercises control and determines how business is done. Court-wide decisions tend to be more haphazard. Because management decision making is viewed negatively as an unwanted chore by judges who would rather be judging in courtrooms, the unpleasant task of administration is addressed as little as possible. Certainly there can be mutual respect among judges and a willingness to listen to ideas from other judges who are acknowledged to be skillful and effective decision makers. However, court-wide policy exists if and only if all judges agree. Use of the rule of unanimity in making administrative decisions restricts the scope and depth of policies, and makes achievement conditional on each judge being willing and able to pursue the same end.

The most obvious evidence of the *autonomous* court's shortcoming is the range of performance among different judges. Disparity in performance will likely be the greatest in an *autonomous* culture due to the presiding judge and court administrator's limited authority in formulating and setting policy. Hence, despite the fact that some disparities might be quite undesirable, their elimination or minimization is not the common subject of administrative conferences.

Internal Organization

The *internal organization* of the *autonomous* culture emphasizes the sovereignty of the individual judges. Courtroom practices and policies reflect the desires of individual judges, with change typically resisted and idiosyncratic practices remaining in place as long as a given judge is on the bench. In one autonomous court, attendance at the "mandatory" monthly judges meeting is sporadic. One judge who attends the meetings sits with his back to the conference table to show he is not part of the organization. The primary reason for attending is to make sure that no procedures and policies change. Thus, an appropriate metaphor for the organization of the *autonomous* court is individual judicial fiefdoms or small law firm-like coalitions.

Hierarchical Courts

The *hierarchical* court is organized in such a way that the chain of command is clear. There are explicit lines of authority among judges, administrative staff, and courtroom staff. The division of labor is clear and the expectations of all employees are formalized. As a result, the *hierarchical* court will be efficient through the application of modern management techniques.

Primary Roles

Court Administrator. The *hierarchical* court is hospitable to a court administrator seeking to use the principles of case management. Gallas (1987, p. 44) argues that in this context, the most basic function of the administrator is to establish and maintain clear case-processing routines. "Routines build predictability and stability, along with power to those who manage the system.... The quality of these routines is clearly evident in case disposition time and the consistency of case disposition times." Court managers in this type of court are particularly attuned to the use of automation to enhance information available to judges and improve the administration of the courts.

Judge. The judge in the *hierarchical* culture is first and foremost a manager, expected to follow prescribed processes and procedures. Interestingly, Butler (1977, p. 189) reports that presiding judges rank case management as a critical "managerial function," yet his findings also show that many presiding judges are reluctant to give authority over case management to their court administrator. This suggests, in turn, that *hierarchical* culture will be difficult to implement and maintain if the roles and responsibilities of the presiding judge and the court administrator are not well integrated.

Case Management Style

There is clarity in the purpose of case management and explicit recognition of the benefits. The goal of responsible managers is an efficient use of public resources to provide a high level of service to litigants, attorneys, and taxpayers. And this task begins in the courtroom with the effective management of the scarcest resource in every court: judge time. To optimize available decision-making time in an era of rising caseloads, judges are expected to follow prescribed methods deemed useful in the resolution of disputes before trial. "The whole thrust of case-flow management is to minimize the number of trials and devise ways to force cases to exit the system quickly through settlement, entry of plea, or some other disposition" (Tobin, 1999, p. 212). The key assumption is that judicial orders that require attorneys to prepare and meet early in the life of the case will lead to case resolutions both timely and fair. Many cases do not require trial; rather, a negotiated plea can benefit both parties. Meaningful plea negotiations are more likely when attorneys have pretrial deadlines and firm trial dates. The *hierarchical* court is also cognizant of the costs of failing to engage in case management: "courts manage the cases filed with them, or they become engulfed and devoured by the case-flow process" (Saari 1982, p. 70).

For the effective pursuit of efficiency, it is incumbent on court leadership to provide the bench with a persuasive rationale for the benefits of the *hierarchical* approach. The utility of judicial case management is not universally recognized or accepted. As one judge in a *hierarchical* court said, "Initially some judges found it difficult to understand why case management was 'our problem.' There was some feeling that the cases belonged to the attorneys, and management was their responsibility." Another issue is that too much emphasis might be placed on the benefits to the court and too little emphasis placed on the benefits to other participants in the legal process. Prosecutors and criminal defense attorneys might not be shown how case management policies encourage early preparation by both sides, fewer continuances, and more control over their own resources. Success clearly depends on system-wide commitment to the substance of case-flow management: policies cannot be enforced without cooperation from everyone involved. Without commitment and cooperation, case management might be statements of lofty goals but fail to effectuate case processing.

Judge–Staff Relations

The structured approach to case management extends to *judge–staff relations*. Just as judges are expected to follow rules, court staff has clear case-processing duties and routines. To make the best use of staff resources, court managers often employ sophisticated staffing models. Attention to staffing patterns and workload helps management assess return on investment in new technologies, reengineering of business practices, staff training, or the adoption of *best practices*. It also helps determine where court operations may be slack, including inefficient procedures or underutilized staff.

Because *hierarchical* courts are lower on sociability, they may suffer from a lack of loyalty and trust in the relations between judges and staff. The chain of command does not necessarily induce a respectful willingness to cooperate. In fact, a *hierarchical* court might have few opportunities in which everyone can voice ideas. Consequently, only a restrained feeling might exist among judges and staff to pull together. Courts moving to adopt more *hierarchical* case management principles (e.g., early and continuous judicial control) must avoid the phenomenon analogous to the *white tornado*. This situation occurs when judges, suddenly realizing they are plagued by delay and backlogs, suspend normal case processing and frantically engage in a crash program. Periodic panic followed by crisis-oriented delay reduction is not a sustainable and effective strategy.

Change Management

Change management is an active area in a *hierarchical* court. Because automation is seen as essential to efficient case processing, court administration pays close attention to how the expanded use of technologies can aid in providing services to the public. A primary focus is on how to enhance the business processes in courts. This concern extends to the judges, especially presiding judges, as they seek ways to improve court performance. However, the area of emphasis is on case management, with a central theme of bench meetings being what can be done to improve the handling of cases. Court leaders seek the involvement of the entire bench in their ongoing efforts to create an efficient case resolution system. As one *hierarchical* court manager said, "Gaining broad judicial agreement for change is paramount. You don't sink ships you help build."

Hierarchical courts can become rigid and unreceptive to fresh ideas. Excessive formalization of structure and process can stymie professional creativity of judges and staff. "Nothing has more destructive potential for professional drive and creativity than a heavy-handed bureaucrat in the role of presiding judges" (Saari 1982, p. 55). Thus, a *hierarchical* court can become petrified with limited opportunities for court-wide discussion of emerging problems and appropriate solutions.

Courts moving to adopt more *hierarchical* strategies typically begin with the application of technology to case management. Reformers may assume that systematic change will occur because computerized data and scheduling provide more information and allow more time for contemplation. However, not only must data be accurate and available, people must change their behavior in response to the increased, readily available information. Success of automated applications depends on whether people are willing to modify their behavior.

Courthouse Leadership

Concerning courthouse leadership, great emphasis is placed on the formal positions of the presiding judge and court administrator to gain necessary resources, establish calendars, and set performance goals. Court members are expected to follow the policies prescribed by the administrative leadership to achieve ends the court has chosen for itself.

Hierarchical courts are beset by two problems in this area. First, court rules and polices might not be viewed by some judges as helpful in handling the specific circumstances surrounding individual cases. As a result, not all rule-oriented cultures are equally effective in achieving either the desired uniform behavior of judges or the widespread acceptance of rules among judges and attorneys. Second, a rule-oriented court encounters difficulties in squaring general guidelines with the expectations of both litigants and attorneys who want to speak, to be heard, and for the court to understand the issues and circumstances in their cases. As a result, *hierarchical* courts might appear to be uninterested in administering justice in individual cases and devoted only to handling cases in the aggregate, leading to the criticism that the courts and its leaders neglect quality.

Internal Organization

The *hierarchical* court culture places a high priority on the efficient and harmonious handling of cases within the administrative framework. This structure not only contributes to delay reduction, but also minimizes friction between judges by encouraging the orderly handling of cases. Timely resolution of the entire caseload is of central importance. If some nontraditional adjudication procedure (e.g., a special calendar) can enhance expeditiousness, it will be considered for adoption. As Boyum demonstrated (1979), judges who see their role as contributing to sound administration resolve their assigned caseloads more quickly than other judges.

Hierarchical courts seek to achieve the advantages of order and efficiency, which are deemed essential goals in a world of limited resources, along with calls for increased accountability. The distinctive feature of a *hierarchical* court is how these goals are to be reached. Basically, a structured decision-making environment is created through rules, adoption of court technology, and a monitoring system to assess compliance. Rules and timely information are viewed as mechanisms for reducing uncertainty, confusion, and conflict in how judges and court staff make decisions.

Success with the *hierarchical* approach to court management requires firm and consistent application of the rules as well as clear lines of authority. Problems arise when insufficient attention is given to ensuring both judges and staff members have proper incentives to carry out court policies. Once established, policies might be assumed erroneously to be self-executing.

Summary

The four culture types provide a framework to discuss general characteristics that define and differentiate how courts see and organize themselves. For example, those favoring a *hierarchical* approach see more planning, more control, and more standard practices as most conducive to producing effectiveness and goal attainment. In contrast, proponents of a *communal* approach view the spirit of accommodation, concern about motivation, and attention to the needs of workers as the means for greater effectiveness. Many of the ideas and alternatives present in a contemporary discussion of court culture have been familiar to court practitioners and observers for many years. In this review, the focus has been on broad patterns and characteristics in each culture as a means to present the diversity of courts.

The four culture types operate on many different levels. They reflect deep-seated views on the appropriate role of the judiciary in the adversary system; how judges, court administrators, and staff organize their work; and the extent to which the court cooperates and collaborates with the wider criminal justice system. There is no intent to suggest that every judge and administrator working in a particular court holds the same views and values. The four cultures are not like blood types with every court typed by one and only one label. Organizational cultures rarely become manifest as a *pure* type in the real world, with judges and administrators wholly wrapped up in the ideas and values of just one culture. Rather, this conception of court culture taps into generally recognized ways of doing business. The culture framework provides a short hand for discussing and comparing relative emphases among different types of courts.

The elaborations offered in this chapter suggest ways courts in each of the four cultures operate in areas of work ranging from *case management style* to *internal organization*. Implicit in the discussion are a number of hypotheses about how trial courts function under different cultural regimes. In the next chapter, the relationship between culture and performance is investigated in several ways.

5 Consequences of Court Culture

Introduction

The profound significance of culture lies in its consequences. According to the data from the courts in this study, culture varies both among and within judicial bodies: No one culture dominates all work areas and there is no dominant cultural mosaic across the twelve courts. A logical question arises: Does this cultural variation have differential performance consequences? Public management experts contend that, in general, culture shapes institutional performance. For example, DiIulio (1989, p. 127) notes:

> Although a disputatious lot, public management scholars tend to agree strongly (if implicitly) on one thing: public management matters. They share a belief ("faith" might be a better word) that how public organizations are managed has a significant bearing on how, and how well, these organizations perform.

Because of the varieties of cultures within a court across the five work areas, an overall cultural type serves as the *public management variable* that permits the comparison of courts. In this chapter, the overall culture type will be used as a surrogate public management variable to test a set of hypotheses about the performance consequences of different cultural orientations.

Performance Measures for Trial Courts

There is widespread agreement that public organizations do not have a clear bottom line. In fact, it is often the case that public organizations have multiple, ambiguous, and inherently nonoperational goals. But as DiIulio (1994) notes: "In recent years a number of major public policy reforms were launched as efforts to define appropriate measures for the goals of government agencies." In the area of American trial courts, the *Trial Court Performance Standards* (TCPS) are a clear example.

In 1987, the trial court community took a major stride toward expanding its ability to measure and assess its performance through the initiation of the TCPS. "The program's objective was to increase the capacity of the nation's trial courts to provide fair and efficient adjudication and disposition of cases...[based on] the theme of the *court as an organization accountable for its performance*" (Trial Court Performance Standards, 1997, p. 1) [emphasis added]. The TCPS provides a framework to assess court performance in general areas, including *access to justice, expedition and timeliness, and equality, fairness, and integrity*.

These groupings represent ways of viewing fundamental responsibilities and purposes of courts. An operational definition of trial court performance thus focuses on a court's ability to reduce delay, provide access to justice, and ensure fairness, as well as other success factors relevant to all public institutions, such as client-customer satisfaction and efficiency of internal processes. In this chapter, the work of the TCPS and other court management experts is drawn upon to construct an observable and measurable set of performance indicators that will help clarify the extent to which culture matters. This is by no means an exhaustive set of factors, but it is a set of measurable elements from which it is possible to obtain a systematic assessment of the court's performance. Two primary consequences of the linkage between cultural orientations and performance seem especially important to explore and document.

One activity likely shaped by culture concerns the way a court carries out its business processing cases. The basic intuitive notion that a connection exists between how practitioners say they are organized to get work done and how cases are, in fact, resolved, needs to be evaluated empirically. The validity of this relationship cannot be assumed automatically because judges might very well assert they are mobilized to act in some particular fashion and then fail to execute intended work plans because not everyone truly embraces the rhetoric of court leaders.

To examine the correspondence between organizational culture and how work is in fact accomplished, timeliness of case resolution is offered as a measure of how courts carry out their business. The research question is: Do courts with different overall culture types resolve cases with similar or different degrees of expeditiousness?

Timeliness is a valid and fair indicator of how business is carried out for several reasons. This measure is consistent with the focus of previous research on the consequences of *local legal culture*."[1] In addition, national organizations, such as the American Bar Association (ABA) (1987), the Conference of State Court Administrators (1983), and the Trial Court Performance Standards Commission (1990), have raised timeliness as a national standard all courts should be expected to meet. The ABA offers no other measure of court performance than timeliness, suggesting it is among the most fundamental indicators. Finally, the importance of timeliness is enshrined in the U.S. Constitution's Sixth Amendment guaranteeing the "right to a fair and speedy trial." The extent to which this provision is meaningful depends on the ability of courts to resolve cases expeditiously.

A second area of culture's potential impact concerns the important performance goals of access to justice, fairness, and the managerial effectiveness of the court. The first two values are pillars of performance, according to the *Trial Court Performance Standards* (1997). Access and fairness are two of the five performance areas around which the Standards are organized. Moreover, numerous commissions and reform efforts in the last twenty years have used these values as their central organizing focus. Fairness, as measured by subjective assessments by participants in the process, also has become an established area of evaluation research, although the studies have contributed more to establish systematic measures than criteria of fairness (Tyler 1998). The managerial effectiveness of the court focuses on the concerns and cooperation courts show toward other organizations (e.g., institutional offices of prosecutors and public defenders) and individuals (e.g., victims) participating in the criminal trial process. As such, the court's managerial effectiveness concerns a court's sense and sensibility as a member of the more broadly construed criminal justice system.[2]

In measuring access, fairness, and managerial effectiveness, perspectives of other participants in the criminal trial process are useful gauges. Previous evaluation research has inquired into the reactions of practicing attorneys on how court actions affect the justice system.[3] Prosecutors and public defense attorneys have daily contact with the judiciary and are in a position to observe the interactions between criminal court judges and defendants, witnesses, jurors, and courtroom staff members. They are able to evaluate how a court carries out its business above and beyond clearing calendars, holding trials as scheduled, and adhering to tight continuance policies all in the name of expedition and timeliness. Attorneys' views constitute a valid and reliable basis for assessing how the actions of judges and administrators affect the important performance goals of access to justice, fairness, and the managerial effectiveness of the court.

Time to Disposition

Hypotheses

A basic organizing hypothesis on how culture affects the timeliness with which courts carry out their business revolves around the joint effect of the two basic dimensions of culture. The higher courts are on the *solidarity dimension*, the more expeditious they are and the higher courts are on the *sociability dimension*, the less expeditious they are. Hence, the combined effect of the two assumptions suggests the following ordering of cultures from the most to the least timely.

1. Hierarchical (e.g., Hennepin, Contra Costa)
2. Networked (e.g., Ventura, Napa, Ramsey)
3. Autonomous (e.g., Dakota, Duval, Duluth, Pinellas)
4. Communal (e.g., Olmsted, Kandiyohi, Virginia)

The *hierarchical* courts are low on *sociability* and high on *solidarity*, which means they pursue case-flow management (e.g., early case control, case coordination, and firm trial dates) with the support of administrative and courtroom staff. These courts use the best practices and innovative procedures available to reduce overall court delay. Moreover, discretion in the timing of key procedural events is constrained by rules; all judges are expected to handle their dockets in a similar manner.

In the *networked* courts, judicial expectations concerning case management derive from a working policy developed through the involvement and planning of the entire bench, and not necessarily the adoption of national standards. Being that *networked* courts are high on *sociability*, timeliness is to be achieved by judges and staff following guidelines rather than uniform rules. Timeliness is an aspirational goal; it is a local community standard rather than an externally imposed one.

In the *autonomous* courts, the importance of court-wide timeliness goals is limited. Individual judges are relatively free to make their own determinations concerning when key procedural events are to be completed. Considerable variation in the time to resolution in these courts is likely. Some judges focus on delay reduction, whereas others emphasize other aspects of court performance. As a result, the *autonomous* courts should be somewhat slower than the two culture types emphasizing *solidarity* and should exhibit substantial variation.

Finally, in the *communal* courts, the limited degree of *solidarity* downplays centralized judicial and administrative leadership. Moreover, being high on *sociability*, the *communal* courts might achieve a consensus that timeliness is not vitally important and, instead, the court might choose to focus primarily on goals other than the pace of litigation. As a result, *communal* courts are expected to be the least expeditious in resolving court business.

Results

The American Bar Association (ABA) Time Standards (1987) are suitable criteria for determining whether culture makes some courts more expeditious than others. According to the ABA, specific percentages of cases should be resolved within certain time-frames. Ninety percent should be resolved within 120 days or fewer, 98 percent within 180 days or fewer, and 100 percent within 356 days or fewer after arrest. A key question is: can differences in court culture account for variation in the percentage of cases resolved within 120, 180, and 365 days, respectively.

As expected, the percentage of cases resolved within 120, 180, and 365 days after arrest coincides with the degree courts emphasize *solidarity* and de-emphasize *sociability*. The time-frames for resolving felony criminal cases expand in the following order of cultures: *hierarchical*, *networked*, *autonomous*, and *communal*, as shown in Table 5-1.

TABLE 5-1. PERCENTAGE OF FELONY CRIMINAL CASES RESOLVED WITHIN AMERICAN BAR ASSOCIATION (ABA) TIME FRAMES

Individual Courts

		Cases Resolved within (days)			
Culture Type	Court	120	180	365	Felonies
Hierarchical	Hennepin	74%	87%	95%	5,307
	Contra Costa	58%	70%	87%	4,973
Networked	Ventura	49%	64%	91%	2,586
	Ramsey	72%	91%	96%	2,370
	Napa	51%	67%	88%	1,081
Autonomous	Dakota	67%	82%	94%	1,265
	Duluth	54%	72%	93%	520
	Pinellas	41%	55%	79%	11,002
	Duval	68%	76%	82%	6,496
Communal	Olmsted	33%	52%	84%	472
	Kandiyohi	55%	70%	89%	193
	Virginia	62%	87%	98%	189
	ABA Standards	**90%**	**98%**	**100%**	

Courts with Similar Cultures Combined

		Cases Resolved within (days)			
Culture Type	Confidence interval	120	180	365	Felonies
Hierarchical		66.3%	78.8%	91.1%	10,280
	(95% CI)	(+/-0.9%)	(+/-0.8%)	(+/-0.5%)	
Networked		58.4%	75.1%	92.4%	6,037
	(95% CI)	(+/-1.2%)	(+/-1.1%)	(+/-0.7%)	
Autonomous		52.2%	64.3%	81.4%	19,283
	(95% CI)	(+/-0.7%)	(+/-0.7%)	(+/-0.5%)	
Communal		44.4%	63.8%	88.2%	854
	(95% CI)	(+/-3.3%)	(+/-3.2%)	(+/-2.2%)	

Turning to an evaluation of *hierarchical* court culture type, we noted that Hennepin County has relatively more cases resolved within 120 days than any other court. It has the second largest percentage at the 180-day marker and the third largest percentage of resolved cases at the 365-day benchmark.[4]

Among the *networked* courts, Ramsey County is among the most expeditious in resolving cases. In fact, Ramsey approximates the ABA criterion for resolving all cases within 365 days or fewer more closely than any other court but Virginia.[5] Ventura is more expeditious, as expected, than most *communal* and *autonomous* courts.

Among the *autonomous* courts, there is a great deal of variation, as expected. For example, at the 120-day benchmark, Duval and Dakota have resolved 68 percent and 67 percent of their filings, respectfully, whereas Duluth and Pinellas are substantially less successful. At 180 days, Dakota, Duluth, and Duval have resolved at least 72 percent of their cases, whereas Pinellas has resolved only 55 percent. At 365 days, the two Minnesota courts have resolved at least 90 percent of their cases, whereas the Florida courts have resolved no more than 82 percent.

The *communal* Courts—Olmsted, Kandiyohi, and Virginia—tend to resolve smaller percentages at the 120- and 180-day markers than the *hierarchical* or *networked* courts. In fact, Olmsted County is the least expeditious of all the courts under study at the first two ABA points of demarcation.

Hence, substantial support exists for the hypothesis that culture matters in how expeditiously courts conduct their business of resolving cases. Cultures that emphasize *solidarity* are more likely to resolve cases with greater expedition than those courts that do not have a *solidarity* emphasis. However, there is not a one-to-one correspondence between a court's cultural orientation and how quickly it executes the task of resolving cases. Virginia, for example, resolves a higher percentage of its cases within 365 days or fewer than any court, including the *hierarchical* courts of Hennepin and Contra Costa. One likely reason is that Virginia has very few felony filings to resolve. Yet, Virginia is a *communal* court, which is hypothesized to be the least expeditious. The single counter-example does not disconfirm the basic hypothesis especially given the very small number of felonies.

To get a better idea of the relationship between culture and timeliness, we combined the results for all courts of a similar cultural type. These results are presented at the bottom of Table 5-1. In addition to providing the combined mean percentages, we also present the 95% confidence intervals for each of the percentages. At the 120-day marker, the hypothesized rank order is clear and all differences are statistically significant (i.e., there is no overlap in the confidence intervals). At the 180-day marker, there is a statistically significant difference between *hierarchical/networked* and *networked/autonomous* but not between *autonomous* and *communal*. At the 365-day marker, there is no significant difference between *hierarchical* and *networked* courts but both are significantly faster than either *autonomous* or *communal*. Hence, when combining the results, we find robust and statistically significant indications that the hypothesized timeliness rank order is supported by data. Timeliness tends to be achieved according to particular ordering of cultures. The courts under study confirm this relationship.

In-Depth Focus on Minnesota

Due to the fact that Minnesota has a well-functioning statewide automated case management system, it is possible to extract more finely grained data with which to investigate the current hypothesis. A separate examination of criminal cases in Minnesota, which includes the largest number of courts in the study and exemplars from each of the four culture types, provides a more refined means to test the connection between court culture and timeliness. The data are presented in Table 5-2 and the median, rather than the mean, is used as the primary indicator of timeliness. The number of cases in many of the cells is quite small (e.g., 5th-degree misdemeanors) and hence the mean—in these cells—is susceptible to outliers. To avoid the undue potential influence of a small number of outliers, the median is used to measure the average amount of time from filing to disposition.

Hennepin, the single *hierarchical* court in Minnesota is substantially more expedient in case resolution than the other six courts, as shown in Table 5-2. The median number of days from the date of arrest to resolution is fewer in misdemeanors (21), gross misdemeanors (28), and felonies (64) than any other court.[6] Ramsey is the second most timely in each of the categories with a median of 44 days in misdemeanors, 41 days in gross misdemeanors, and 80 days in felonies. As expected, Ramsey, which has a *networked* culture, is not as expeditious as Hennepin, but it is more expeditious than all other courts.

The two autonomous courts, Dakota and Duluth, are substantially slower than Hennepin and Ramsey in both the misdemeanor and gross misdemeanor categories. With the exception of Virginia, the *communal* courts are the least expeditious courts. Kandiyohi has a median of 87 days in misdemeanors, 77 days in gross misdemeanors, and 113 days in felonies, whereas Olmsted has a median of 102 days in misdemeanors, 54 days in gross misdemeanors, and 174 days in felonies. The differences between these two courts and the two courts emphasizing *solidarity* in their culture are dramatic.

One important policy question arising from these results is whether courts that accentuate *solidarity* spend less time overall on

TABLE 5-2. MEDIAN NUMBER OF ELAPSED DAYS FROM THE DATE OF ARREST TO RESOLUTION

	Hierarchical		Networked		Autonomous				Communal					
	Hennepin		Ramsey		Dakota		Duluth		Kandiyohi		Olmsted		Virginia	
Current Case type	Median	N	Median	N	Median	N	Median	N	Median	N	Median	N	Median	N
Misdemeanor	21	986	42	684	52	509	84	78	87	102	96	102	66	50
Petty Misdemeanor	1	65	25	24	77	30	95	1	101	3	175	2	57	2
Misdemeanor - Domestic Assault	24	20	85	44	101	46	69	14	68	3	68	6	59	3
Misdemeanor - DWI	28	140	33	59	43	217	41	44	22	5	156	6	26	14
Misdemeanor - Fifth Degree	52	11	95	18	97	22	56	7			158	5	88	5
Misdemeanor Average	**21**	**1,222**	**44**	**829**	**52**	**824**	**65**	**144**	**87**	**113**	**102**	**121**	**64**	**74**
Gross Misdemeanor Domestic Assault	31	176	66	39	101	73	77	27	57	1	96	8	74	8
Gross Misdemeanor DWI	25	2,538	36	1,023	51	830	76	356	53	103	53	291	44	152
Gross Misdemeanor - Fifth Degree	31	35	84	45	122	15	71	6			355	2	109	3
Gross Misdemeanor	29	3,032	42	1,240	54	609	69	193	89	161	52	288	49	105
Gross Misdemeanor Average	**28**	**5,781**	**41**	**2,347**	**53**	**1,527**	**73**	**582**	**77**	**265**	**54**	**589**	**47**	**268**
Serious Felony	126	289	132	95	181	46	178	32	190	8	228	42	142	13
Felony	60	4,984	88	2,270	78	1,191	98	462	111	184	173	424	98	172
Felony - Fifth Degree	54	16												
Felony - Domestic Assault	110	10	97	4	71	28	165	14			170	6	114	1
Felony - EJJ		8		1						1				
Felony Average	**64**	**5,307**	**80**	**2,370**	**81**	**1,265**	**105**	**508**	**113**	**193**	**174**	**472**	**99**	**186**
Overall Average	**36**	**12,310**	**66**	**5,546**	**60**	**3,616**	**84**	**1,234**	**88**	**571**	**96**	**1,182**	**64**	**528**

DWI = Driving While Intoxicated and EJJ = Extended Jurisdiction Juvenile.

their cases than do the other courts. Table 5-3 presents pertinent information on *case weights* based on a separate workload study on the Minnesota courts.[7]

In the domain of less serious criminal cases, Hennepin County judges spend less work time than any of the other courts. However, in the handling of major criminal cases, the 102 minutes on average that judges in Hennepin County spend is at the top. This finding suggests that Hennepin has put procedures and policies in place that enable judges to spend time more directly proportional to the seriousness of the cases than the other courts. Consequently, Hennepin's timely case resolution is not accomplished simply by giving less attention to all cases, but, instead, by emphasizing *solidarity*, available work time is distributed more closely with case seriousness than in the other five courts.[8]

Taken together, the evidence in Tables 5-2 and 5-3 provides additional support for the hypothesis that court culture plays a role in the timeliness aspect of court performance. Courts accentuating *solidarity* have a faster time to resolution than do those bodies not having a *solidarity* emphasis, but expeditiousness does not automatically mean less judge time is being spent on cases. Rather time is being apportioned according to seriousness—this may, in fact, be the hallmark of the well-functioning *hierarchical* court culture.

Access, Fairness, and Managerial Effectiveness

Hypotheses

It is anticipated that court culture plays a role in shaping attorneys' assessments of how closely the courts in which they practice achieve access, fairness, and managerial effectiveness. Because these three values involve the rights and concerns of participants in the trial process other than judges and administrators, courts accenting *sociability* and downplaying *solidarity* should likely garner relatively greater positive assessments from attorneys. Concern for others and willingness to cooperate promote these values, and limited *solidarity* avoids the perception that a court is interested only in championing its own needs and interests (e.g., meeting time standards).

Attorneys' views on how closely courts approximate the ideals of access, fairness, and managerial effectiveness reflect the nature of the adversary system. These lawyers are not disinterested observers of

TABLE 5-3. AVERAGE AMOUNT OF TIME SPENT BY JUDGES IN MINUTES

	District Case Weights for Major and Minor Criminal from 2002 Time Study					
Case Type	Hennepin 4th District	Ramsey 2nd District	Dakota 1st District	Duluth/Virginia 6th District	Olmsted 3rd District	Kandiyohi 8th District
Fifth Degree Assault (27)	13	31	26	30	74	30
Nontraffic MSD/ petty (6)	4	11	5	7	7	8
MSD DWI (14)	6	12	10	20	23	37
Minor Criminal (8.4)	**5**	**12.5**	**7**	**9.4**	**12.9**	**11.6**
Serious Felony (852)	1,211	714	1,199	137	912	262
Other Felony (106)	124	113	101	97	113	116
Gross MSD DWI (47)	48	33	37	54	65	69
Other Gross MSD (38)	33	24	43	49	43	67
Major Criminal (87)	**102**	**78**	**86**	**75**	**103**	**96**

DWI = Driving while Intoxicated and MSD = Misdemeanor.

how a court affects litigants and victims. They have their own stake in how court business is conducted. A well-established proposition about criminal trial courts is that they are organized in terms of individual "courtroom work groups" (Eisenstein and Jacob 1977).

The same group of prosecutors, public defenders, judges, and courtroom staff assigned to the same courtroom develop norms over time on how cases are to be resolved (e.g., what cases should go to trial, what is a reasonable punishment for particular offenses, what are reasonable mitigating circumstances, and so forth). This setting fosters predictability in court decisions, which is a benefit to everyone, including both prosecutors and attorneys. As a result, there are special advantages to *autonomous* cultures from the perspectives of both sets of attorneys. In courts with highly *autonomous* cultures, the attorneys need not consult or adhere to court-wide administrative controls; they can operate by relying on the agreed-upon practices formed in the immediate setting where they work every day. In fact, they likely have internalized the agreed-upon procedures and may be quite resistant to *outside intervention*. Hence, courts with *autonomous* cultures are expected to best approximate the values of access, fairness, and managerial effectiveness more closely than those with *hierarchical* cultures from the perspective of the practicing attorneys.

The presence of a *hierarchical* culture does not automatically doom a court to negative assessments on values other than timeliness. However, if timeliness is extolled by judges and administrators as the ultimate mark of a *good* court and advantages to attorneys and litigants are not stressed and communicated, a court very well might be seen as interested only in its own agenda and status. Furthermore, if courts with *hierarchical* cultures never measure or even show an interest in measuring access, fairness, or managerial effectiveness, attorneys are likely to perceive that the court is interested in counting only what it considers important (e.g., the elapsed number of days from arrest to case resolution). Attorneys might view courts with *hierarchical* cultures positively in terms of achieving timeliness, but they might find those same courts to be ineffective in achieving other important performance values.

Despite the existence of courtroom work groups, and their effect in attenuating the clashes among judges and attorneys in an adversary legal system, prosecutors and public defenders will not agree completely on what sorts of court cultures are most conducive to access, fairness, and managerial effectiveness. They each have their own missions and agendas. Protection of society and protection of constitutional rights are contending perspectives between these two adversaries. As a result, a *networked* culture is more conducive to the former and a *communal* culture to the latter. The greater spotlight on rules in *networked* cultures is more hospitable to prosecutors who seek convictions on the basis of what they consider appropriate charges under existing law. Conversely, public defenders who seek through negotiation to minimize the loss of liberty for their clients see the virtues of *sociability* in *communal* cultures as conducive to working out what is in their client's best interest. Hence, whereas prosecutors and public defenders might agree that an *autonomous* culture promotes access, fairness, and managerial effectiveness better than a *hierarchical* culture, they will have different cultural preferences concerning *networked* and *communal* cultures.

In fact, prosecutors are likely to rate courts in *communal* cultures as the least effective in achieving access, fairness, and managerial effectiveness, whereas public defenders will rate these courts mostly favorably. Public defenders are likely to view courts operating in *networked* cultures to be the least effective because they are more prone than courts with other court cultures to take into account the rights and interests of individuals (e.g., victims) and organizations (e.g., Mothers Against Drunk Drivers [MADD]) that might possibly conflict with those of criminal defendants.[9] For prosecutors, *networked* courts will be second only to *autonomous* bodies because they have no quarrel with a court's efforts to be responsive to victims and victims' rights organizations.

Thus, court cultures will be rated in the following order from the most to the least effective in achieving access, fairness, and managerial effectiveness. For prosecutors the anticipated ranking is: (1) *autonomous*, (2) *networked*, (3) *hierarchical*, and (4) *communal*. For public defenders the anticipated ranking is: (1) *communal*, (2) *autonomous*, (3) *hierarchical*, and (4) *networked*.

Measuring Attorneys' Views

Attitude surveys consisting of forty-six questions were administered to 590 prosecutors and public defenders with at least two years of practice in each of the twelve courts under study. The foundation of the survey instrument is drawn from the work conducted by Ostrom and Hanson (1999). A copy of the instrument used in the twelve courts is presented in Appendix 5 (the average responses for both prosecuting attorneys and defense attorneys for all items in the survey instrument are available at http://www.ncsconline.org/courtculture/).

To discern patterns across the courts of the attorneys' views on the degree to which culture influences the promotion of access, fairness, and effective management, the responses by the public defenders and prosecuting attorneys are synthesized into coherent categories by creating three statistical scales—*access*, *fairness*, and *managerial effectiveness*.

The *court access scale* is designed to measure multiple facets of a court's availability and accessibility to the public and to attorneys' access to a court. The court access scale is constructed using the following six items from the *attorney survey*: The court takes adequate steps to ensure accuracy and availability of court records (Item 25); Public areas of the courthouse are safe and accessible (Item 32); Information can be obtained on a case quickly and easily (Item 33); Court proceedings are easy to understand and follow (Item 35); The court is sensitive to the concerns of the average citizen (Item 36); and Court personnel are helpful and courteous (Item 37).[10] The Cronbach alpha statistics for the court access scale are .73 and .70 for the prosecutors and public defenders, respectively.[11]

The *procedural fairness scale* is constructed using the following eight items from the *attorney survey*: The amount of time judges give to cases is proportional to the amount of time the case merits (Item 18); Most juries are representative of the community (Item 19); The court protects criminal defendants' constitutional rights (Item 20); There is effective legal representation at all critical stages of the legal process for criminal indigent defendants (Item 21); Judges give adequate time and attention to the circumstances of individual criminal defendants (Item 22); Criminal defendants understand the court's rulings (Item 29); The court is able to process cases efficiently without sacrificing equity and justice (Item 30); and The court takes appropriate responsibility for enforcement of its orders (Item 31). The Cronbach alpha statistics for the procedural fairness scale are 0.67 and 0.75 for the prosecutors and public defenders, respectively.

The *managerial effectiveness scale* is designed to draw attention to the court's effectiveness in communication, leadership, victim awareness, and expenditure of public resources. The management effectiveness scale is constructed using the following six items from the *attorney survey*: There is good communication among the court, prosecutor, and public defender when case management problems arise (Item 11); Effective judicial leadership is one of the strengths of the criminal justice system in this jurisdiction (Item 12); Effective leadership by the prosecutor is one of the strengths of the criminal justice system in this jurisdiction (Item 13); Effective leadership among indigent criminal defense attorneys is one of the strengths of the criminal justice system in this jurisdiction (Item 14); Victims of crime are kept informed of all court settings and offender bond status (Item 24); The court works well with other components of the criminal justice system (Item 26); and The court spends its funds wisely (Item 34). The Cronbach alpha statistics for the managerial effectiveness scale are 0.66 and 0.64 for the prosecutors and public defenders, respectively.

Results. Attorneys' views on the three scales are standardized statistically.[12] The more positive the evaluation, the higher the standardized score; the more critical the evaluation, the lower the negative score. The courts have been organized by the overall culture type to facilitate the drawing of inferences. For both sets of attorneys, a neutral point of view is shown as "0." Thus, when both prosecutors and defense counsel rate a court positively, both types of attorneys view the court as above average. If both have negative views, both types of attorneys view the court as below average. The results are displayed in Table 5-4.

Survey scale results generally confirm expectations: courts with similar cultures tend to foster similar attorney attitudes. Looking at the results for the prosecutors, it is clear that they have negative evaluations of all three scales for *hierarchical* (6 of 6 possible ratings) and *networked* (8 of 9) courts, and strong positive evaluations for *autonomous* (10 of 12 possible ratings) courts, as shown in Table 5-4. Turning our attention to the defense attorneys, it is noted that they rate *hierarchical* courts low on all three performance scales (6 of 6 possible ratings), whereas they rated *autonomous* courts high on all three performance scales (9 of 12 possible ratings).

Results for individual courts are more mixed. Three courts—Virginia (*communal*), Pinellas (*autonomous*), and Duluth (*autonomous*)—received positive evaluations from both types of attorneys across all three performance scales. Four courts—Contra Costa (*hierarchical*), Hennepin (*hierarchical*), Napa (*networked*), and Kandiyohi (*communal*)—received negative evaluations from both types of attorneys across all three values. In three courts—Duval

TABLE 5-4. PROSECUTORS' AND PUBLIC DEFENDERS' VIEWS ON COURT PERFORMANCE

		Access Scale		Fairness Scale		Management Scale	
Overall Culture Type		Prosecutor	Public Defender	Prosecutor	Public Defender	Prosecutor	Public Defender
Hierarchical	Hennepin	–0.25	–0.62	–0.13	–0.41	–0.15	–0.48
	Contra Costa	–0.18	–0.28	–0.56	–0.24	–0.45	–0.64
Networked	Ventura	–0.30	0.19	–0.39	0.25	–0.27	0.21
	Ramsey	0.01	0.10	–0.43	0.10	–0.39	0.36
	Napa	–0.83	–0.12	–0.50	–0.12	-1.41	–0.42
Autonomous	Dakota	0.78	0.09	0.47	–0.13	0.27	–0.09
	Duluth	0.38	–0.30	0.86	0.58	0.77	0.10
	Pinellas	0.66	0.81	0.55	0.39	0.57	0.67
	Duval	–0.32	0.0	–0.05	0.19	0.10	0.39
Communal	Olmsted	0.84	–0.20	0.83	–0.77	0.33	-1.16
	Kandiyohi	–0.69	–0.07	–0.38	–0.04	–0.44	–0.35
	Virginia	1.34	0.18	1.96	1.40	1.99	1.25

The cell entries are standardized scores (mean 0, standard deviation 1) for each scale.

(*autonomous*), Ramsey (*networked*), and Ventura (*networked*)—the views are mixed, with the public defenders positive and the prosecutors negative. In two courts—Olmsted (*communal*) and Dakota (*autonomous*)—the results are mixed in the opposite direction, with the public defenders negative and the prosecutors positive.

A refined perspective on the linkage between culture and performance is gained by combining attorneys from each of the four court culture types and determining if prosecutors (or public defenders) have consistent views on the courts' efforts to achieve access, fairness, and managerial effectiveness as hypothesized.

Substantial correspondence between the expected and the observed outcomes is evident by attorneys from *autonomous* courts rating the efforts of their courts in promoting access, fairness, and managerial effectiveness positively, as shown in Table 5-5. At the same time, both types of attorneys in courts with *hierarchical* cultures rated their courts' efforts negatively. *Networked* courts received relatively high marks from the prosecuting attorneys and below average evaluations from the public defenders. The *communal* courts received relatively high marks from the public defenders and relative low evaluations from the prosecuting attorneys, as expected.

Attorneys' views that *hierarchical* cultures promote access, fairness, and managerial effectiveness less adequately than they promote

TABLE 5-5. PROSECUTORS' AND PUBLIC DEFENDERS' VIEWS ON COURT PERFORMANCE GROUPED BY OVERALL CULTURE TYPE

	Access Scale		Fairness Scale		Management Scale	
	Public Defender	Prosecutor	Public Defender	Prosecutor	Public Defender	Prosecutor
Communal	0.58	–0.12	0.89	–0.36	0.60	–0.68
Networked	–0.31	0.11	–0.42	0.13	–0.54	0.19
Autonomous	0.26	0.39	0.35	0.30	0.37	0.48
Hierarchical	–0.22	–0.48	–0.32	–0.34	–0.27	–0.54

timeliness are consistent with academic critiques of courts. A school of thought contends that courts are interested only in aggregate level concepts and have forgotten the meaning of justice as rendering attention to individual cases.[13] Such criticism should alert courts to avoid extolling and heralding timeliness and neglecting other values, such as access and fairness.

Returning to the hypotheses concerning the ordering of culture by attorneys, they compare well with actual orderings obtained through the attorney surveys, as shown in Table 5-6. *Autonomous* cultures are viewed more favorably than *hierarchical* cultures in promoting access, fairness, and managerial effectiveness, which is surprising perhaps to advocates of strong case-flow management. *Hierarchical* culture with its high emphasis on *solidarity* and low emphasis on *sociability*, puts a court in a position in which it is seen as concerned only with its own needs and circumstances. Timeliness is perceived to be strictly for a court's benefit, with little judicial interest in the rights and circumstances of litigants, victims, or attorneys. Hence, attorneys rate such courts low in the areas of access, fairness, and managerial effectiveness.

TABLE 5-6. PROSECUTORS' AND PUBLIC DEFENDERS' CULTURAL RANK ORDERINGS

Procedural Fairness		Access to Courts		Management	
Prosecutor	Defense	Prosecutor	Defense	Prosecutor	Defense
A	C	A	C	A	C
N	A	N	A	N	A
H	H	C	H	H	H
C	N	H	N	C	N

Note: C = *Communal*; N = *Networked*; A = *Autonomous*; H = *Hierarchical*.

The attorneys' positive views of *autonomous* cultures are understandable given that they reap the advantages of "court room work group relations". They benefit from the predictability of working daily with the same judge, opposing counsel, and court staff and coming to arrive at mutually agreed upon ways of resolving cases free from the intervention of rules, norms, or values outside *their* courtroom. The familiarity of courtroom work group relations leads attorneys to see litigants and themselves treated better in terms of access, fairness, and managerial effectiveness than in cultures not as conducive to maintaining the work group.

However, understandable differences between prosecutors and public defenders in their assessments of the performance consequences of cultural orientations also arise. The prosecutorial mission of protecting society, bringing only provable charges, and gaining convictions is more consistent with a *solidarity*-based culture than with a *sociability*-based one. Emphasis on procedures, and compliance to them, emanating from *solidarity*, is much more appealing to prosecutors than are the court practices in *communal* cultures. As a result, prosecutors see *autonomous* cultures most favorably and communal cultures least favorably. Their culture preference ordering for prosecutors is *networked* followed by *hierarchical* with *communal* rated last.

The mission of protecting individual constitutional rights, minimizing the loss of liberty, and negotiating the favorable outcomes for individual defendants draw public defenders to *communal* courts. *Communal* courts offer less confrontation, more relaxed rules, and a desire for mutually beneficial outcomes, all of which are more in-line with a public defender's posture. Hence, courts in *communal* cultures are rated by public defenders most positively in achieving access, fairness, and managerial effectiveness, followed by courts in *autonomous* cultures. *Networked* cultures are likely to be seen by public defenders as the least conducive to access, fairness, and managerial effectiveness because the interests of victims and victims' rights organizations are seen as possibly advanced above those of criminal defendants.

Documenting competing opinions of prosecutors and public defenders about preferred organizational arrangements underscores the nature of the management challenge facing court administration. Prosecutors and public defenders prefer a cultural environment that makes it easier to achieve their respective ends by maximizing their influence over how cases are handled and resolved. In other words, self-interest leads these practitioners to favor courts low on *solidarity*.

Of course, judges and court administrators have their own legitimate views over what constitutes effective case processing and who should determine the pace of litigation. And these perspectives may or may not align with the interests of other institutional actors. Where a particular court falls on the dimension of *solidarity* illuminates how potential differences (dividing judges, court administrators, prosecutors, and public defenders) on issues of court management issues are being resolved. Does the court lean toward allegiance to individual courtroom norms or standardized court-wide rules? Do judges prefer diffusion of decision making authority or consolidation within a judicial leadership team? How a court answers these questions indicates the strength and responsibilities of the presiding judge and the role of the court executive. Moreover, efforts to achieve a particular vision of case management, change management, and courthouse leadership that emphasize greater *solidarity* put considerable weight on the court leadership team to explain, persuade, and communicate the benefits to all relevant parties. The next chapter brings this issue into sharper focus when current culture is compared to the preferred way of organizing and conducting court business.

Summary

Cultural orientations in the courthouse make a difference in the degree that courts achieve important goals, such as timeliness, access, fairness, and managerial leadership. Courts with *hierarchical* predispositions are associated with more timely resolution of cases relative to other court cultures, but they tend to be assessed less favorably in promoting access, fairness, and managerial leadership by prosecutors and public defenders practicing in the courts.

Both sets of attorneys see courts with *autonomous* cultures providing a greater degree of access, fairness, and managerial effectiveness than courts with *hierarchical* cultures. The attorneys' interests in maintaining the advantages of courtroom work groups lead them to see *autonomous* cultures more favorably than *hierarchical* cultures when it comes to key court performance values. The pull of maintaining the courtroom work group relationships will slant the attorneys' views on how best to achieve high performance. Attorneys will see themselves and litigants as having greater access, being treated more fairly, and courts acting more effectively in cultures where the attorneys have a greater say in how business is conducted.

However, prosecutors and public defenders differ in their views about the relative merits of other cultures. Prosecutors prefer the solidarity of *networked* and *hierarchical* cultures more than the *sociability* of *communal* cultures. Conversely, public defenders value the *sociability* of *communal* courts because this culture likely enhances their role in gaining the best resolution for their clients. Managing the competing interests of prosecutors and public defenders, while maintaining an effective internal work environment for judges and court staff, highlights the management challenge facing court leaders.

The bottom line is that culture matters to trial court performance. The way a public organization organizes itself—in other words, its social architecture—clearly shapes the way the organization performs. In the next chapter, we explore whether judges and senior administrators make this connection in formulating their desire for their preferred cultural orientation.

6 Preferences for Court Culture

Introduction

Courts are regarded as conservative bodies wedded to precedent, both in substantive and procedural law. With very limited research and development capacities, they lack the wherewithal to keep up with innovations and emerging trends, in contrast to other organizations that continually monitor the outside world to remain vibrant and vital. If the conventional wisdom is true, courts might be stuck in the cultural tradition in which they find themselves, with little thought given to how practices might be improved. However, as some judges and court administrators have demonstrated, they are not as bound to the status quo as the classic model of courts moving with glacial speed suggests. For the last thirty years, planned changes have occurred. Conscious decisions have been the basis for the adoption of new forums, including a wide variety of specialized courts, new dispute resolution techniques, mediation and therapeutic justice, and new goals (including both those embodied by performance standards and by commissions to eliminate racial, gender, and other forms of discrimination).

Several questions revolve around the issue of whether courts want to alter their current cultural configurations in pursuit of these new objectives. Are practitioners so accustomed to past practices that they cannot envision alternative ways of organizing themselves and their work? Or is a court's cultural orientation sufficiently flexible to permit judges and administrators to envision more preferred configurations in the future? If so, what is the nature of preferred cultures?

The paths that practitioners aspire to follow are essential to establish. Knowing where a court currently stands and where it seeks to move will be helpful in clarifying what areas of business will have to undergo change as well as the content of the changes. On a broader scale, policy makers and attorneys should be interested in ascertaining the direction courts want to chart for themselves. State courts are the forums for the resolution of almost all criminal cases in the United States. Because culture is as much a part of institutional character as are structure, resources, and technology, one should be alert to cultural changes possibly propelling greater timeliness, access, fairness, managerial effectiveness, and related values.

Preferred Court Culture

Hypotheses

Three hypotheses suggest the nature of practitioners' preferences for the culture they would like to see evolve. First, it is anticipated that all of the courts desire a culture different from what they believe to be their current culture. In Chapter 3, it was suggested that a primary reason for fuzziness or diversity in culture within work areas is due to little, if any, thought being given to the *meta-analysis* of cultural norms and values. When asked to consider where they would like to be in five years, judges and senior administrators are given the opportunity to think reflectively about culture. They can begin to identify elements of what it means to be a high-performance court, the demands they will face in the future, and in which areas the court is currently underdeveloped. Consideration of these issues will likely produce a preferred culture more highly defined in terms of more or less *sociability* and *solidarity*. Despite the benefits of familiarity, judges and court administrators embrace change for its potential in improving performance and work relations. Maintaining the existing way of doing business is not seen as the path to doing better.

Second, it is anticipated that the direction in which the courts want to move will vary across the five areas of work. Differences in the substantive nature of the work areas will lead judges and court administrators to seek a combination of distinct cultures. Multiple cultures mean, of course, that the preferred configurations are not congruent. *Hierarchical* culture might be preferred in one area and *networked* culture in another, and so on.

Third, a similarity in the type of cultural mosaic that trial courts aspire to develop is anticipated. Judges and court administrators agree that some cultural orientations foster the sorts of values they wish to promote and achieve more than others. This agreement is not necessarily because judges and administrators have a common model (or ideal) of a good court. Rather, it is likely the result of over 200 years of common law experience. Judges have come to know and agree upon what sorts of approaches and guidelines should orient the work of courts. They simply have limited occasions to reflect on the possibilities or to express their views on such matters and to try to put them into place.

In terms of the third hypothesis, the desired mosaic is expected to have a particular composition because judges and administrators share views on what orientations should govern what work areas. It is anticipated that courts will seek to move toward greater *hierarchical* culture in both *case management style* and *change management*. These two dimensions involve social relations minimally and are the least individualistic of the five dimensions. Being more case based, and involving aggregate concepts such as caseload sizes, backlogs, and clearance rates, these two work areas focus on procedural events and dates amenable to the use of automated case management systems. As a result, the interest in greater *solidarity* will prompt judges and court administrators to want business done on the basis of clear and orderly rules, expertise, and modern management techniques.[1] *Hierarchical* cultures highlight these business-like values in the areas of *case management style* and *change management* to a greater extent than the other cultures, which tend to involve decision making by consensus and a tolerance for *second-best* solutions to accommodate all view points. *Hierarchical* culture exudes professionalism, which judges and court administrators are likely to think warrants priority in handling cases and creating a modern court.

In the work areas of *judge–staff relations* and *internal organization*, it is anticipated that judges and court administrators will seek *networked* cultures in which *sociability* is more valued. These two areas prompt judges and court administrators to want business done on the basis of inclusiveness. Because judges and court administrators have ongoing relationships and must consult each other to discuss ways to implement policies, allocate resources, and configure court staff, they naturally want *judge–staff relations* and *internal organization* to combine individualism and diversity. *Networked* cultures promote the democratic values that each individual court worker counts and every worker should be consulted. Hence, *networked* cultures will seem especially desirable because of their promise that personnel conflicts will be minimal.

Finally, it is anticipated that judges and court administrators will prefer a *communal* culture in the work area of *courthouse leadership*. This area sets the tone for how the business of the court is to be done. It is neither exclusively nor primarily case- or people-oriented. It is a hybrid governing the mechanics of how the court is to operate and the manner in which court personnel are to treat one another. *Courthouse leadership* is a dimension permeating and guiding the other four work areas. Judges and court administrators want court business done on a collegial basis, where trust and mutual respect reign axiomatically. If these two values are present, then the groundwork is laid for the roles of *hierarchical case management style* and *change management*. Trust ensures policies will be carried out as intended, overcoming the problem that policies are not self-executing. Moreover, mutual respect is the foundation for inclusiveness in the areas of *judge–staff relations* and *internal organization*. This value ensures that everyone's views are taken into account in improving the quality of decisions, policies, and programs. Hence, *communal* courthouse leadership enables other cultural values to govern *case management style*, *change management*, *judge–staff relations*, and *internal organization*.

Little, if any, movement toward an *autonomous* orientation is preferred because the other cultures are deemed superior in each particular work area. The movement away from *autonomous* cultures should be striking. Conventional wisdom suggests that such cultures are currently dominant and likely to continue to exist because of the substantial resistance to administrative controls as well as the lack of opportunity to think reflectively on culture. However, when asked, judges and court administrators are likely to see the pitfalls of continuing this culture.

Consequently, no one cultural orientation is likely to dominate the direction in which courts seek to move. Judges and administrators are apt to believe that success along different cultural content dimensions will call for different cultural orientations. Specifically, it is expected that judges and court administrators prefer the following cultural mosaic—*hierarchical case management style* and *change management*; *networked judge–staff relations* and *internal organization*; and *communal courthouse leadership*.

Results

To address the question of cultural change, respondents in the twelve courts were asked to indicate how they would like to see their organization develop in the near future. For example, would they like to be more like a *hierarchical* court than they are now in managing cases? Or would they like to be more *communal* in how courthouse leadership is exercised? The data were gathered from the Preferred Column of the CCAI (See Appendix 3-1).

The results of the Court Culture Assessment Instrument (CCAI) preferred part of the questionnaire—presented as the average number of points for each culture type—are displayed in Table 6-1. These mean values show the central tendency for each court on each culture type (the standard deviations, median, and coefficient of variation for each of the means is presented in Appendix 6-1).

To gauge the direction and size of the desired changes as well as to make comparisons among courts, Table 6-2 presents the differences between the *current* culture in Table 3-2 and the *preferred* culture in Table 6-1. Negative values indicate a court wants to *decrease* the future emphasis of that culture type for a particular work area, whereas positive values indicate a court wants to *increase* the future emphasis of that culture for the given work area. The differences indicate the strength and type of desired culture change.

Judges and court administrators know the type of culture they prefer. Conversely, they know the aspects of culture they would like to minimize, if not eliminate. In fact, there are twenty-four instances in which a culture type receives a negligible score (i.e., less than 10 points on Table 6-1). As a counterpoint, there are thirty-three instances of average scores greater than or equal to 40, as well as six instances above the 50-point threshold. When it comes to future culture, there is significant strength and clarity of perspective.

As an example, consider Napa County where the average scores on *case management style* reveal that the preferred cultural emphasis is extremely high on the *solidarity* dimension. Of a total of 100 points, Napa County has average scores of 4 for *autonomous* and

TABLE 6-1. RELATIVE EMPHASIS OF PREFERRED COURT CULTURE ON WORK AREAS

Content Dimension	Culture Type	California			Florida		Minnesota						
		Contra Costa	Napa	Ventura	Duval	Pinellas	Dakota	Hennepin	Kandiyohi	Olmsted	Ramsey	Duluth	Virginia
Case Management Style	*Communal*	15	13	22	26	27	20	17	15	15	20	20	20
	Networked	33	38	29	29	15	22	33	36	31	29	23	26
	Autonomous	10	4	11	22	22	16	12	16	8	12	10	16
	Hierarchical	43	46	38	23	36	42	38	34	47	40	48	39
Judge–Staff Relations	*C*	21	10	9	24	18	27	19	18	21	13	21	19
	N	41	43	39	32	33	40	37	45	39	39	40	32
	A	11	3	14	24	33	13	20	8	16	28	21	9
	H	27	43	38	20	16	20	24	29	25	21	19	41
Change Management	*C*	19	14	12	18	26	20	19	21	25	17	13	28
	N	34	36	30	24	24	30	35	39	37	40	54	30
	A	11	3	5	27	13	12	12	7	6	8	6	11
	H	36	47	52	31	38	37	34	33	32	36	28	31
Courthouse Leadership	*C*	41	42	47	34	33	50	36	56	39	32	42	44
	N	34	29	32	25	30	25	39	30	43	42	37	28
	A	7	4	8	19	24	8	11	6	4	9	4	11
	H	18	26	13	21	14	16	15	8	15	18	18	18
Internal Organization	*C*	28	18	24	26	33	31	24	30	27	24	26	26
	N	44	54	49	26	33	35	48	40	44	36	51	34
	A	11	5	9	26	17	18	12	11	12	12	6	11
	H	17	23	18	22	18	16	16	19	18	29	18	29

TABLE 6-2. DIFFERENCES BETWEEN THE AVERAGE SCORES ON CURRENT AND PREFERRED CULTURES

		California			Florida		Minnesota						
Content Dimension	Culture Type	Contra Costa	Napa	Ventura	Duval	Pinellas	Dakota	Hennepin	Kandiyohi	Olmsted	Ramsey	Duluth	Virginia
Case Management Style	*Communal*	0	–1	5	–2	–3	–8	–3	–15	–14	0	–13	–11
	Network	12	7	3	7	0	7	8	12	11	3	13	11
	Autonomous	–22	–15	–14	–12	–15	–19	–15	–6	–12	–8	–27	–7
	Hierarchical	10	9	6	7	18	20	10	9	16	5	27	6
Judge–Staff Relations	*C*	–4	–11	–2	–3	0	–3	1	4	–3	–9	3	–3
	N	15	10	–1	2	–2	12	17	9	5	8	5	6
	A	–12	–8	–4	–2	0	–9	–26	–11	0	–3	–2	–10
	H	2	9	7	4	2	0	9	–1	–2	4	–7	6
Change Management	*C*	–5	–11	–5	–10	–6	–17	–6	–5	–10	–11	–18	–4
	N	12	10	4	9	6	15	11	6	0	11	31	6
	A	–21	–8	–5	–3	–10	–16	–19	–9	–4	–9	–28	–4
	H	15	9	7	4	10	17	14	8	15	9	15	1
Courthouse Leadership	*C*	18	3	7	1	14	18	16	18	2	3	11	4
	N	17	9	3	6	12	7	16	4	7	14	21	9
	A	–29	–12	–9	–7	–25	–23	–26	–18	–7	–21	–39	–6
	H	–6	–1	–1	1	–1	–2	–6	–4	–2	4	8	–6
Internal Organization	*C*	9	–9	0	1	9	7	2	–1	1	–1	6	1
	N	22	22	13	4	13	16	25	6	12	11	22	8
	A	–15	–13	–11	–3	–16	–13	–22	–5	–13	–13	–32	–14
	H	–15	–1	–2	–3	–6	–9	–4	–1	–1	4	5	5

13 for *communal* (low *solidarity*), whereas this county averages 46 for *hierarchical* and 38 for *networked* (high *solidarity*). Napa's scores for *courthouse leadership* show a preference for *sociability*, with average scores of 4 for *autonomous* and 26 for *hierarchical* (low *sociability*), whereas they average 42 for *communal* and 29 for *networked* (high *sociability*). Members of the court are clear on how they must move in the area of *courthouse leadership*: build a more *communal* work environment by minimizing aspects of *autonomous* culture.

Table 6-2 shows the direction and size of the desired changes in all twelve courts. Looking first at *case management style*, every court wants to reduce the *autonomous* component of their culture. There are negative values in the *autonomous* row under *case management style* beginning with Contra Costa (−22) and ending with Virginia (−7). Nine of the twelve courts desire to reduce the *communal* component as well. All of the courts desire a marked increase in both the *hierarchical* and *networked* aspects of their culture. The overwhelming—and widespread—desire is to increase *solidarity*.

The preferred character of *change management* bears many similarities to *case management style*. All of the courts want to decrease the *autonomous* component. Some of the desired changes are substantial and in the direction of *hierarchical* culture. Finally, all but Olmsted desires an increase in the *networked* component of their culture. Therefore, as with *case management*, the courts want to increase *solidarity* in *change management*.

Turning to *judge–staff relations*, all courts, except for Pinellas (no change) and Olmsted (no change), desire to decrease the *autonomous* aspects of their culture in this area, and ten courts desire an increase in the *networked* aspect of culture. In addition, eight of the courts desire an increase in the *hierarchical* component in this area, although the magnitudes are small. Hence, whereas the move toward *networked* cultures is expected, there also is a minor unanticipated move toward *hierarchical* cultures.

Looking at the results for *internal organization*, all the courts want to decrease the *autonomous* culture, whereas nine courts desire to decrease the *hierarchical* culture, as expected. All of the courts seek a substantial increase in the *networked* component and eight of the twelve desire modest increases in the *communal* component. Consequently, whereas the move toward *networked* cultures is as expected, there is also a slight unanticipated move toward *communal* culture.

Patterns in the direction of desired change largely confirm the previously discussed hypotheses. All of the courts wish to develop a culture with greater *solidarity* when it comes to managing cases and managing change. In these domains, the dominant desire is on developing and using modern management techniques. In contrast, all of the courts wish to develop a culture that has more *sociability* and *solidarity* when it comes to *judge–staff relations* and *internal organization*. In these areas, the courts appear to want a culture emphasizing the core values of a *networked* culture. Finally, when it comes to *courthouse leadership*, there is a common desire among all twelve of the courts for a culture that is more *communal* in nature. Taken together, the courts in this study do not aspire to a single cultural type. Instead, they wish to align particular cultural values with particular work areas.

Culture kites create a graphic display of the results in Tables 6-1 and 6-2 and, hence, provide a visualization of the desired changes. Court culture kites can be used both to illuminate the preferred culture and to compare it to the current culture. To gain insight into the preferred cultures, attention is focused on the five work areas in Contra Costa (CA).[2] The original culture for *case management* has a trapezoid-like shape, whereas the preferred culture is more kite-like, as shown in Figure 6-1. The desired movement is toward more *solidarity* and somewhat more *sociability*. The preferred culture is *hierarchical*, with a strength in excess of 40. Therefore, in this work area, there is both a movement and sharpening of cultural values.

Figure 6-2 presents the current and preferred cultures for the *judge–staff relations* work area. Although the current culture has a distinctly square shape, the preferred culture is again more kite-like. The movement is decidedly toward more *sociability* and somewhat more *solidarity*. The primary culture type is *networked* with a strength of approximately 40 points. Again, one finds both cultural movement as well as cultural sharpening.

For *change management*, there is a shift from the current amorphous culture *square* to a preferred trapezoid-like structure (Figure 6-3). The preferred culture type is a combination of *hierarchical* and *networked*, each with a strength of 35 points. Although there is a clear desire for more *solidarity*, there is no clear preference for a single primary culture type.

The current culture for *courthouse leadership* is *autonomous*; however, the desired culture is a marked shift toward *communal*, as shown

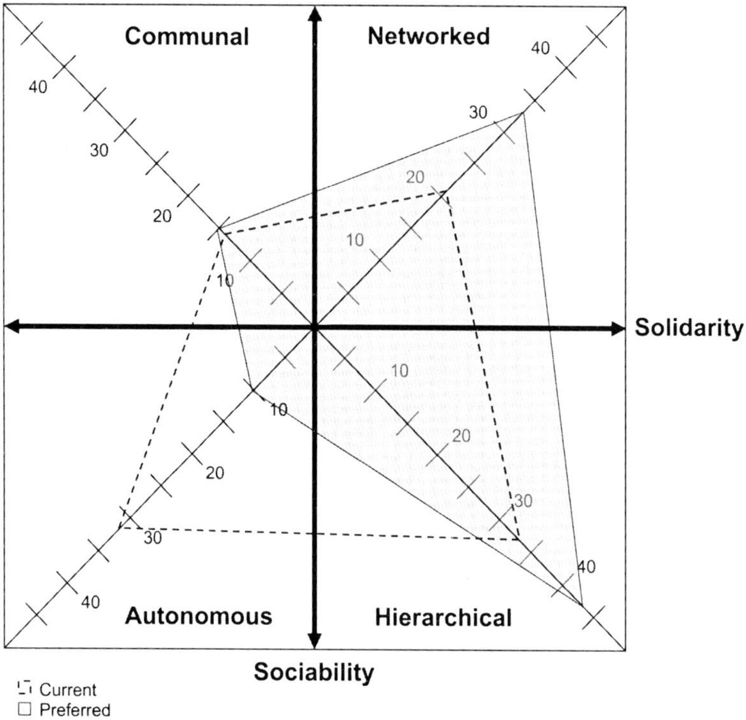

Fig 6.1 Current and Preferred Contra Costa Case Management Style

in Figure 6-4. Not only is there is a clear preference for increasing the *sociability* of the culture in this important work area, but there is a desire for a strong primary *communal* culture (strength of 40).

In the area of *internal organization*, the current culture has a square-like shape, whereas the preferred culture has a distinctly kite shape with a rather long tail (Figure 6-5). The preferred culture is *networked*, with a strength of 44. There is a clear desire for a dominant primary culture in this work area.

Looking at the five kites together, it is readily apparent that the Contra Costa judges and administrators prefer a cultural mosaic that is substantially different from the current cultural configuration. In some instances the changes reflect a desire for more *solidarity* or *sociability*, whereas in others there is a desire for a strong primary culture. In every instance, the court desires change.

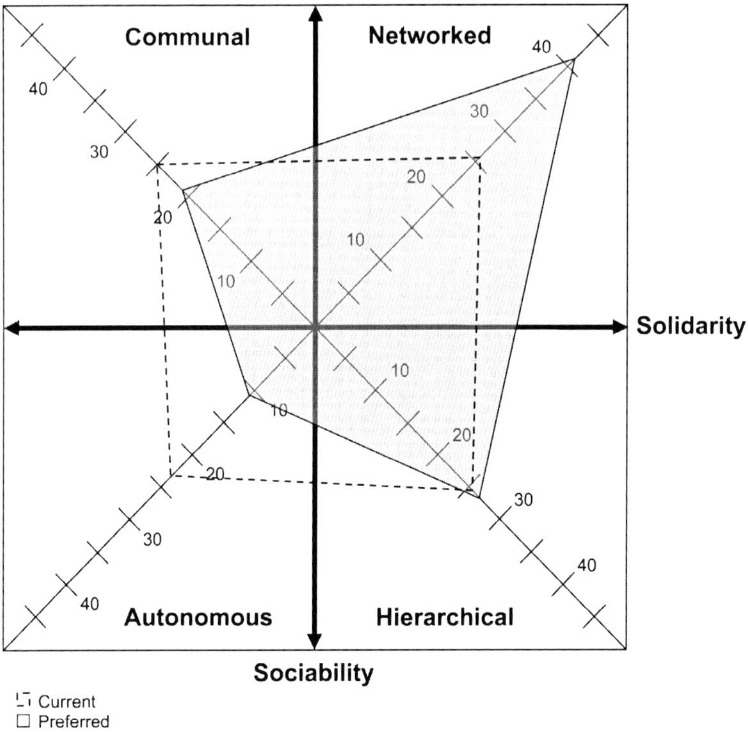

Fig 6.2 Current and Preferred Contra Costa Judge Staff-Relations

The third hypothesis presented at the beginning of this chapter, proposes a high degree of similarity in the type of cultural mosaic that courts aspire to. To test this hypothesis, Table 6-3 presents the product moment correlations between the preferred cultural patterns in each of the courts and can be compared with current cultural patterns described in Table 3-4 in Chapter 3. In terms of current culture, recall only 16 of the 66 correlations were statistically significant and positive, whereas 4 were statistically significant and negative. In Table 6-3, 56 of the 66 correlations are significant ($p < 0.05$) and positive; in fact, more than half of the correlations are greater than 0.80. With the exception of the two Florida courts, where Table 6-3 shows the two courts to have low correlations with other courts as well as between themselves, there is a great deal of homogeneity in the desired cultural configurations in the trial courts.

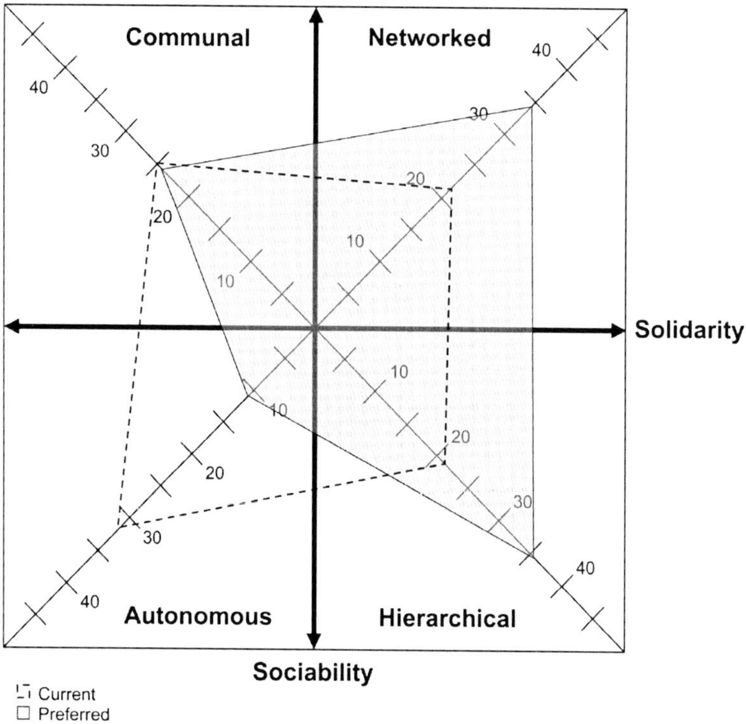

Fig 6.3 Current and Preferred Contra Costa Change Management

The Florida courts are not only different from the courts in California and Minnesota, they are also not correlated significantly with one another. The reason for this finding may lie in the electoral process. The electoral process in Florida affects both the court and the system in which the judiciary is expected to exert a leadership role. Florida's judges emphasize their independence from each other and from the court's presiding judge in deciding how to handle their cases purposefully and deliberatively. Moreover, the primacy of elections in Florida accentuates the respective missions of prosecutors and defense attorneys in protecting society versus protecting the constitutional rights of defendants. Prosecutors and defense counsel truly see themselves representing different institutions because of their elected constitutional officer status. Simply stated, the independence grounded in the electoral process along with the local form

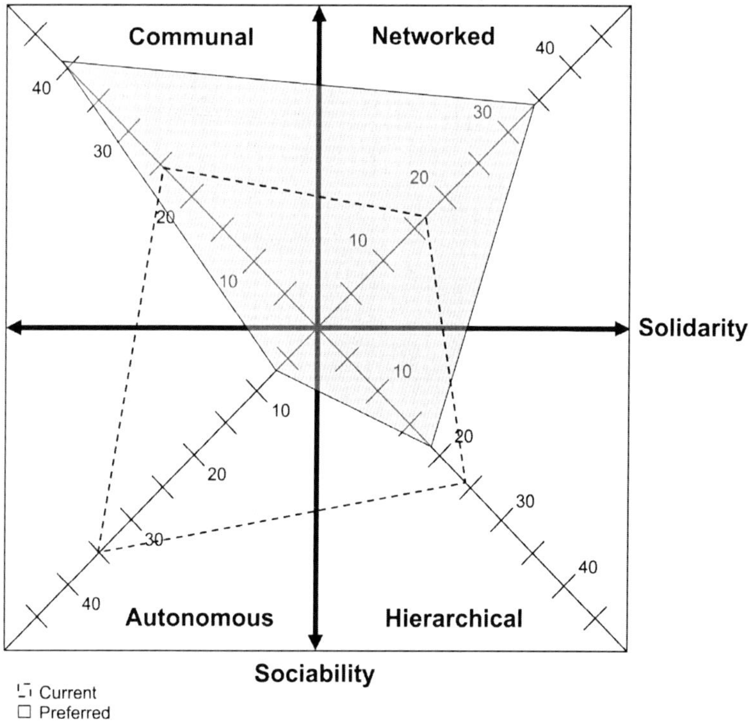

Fig 6.4 Current and Preferred Contra Costa Courthouse Leadership

of court financing in Florida, appears to have some marked cultural consequences.

Concerning the primary type and strength of *preferred* court culture type, the pattern of preferred cultures is consistent with hypothesized preference for a *hierarchical* culture in both *case management style* and *change management*. Eleven of the courts have a preference for a *hierarchical* culture in the *case management style* work area, whereas six of the courts have that preference in *change management*, as shown in Table 6-4. In the case of *change management*, the second choice is the other culture that is high on the *solidarity* dimension—*networked*. It was hypothesized that there would be a preference for a *networked* culture in both *judge–staff relations* and *internal organization*. As can be seen, all the courts have a preference for a *networked* culture in the *judge–staff relations* work area, whereas all but one

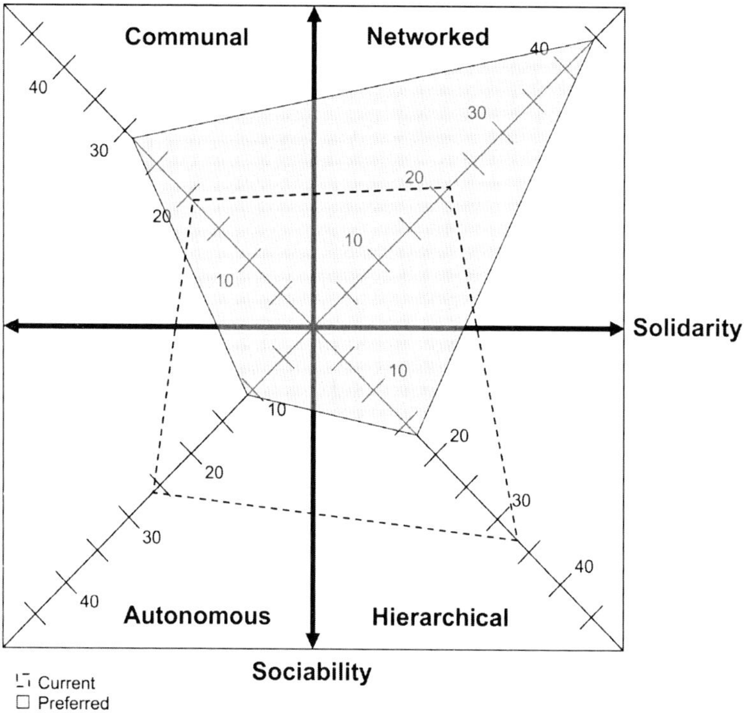

Fig 6.5 Current and Preferred Contra Costa Internal Organization

court (Duval) has that preference in the *internal organization* work area. Finally, it was hypothesized that there would be a preference for a *communal* culture in the *courthouse leadership* work area. As can be seen, with one exception (Hennepin), this hypothesis is supported by the data.

Concerning the strength of the preferred cultures, 33 of the preferred cultures have an average score of 40 or greater; this compares to only six such averages for current cultures, as shown in Table 3-3. It is also interesting to note that in Table 6-1, 24 of the average scores are less than 10, whereas Table 3-3 had no such low numbers. Therefore, desired cultural preferences are stronger than their current counterparts.

Courts prefer different culture types for different work areas, as seen in Table 6-4. What is surprising is the degree of uniformity across

TABLE 6-3. PRODUCT MOMENT CORRELATION—PREFERRED CULTURE AVERAGE SCORES BY WORK AREA

	Contra Costa	Napa	Ventura	Duval	Pinellas	Dakota	Hennepin	Kandiyohi	Olmsted	Ramsey	Duluth	Virginia
Contra Costa	1.000											
Napa	**0.924**	1.000										
Ventura	**0.900**	**0.928**	1.000									
Duval	**0.532**	0.406	**0.556**	1.000								
Pinellas	**0.558**	0.405	**0.624**	0.379	1.000							
Dakota	**0.893**	**0.752**	**0.812**	**0.650**	**0.661**	1.000						
Hennepin	**0.957**	**0.871**	**0.883**	**0.499**	**0.612**	**0.797**	1.000					
Kandiyohi	**0.922**	**0.834**	**0.862**	**0.609**	**0.512**	**0.891**	**0.865**	1.000				
Olmsted	**0.963**	**0.852**	**0.834**	0.414	**0.600**	**0.840**	**0.959**	**0.872**	1.000			
Ramsey	**0.843**	**0.785**	**0.802**	0.429	**0.640**	**0.695**	**0.890**	**0.756**	**0.894**	1.000		
Duluth	**0.891**	**0.786**	**0.776**	0.407	**0.598**	**0.807**	**0.912**	**0.815**	**0.913**	**0.887**	1.000	
Virginia	**0.846**	**0.871**	**0.838**	0.283	0.404	**0.778**	**0.740**	**0.865**	**0.814**	**0.675**	**0.707**	1.000

Correlation coefficients $p<.05$ are in bold.

TABLE 6-4. PRIMARY PREFERRED COURT CULTURE TYPES

		Case Management Style		Judge–Staff Relations		Change Management		Courthouse Leadership		Internal Organization	
		Primary Culture	Strength	Primary Culture	Strength	Primary Culture	Strength	Primary Culture	Strength	Primary Culture	Strength
California	**Contra Costa**	H	43	N	41	H	36	C	41	N	44
	Napa	H	46	N/A	43	H	47	C	42	N	54
	Ventura	H	38	N	39	H	52	C	47	N	49
Florida	**Duval**	N	29	N	32	H	31	C	34	*	*
	Pinellas	H	36	N/A	33	H	38	C	33	N/C	33
Minnesota	**Dakota**	H	42	N	40	H	37	C	50	N	35
	Hennepin	H	38	N	37	N	35	N	39	N	48
	Kandiyohi	H	36	N	45	N	39	C	56	N	40
	Olmsted	H	47	N	39	N	37	N	43	N	44
	Ramsey	H	40	N	39	N	40	N	42	N	36
	Duluth	H	48	N	40	N	54	C	42	N	51
	Virginia	H	39	N	41	C	31	C	44	N	34

Note: C = Communal; N = Networked; A = Autonomous; H = Hierachical.
* = No primary culture.

courts in terms of their preferences. Thus, not only do courts desire a cultural mosaic, they prefer moving toward a mosaic that bears striking similarity across courts. This raises the possibility that there may be a mental picture of an ideal mixture of the various culture types.

However, given that courts desire a mosaic of culture types across the work areas, does the preferred incongruence suggest that courts will find effective management extremely difficult, if not virtually impossible? When one looks at the type of cultural incongruence desired, it is important to see that—with the exception of *courthouse leadership*—respondents desire cultures with a high degree of *solidarity*. Multiple cultures arise because judges and court administrators believe different degrees of *sociability* also are required in individual work areas. As a result, the cultures making up the mosaic are different but adjacent to one another. This situation is likely more manageable than if the cultures were diagonally opposed to one another.

But perhaps of greater relevance to court management is whether a reform agenda set by internal court leadership can overcome traditional concerns about resistance to change by judicial institutions. Some experts contend that almost all efforts to reform courts through administrative means fail, and do so because of the fragmentary nature of courts. A leading exponent of this view argues courts are not "bureaucratic structures" that can be induced to accept and implement change through "greater coordination and management" (Feeley 1983, p. 205).

Without questioning the merits of Feeley's thesis, his assertion that judges resist change because of a common desire to be free from external influence is less in direct conflict with the preferred mosaic than what might appear at first glance. Feeley takes great pains to identify and document outsiders, such as legislators, the public, the press, and scholars, as the sources of the attempted reforms he examines. He focuses on planned changes, such as sentence reform and speedy trial rules, both of which were inspirations emanating from outside the courthouse.

In contrast, the source for preferred change in court culture emanates from inside the courthouse. Judges and administrators were asked to state how they would like to see their court operate in the future. Their views were the basis for the emergent cultural mosaic. Moreover, the work areas subject to culture's effect are themselves internal to court operations. Therefore, Feeley's sound commentary on the problematic nature of externally based changes in how courts function, does not clash with current research results or reasoning. In fact, Feeley's acute insight implies that the internally generated desire by judges and administrators for a cultural mosaic stands a fair chance of taking hold and directing a major portion of future court agendas. Of course, this does not suggest the road of change is easy to navigate.

Summary

Despite differences among courts in the nature of current culture, all courts prefer a strikingly similar future culture. Courts envision a *cultural mosaic* that assigns a particular culture to a particular work area: *communal courthouse leadership*, *hierarchical case management style* and *change management*, *networked judge–staff relations* and *internal organization*, and virtually no *autonomous* culture. This preferred combination of cultural orientations places considerable responsibilities on the presiding judge to lead the court by fostering agreement among members and staff of the court in a collegial manner. And the presiding judge needs to encourage other judges and staff to embrace one set of cultural orientations in *case management style* and *change management* and another set in *judge–staff relations* and *internal organization*. Clearly, this role calls for the presiding judge to be deft in building agreement and not asserting authority unilaterally or collaborating with a particular coalition on the court. Such skills are needed to move the culturally diverse court steadily forward.

Experts on private sector organizations would say the pursuit of multiple cultures is a sign of incongruence and possibly inhibits positive performance (Cameron and Quinn 1999, p. 64). However, this issue strikes at the heart of the difference between private and public sector organizations. Whereas the pursuit of profit and minimization of cost binds private organizations into tightly cohesive cultures, public organizations have multiple cultures because they have multiple goals and multiple "clients," including litigants, attorneys, taxpayers, and policy makers in addition to their own needs. Thus, whereas incongruent court cultures will require extensive skill sets to manage, that is likely be the nature and challenge of public sector organizations like courts.

One final observation is that the desired cultural incongruence places a premium on leadership. This means that supervising judges and court administrators must employ multiple policies that work with the multiple cultures and the system dynamics created by the cultural incongruities. This, in turn, makes it imperative for a court to diagnose both its current and preferred cultural makeup. This additional complexity will become an important factor in managing the direction and performance of the court.[3]

7 Conclusions and Implications

Happy Courts are all alike; every unhappy court is unhappy in its own way.

Introduction

We summarize our principal finding—with apologies to Leo Tolstoy and a slight reworking of the famous first line from *Anna Karenina*: "Happy families are all alike; every unhappy family is unhappy in its own way" as an epigraph to this chapter. Jared Diamond initially uses the quotation to illustrate why so few wild animals have been successfully domesticated throughout history—for a species to be domesticated, a great number of factors have to be just right. Success in domestication comes not from a particular positive characteristic of the species, but by avoiding any number of possible negative factors. Diamond (1997, p. 157) also discusses the principle in the context of social relations when he reminds us that what Tolstoy meant was "in order to be happy, a marriage must succeed in many different respects: sexual attraction, agreement about money, child discipline, religion, in-laws, and other vital issues. Failure in any one of these essential respects can doom a marriage even if it has all the other ingredients needed for happiness." Diamond names this notable insight the *Anna Karenina* Principle and states: "This principle can be extended to understanding much else about life besides marriage. We tend to seek easy, single-factor explanations of success. For most important things, though, success actually requires avoiding many separate possible causes of failure" (1997, p. 157).

The *Anna Karenina* Principle operates in trial courts as well. There is no *single* key to success. To be successful across all five trial court work areas, courts must pay attention simultaneously to multiple, and often competing, values. Given the preference for a cultural mosaic, there are many ways in which court leaders can fail. In the concluding chapter, six basic propositions about court culture are offered that summarize the key findings of this research. The management implications that flow from these basic propositions are examined. The chapter concludes by considering how the research fits into the larger public policy picture.

Six Propositions

A contribution of the current research is the use of a conceptual framework and measurement tools that permit the variation in court cultures to be captured and described in a coherent and comprehensible manner. The variety of cultures is reducible to the combination of four cultures operating in five work areas, such as *case management style, judge–staff relations, and courthouse leadership*. As a result, the realities of court cultures are not bewildering and, in fact, can be linked to observable variation in performance. Through the course of this research, six general propositions about culture have emerged as a foundation for thinking managerially about American trial courts:

1. Culture plays an important role in how trial courts function.
2. Culture can be measured, and the competing cultural values can be arrayed in a two-dimensional conceptual framework.
3. Courts are amalgams of the four primary cultural archetypes in each of the work areas.
4. None of the four culture types is either bad or good by definition.
5. Culture has performance consequences.
6. Courts, when asked to consider the future, desire a remarkably similar mosaic of cultural archetypes.

These propositions have many implications for the meaning and scope of management in courts. In particular, a more refined understanding of culture helps clarify how the judge's role in management is interwoven with the work of the court administrator.

Culture Plays an Important Role in How Courts Function

The book begins with a vignette involving a conversation between two court administrators. The two administrators found that despite strong similarities in court size, structure, technology, and processes, there were equally strong differences in organizational relations and performance. Culture was singled out as the distinguishing feature. Court leaders and managers know, at least intuitively, that particular types of cultures form as a result of certain values, assumptions, and priorities becoming dominant in the organization.

Previous research supports, and, in fact, leads judges and administrators to think culture truly explains why courts vary in performance. The notion of *local legal culture*, advanced in the 1970s as a reason for observed differences in court performance and for varied success in adopting new ideas, continues to influence contemporary conversations, as illustrated in the scenario in Chapter 1. However, questions remain about exactly what distinguishes one culture from another and how, why, and to what extent the distinctions actually make a difference in what courts do. Without identifying and measuring the distinctions, no one, including both scholars and practitioners, can point to what makes some courts more closely approximate desired goals than other courts. To suggest certain kinds of cultures lead to success raises the questions: what do you mean and how do you know it?

The current research addresses these two essential questions and offers a conceptual framework based on the organizing ideas of culture, work, and performance. By measuring these concepts and observing how the measures are related, important conclusions are drawn about the consequences of differences in cultural orientations and the type of cultural configuration judges and administrators aspire to achieve in the future. Implications for court management bring the findings directly into the arena for discussion and application by practitioners.

Culture Can Be Measured and the Competing Cultural Values Can Be Arrayed in a Single Conceptual Framework

Four distinct cultural orientations concerning how felony criminal cases are handled in contemporary American trial courts are identified:

(1) *communal*, (2) *networked*, (3) *autonomous*, and (4) *hierarchical*. These four cultures represent particular combinations (high, low) of two foundational dimensions: (1) *solidarity* and (2) *sociability*.

Solidarity represents the extent to which a group of individuals in an organization are bound together, ranging from a loosely knit conglomerate to a cohesive entity unified around explicit roles. *Sociability* captures the nature of the attachment individuals in an organization have toward one another, ranging from close personal ties to little social interaction as the rules and structure determine what is to be done. Taken together, the two dimensions create four quadrants, each of which represents one of the following distinct court culture types:

- *Communal* cultures are low on *solidarity* and high on *sociability*. Judges and administrators are team players but coordinate their actions by following norms that the *team* has agreed are reasonably mutually beneficial. Very few sharp edges exist in this court.
- *Networked* cultures are high on *solidarity* and high on *sociability*. Judges and administrators are drawn to design and apply general rules of behavior, but structured orientations are more like guidelines than rules. Judges and administrators try to accommodate the maximum number of colleagues resulting in the formation of principles permitting departures when an individual deems it appropriate and necessary.
- *Autonomous* cultures are low on *solidarity* and *sociability*, resulting in limited court-wide polices except the idea that the discretion of individual judges and corresponding staff is to be respected. Each chamber takes on the character of a solo legal practitioner, although some chambers might occasionally find they have enough in common to form a small law firm like coalition.
- *Hierarchical* cultures are high on *solidarity* and low on *sociability*. They are organized and mobilized to get the job done and done in a common manner by following an explicit set of rules. Written court policies and procedures are to be applied in a uniform manner by all judges.

These cultural types are not just theoretical abstractions, they capture the distilled essence of trial courts. Each culture type emphasizes a distinct blend of values that represent different ways of seeing the world of judicial administration. Or as Quinn (1988, p. 42) observes in his study of private sector organizations, the different cultural configurations "represent the values that precede the assumptions that people make about what is good and what is bad, the unseen values for whose sake people, programs, policies, and organizations live and die." These archetypes capture the ways work gets done in felony trial courts.

Courts Are Amalgams of the Four Primary Cultural Archetypes in Each of the Work Areas

To bring greater precision and evidence to the discussion of court culture, instruments have been adapted from private sector organizational studies. The result, called the Court Culture Assessment Instrument (CCAI), captures the views of judges and administrators on how they see their court operating in five key work areas: (1) *case management style,* (2) *judge–staff relations,* (3) *change management,* (4) *courthouse leadership, and* (5) *internal organization*. Results obtained from administering the CCAI in the twelve courts are presented graphically in the form of culture kites. These diagrams show the strength, center of gravity, and congruence of court culture across the five work areas.

The fact that in most courts different cultures are strong on different areas of work is striking, unexpected, and divergent with the theory and reality of private sector cultures where congruency is found to be essential for organizational effectiveness. In the well-managed business, one culture tends to dominate all areas of work, although the predominant culture might vary from organization to organization. Building upon insights from James Q. Wilson (1989), it appears that public organizations do not have the luxury of a single culture and instead face multiple and often competing cultures.

Since cultures reflect underlying values, they emerge from choices made by judges and court administrators on how they believe work should be organized and accomplished. Each culture has a particular manner of conducting business in five work areas. The *court culture value matrix* introduced in Chapter 2 provides a summary of the way work is done in each content area according to the ideal form of each culture. However, the conceptual classification of multiple cultures and multiple work areas does not mean courts in the real world will be *pure* types, being characterized completely by a single dominant culture.

Detailed examination of culture within the twelve courts from California, Florida, and Minnesota affirm the existence of all four cultural types. There are examples of the four cultures within the seven courts located in the single state of Minnesota. Hence, this robust framework likely describes the basic cultural orientations that exist in the broader court community beyond the courts under study.

This view is neatly summarized by Quinn when he writes: "[r]eal organizations do not fall neatly into one or the other of these four models. In fact, the models do not contain organizations, organizations contain the models, all of them. In every organization all four models exist" (1988, p. 45). To a greater or lesser extent, all of the values in the *court culture value matrix* are *in play* in every trial court each day. What gives a court its distinctive culture is the relative emphasis given to the combinations of cultural values expressed in different work areas.

None of the Four Culture Types Is Either Bad or Good by Definition

Chapter 4 describes and illustrates the defining characteristics of the four culture types based upon an extensive series of interviews with judges, administrators, and attorneys. In the course of these interviews, it became clear that the values underlying each of the four culture types manifest themselves in both positive and negative ways across the five work areas. The key is that a particular culture type is effective only when it is appropriate to the work area and the goals to be achieved.

The four culture types provide a framework to discuss general characteristics that define and differentiate how courts see and organize themselves. For example, those favoring a *hierarchical* approach in the area of *judge–staff* relations see more planning, more control, and more standard practices as most conducive to clear task focus and goal attainment. Alternatively, a *communal* approach views the spirit of accommodation, concern about motivation, and attention to the psychological nature of workers as the means for greater teamwork and positive accomplishment.

On the negative side, *communal* court cultures often lack monitoring mechanisms and may overlook problems for an unnecessarily long period of time. Because limited centralized leadership exists and personal relationships are valued, it is difficult to rein in personnel problems. Friendship is valued and formal authority is eschewed. Consequently, it is often difficult to change nonproductive behaviors. Because *hierarchical* courts are lower on *sociability*, they may be influenced by a lack of loyalty and trust in the relations between judges and staff. The chain of command does not necessarily induce a respectful willingness to cooperate. In fact, a *hierarchical* court might have few opportunities where everyone can voice ideas. Consequently, only a restrained feeling might exist among judges and staff to pull together.

The four culture types reflect deep-seated views on the appropriate role of the judiciary in the adversary system; how judges, court administrators, and staff organize their work; and the extent to which the court cooperates and collaborates with the wider criminal justice system. Conversations with practitioners in the twelve courts point to the actual cultural amalgam being a dynamic process. Pursuit of one set of cultural values requires the ability to also incorporate directly competing values in order to achieve balance. For example, the *communal* courthouse values the ideals of *sociability* to build high morale and esprit de corps. Yet, to avoid the negative side, there is also a need to adopt positive values from the *hierarchical* culture type. Appropriate planning and use of standardized procedures help tame the more freewheeling flexibility and accommodation of the *communal* culture. Hence, there is a strong sense in which each court desires to embrace the positive aspects of all four cultures to achieve the balance necessary for high performance.

Culture Has Performance Consequences

As noted in Chapter 1, two common features characterize criminal caseloads in American trial courts. First, similarities in cases coming to courts are more prominent than differences. For example, if felony criminal cases are grouped by the seriousness of the offense (e.g., homicide, other crimes against the person, property crimes, drug crimes, and other types of felonies), the rank ordering of the categories is the same in most communities, regardless of population size or geographic location. Second, these similar criminal caseloads are resolved quite differently. The manner of resolution can be measured in alternative ways, but a simple and observable indicator is timeliness. What is striking is the wide variety of case-processing times. Some courts take five or more times as long as the more expeditious courts to resolve cases, despite little difference in caseload composition. Hence, an intriguing question arises: how and why do some courts get the same basic work done in noticeably different time-frames than do other courts? Based upon the current research, the answer lies in organizational culture.

Embracing a culture has consequences. For example, courts with *hierarchical* cultures achieve objective standards of timeliness promoted by the American Bar Association (ABA) and other groups more closely than courts with other dominant cultures do. Interestingly, all of the courts under study exhibit awareness of this connection. Every court, according to the preferences of judges and administrators, seeks to increase its *hierarchical* culture in the area of case management. This common desire likely arises because none of the courts currently meet the ABA-prescribed timeframes. Courts are cognizant of this situation and seek to do better by moving toward a culture more conducive to expedition and timeliness.

Like culture, court performance has multiple dimensions. Moving beyond timeliness, courts can also be judged on how well they achieve other important goals, such as access, fairness, and managerial effectiveness. Expanding the set of performance criteria also increases the management challenge because what it means to be a high performance court can be open to interpretation. As shown in Chapter 5, the parties involved in handling criminal cases, including judges, attorneys, and court administrators, have different opinions on how a court system can best achieve multiple goals.

Prosecutors and public defenders may not see only virtue in a court's emphasis on *solidarity* and a move toward a more hierarchical culture to achieve greater timeliness. Both sets of attorneys see greater benefits to themselves from the courtroom workgroup relations fostered by an autonomous culture's minimal emphasis on solidarity. Vested interest in established work patterns leads attorneys to view courts with autonomous cultures as also doing better when it comes to access, fairness, and managerial effectiveness. Further complexity is introduced because prosecutors and public defenders disagree over the relative merits and limitations of other cultures. The former see the greatest advantage in networked cultures and defense attorneys embrace communal cultures most closely. But both will happily accept *autonomous*—the least preferred by the judges and senior court administrators interested in improving overall court performance. No one culture is obviously going to enjoy the support of everyone.

As a result, judicial administrators confront a process in which the courts, prosecutors, and public defenders all have different views of the kind of court cultures most and least conducive to achieving strong performance. Hence, court managers must take steps to assemble information needed to make a credible and persuasive case for the cultural mosaic they deem most appropriate and at the same time enhance their standing among attorneys on the goals of timeliness, access, fairness, and managerial effectiveness.

For example, courts should avoid reporting timeliness strictly in terms of what percentiles of cases they resolve in particular numbers of days. Instead, courts should demonstrate how the elapsed time taken to resolve cases is proportional to the seriousness, complexity, and difficulty of cases.[1] At the very least, courts should show understanding that it typically takes more time to resolve, say, serious person crimes than property crimes. When courts do not exhibit knowledge and awareness of the sources of variation in case-processing times, attorneys and the public are left to think *delay* was due to omission ("falling between the cracks"), a notoriously inept judge, or lack of managerial attention. Courts need to communicate and demonstrate that they are giving each case individual attention in proportion to what is warranted given the real work constraints of limited resources. To institute a more comprehensive system of performance assessment, court leadership must address not only judicial reactions to change, but also the other key institutional actors. Without appropriate communication and planning, court initiated movement in the direction of, say, greater timeliness risks backlash from attorneys who are being pushed outside their comfort zone.

Courts, When Asked to Consider the Future, Desire a Remarkably Similar Mosaic of Cultural Archetypes

Judges and court managers recognize that no single culture is necessarily the most appropriate or efficacious in all situations. Courts demonstrate sensitivity to the complex nature of culture by preferring a distinct combination of cultures across different work areas. Specifically, the courts under study desire to move to a cultural orientation with a *hierarchical* emphasis in *case management style* and *change management*, a *networked* emphasis in *judge–staff relations* and *internal organization*, and a *communal* emphasis in *courthouse leadership*.

Understandably, judges and administrators want to stress *solidarity* in work areas (*case management style, change management*) whose substantive nature focuses on cases and aggregate concepts such as backlog, size of caseloads, and productivity and stress *sociability* in work areas (*judge–staff relations* and *internal organization*) whose substantive nature focuses on social relations and individual level concepts such as inclusiveness, personal growth and diversity. Moreover, the preference for *communal courthouse leadership* suggests judges and administrators recognize that this area is a hybrid of case flow and social relations, and that the *correct* culture is one that will set the right tone for the court overall and one that can effectively maintain intra-court cultural differences across other, more specific work areas.

The weaving of multiple cultures into a mosaic form undoubtedly will prove to be an internal challenge for any court. Scholars of private sector organizations contend that cultural incongruency, the presence of multiple cultures, with a different one dominating a particular work dimension, poses a daunting test to organizational effectiveness. Many theorists argue that private sector organizations work best when a single culture orients all facets and subunits. Congruency's effect would seem to follow from the common goals of private organizations to remain profitable and maximize shareholder value. Yet, for courts and other public sector organizations, successful performance likely requires the ability to accommodate and manage multiple cultures simultaneously. Neither task is easy nor comfortable; this arrangement underscores the great challenge of professional court administration.

Management Implications

The desire for a cultural mosaic places heightened responsibilities on the administrative leadership of courts, the chief judge and court administrator in particular. Whereas previous research calls on chief judges to lead efforts directed at reform and self-improvement, the implications of a preferred mosaic reveal the contours of leadership to be more challenging than simply exerting the force of personality, leading by example, and occasionally insisting on compliance to agreed policies. Leading a court requires a coherent and innovative management plan.

According to the *Anna Karenina* Principle and the opinions of modern organization experts, it is understandable that American trial courts struggle to achieve organizational effectiveness. Success in trial court management requires purposeful and deliberative leadership rather than forceful tactics or combative reactions. This is particularly true as a court takes steps to implement an organizational culture change effort. Steps must be taken to promote involvement and minimize resistance, to clarify what the new cultural emphases will be, and to establish a plan of action to initiate and encourage momentum for change. One initial question that often arises is "do we really have to go through all the consensus building and planning, isn't there one best court culture that we should seek to implement?"

Members of the legal profession, including some judges and administrators, have gone back and forth on whether there is one best way to organize and manage the courts. Over thirty years ago, in the classic *Managing the Courts*, Friesen et al. (1971, pp. 9–10) observed:

> The courts of the United States reflect an institution in search of viable management models for modernizing their operations. The court environment is identifiable. *Its culture is established.* The courts require a rational but realistic approach to organizing for management purposes... The challenge many courts face is how to develop and operationalize a management model that fits the courts' unique features, yet benefits from the experience of other complex organizations with which they share common problems. [Emphasis added]

The fundamental premise of this argument is that an optimum court management model can be developed because court culture is established and the court environment is clearly identified and understood. The belief in a universalistic model of court administration aligns with the *one size fits all* tradition of rational management.

In contrast, in *American Court Management: Theories and Practice,* David A. Saari (1982, p. 139) declares that "courts cannot be structured or managed in one best way." In place of a single model, Saari states (p. 140):

> [T]here are too many variables in the court environment to achieve an ideal form [of management] . . . it is presumptuous to posit simplicity in structure and clarity in management and responsibility and strive for organizational symmetry for its own sake. *Centralizing power has its virtues and faults, just as decentralizing power has its own virtues and faults.* [Emphasis added]

Saari recognizes that there are too many individual variations among courts to say precisely how they should be organized and run in all circumstances. Successful management depends on knowing that different values (e.g., centralizing power) can reveal themselves in both positive and negative ways. That is, centralization can work in some environments and not in others. The key is to accentuate the aspect of each value that is most appropriate to achieving desired ends in each particular court.

In *Beyond Rational Management*, Quinn (1988) provides many examples of the positive and negative aspects of competing and complementary values. The clear implication is that there is no single culture that is appropriate in all instances.

> Management theory . . . is based on hierarchical logic, and is filled with rules of action. The problem is that as individuals come to better understand the dynamic world of real organizations, they also discover that these rules are insufficient and limiting. They learn to see the world in more dynamic, holistic, and intuitive ways. *They discover the difference between the map and the territory.* [Emphasis added]

The hard fact is that no single map exists to serve all court leaders and managers. There is no *best* culture that offers a shortcut for completing the complex agenda of culture change. Rather, judges and administrators must engage in a systematic process to uncover and document the terrain of the work environment in their own particular court. Fortunately, there are actionable steps that court leaders can follow in deciding how to put a more effective culture into place.

The utility of the framework described in this book is that it provides a means for a court to diagnose and initiate change in its underlying organizational culture. Results from the CCAI reflect an initial take on the basic values and behaviors extant in the court. From the perspective of the five work areas, the instrument measures where the court is and where it wants to be. The first step is to reach consensus by key individuals in the court on the current culture and the desired future culture—these results are necessary to develop and implement an action plan.

Preparing to Implement Cultural Change in Trial Courts

The fourfold typology of culture provides a framework for a court seeking to find new and better ways to organize and conduct business. The architecture framing the four cultures helps steer courts as they work to design their own particular desired configurations. A focused implementation process consists of five basic steps.

First, any court aspiring to cultural change invites an appropriately representative combination of judges, commissioners, administrators, and senior managers to complete the CCAI. After completing the questionnaire, individuals meet together to review the results with the goal of reaching consensus on current court culture. (If a court desires to share more information on the four cultures in advance of the meeting, Chapter 4 provides a solid overview of the pluses and minuses of each culture across the five work areas.). The face-to-face meeting allows alternative perceptions on current culture to be voiced and discussed. Given ongoing work responsibilities and divergent schedules of the participants, it is likely that the court will need to organize separate meetings with each subgroup, establishing their consensual views on culture. A related concern is creating an environment where all people involved feel free to speak. In the traditional world of courts, power is not equally distributed between judges and administrators. It can be difficult for senior administrative members to candidly express opinions in an open forum with judges if they do not believe that they are perceived as valued team members. Because the orientations of judges and administrators may be incompatible, separate meetings may be necessary to encourage open discussion and the surfacing of constructive opinions and ideas.

Second, the process in the first step should be repeated to identify the preferred future culture. By keeping the discussion of preferred culture separate from current culture, participants are able to focus more closely on the emerging demands facing their court, on identifying existing bottlenecks and management challenges, on how to develop greater trust and improved work relationships, and on defining what it means to be a high performing court that is delivering great service to the public. Looking to the future, is there a mosaic of preferred cultures? Again, the goal is to reach consensus on a preferred culture that the organization can commit to and strive to achieve. The conversations on current and preferred culture are likely to be among the best aspects of the entire change process.

Third, the presiding judge convenes a meeting of a *working group*, composed of a representative set of judges and administrators, to draw together the work of the subgroups and generate an overall consensus on current culture. This *working group* is charged with identifying, interpreting, and weaving together the results from both judge and administrator surveys to address a fundamental question: Does the classification of the four cultures and their manifestations across the five work areas make sense? Basically, members of this group must determine if they recognize their court in the numerical and graphic patterns. The results gain essential credibility and thereby enhanced utility if almost everyone agrees that the numbers accurately indicate what cultures are the most and least influential on the separate work areas.

The next phase of the working group meeting (or meetings) should be directed in a parallel manner at the results concerning the court's preferred culture. Just as with the current orientation, the meeting participants should discuss whether the preferred schemata conform to what they think should be the court's future orientations. In addition to noting how the preferred cultures for each work area differ from their current counterpart, the meeting should address: What is the rationale for a desired move from the current situation to a new and different orientation?

Fourth, after the working group meeting(s), the administrative leadership of the court must explore the actions necessary to put their preferred cultural orientation into practice. No two courts have the same set of policies and procedures, but they all have the same basic work areas. Hence, the task is for each court to identify which existing policies, procedures, and practices support desired change and which must be added, modified, or dropped. In future meetings, court leadership can return to these issues, receiving regular reports from individuals with responsibility to define, monitor, and report on changes in the five work areas over time.

Fifth, the administrative leadership of the court convenes to determine how to measure performance so as to document the consequences of culture change. In considering this question, the court administrator working with the presiding judge should address the following questions: What is meant by performance? How might court performance be measured? What sorts of changes in performance can be expected with cultural change? Basic answers to those three queries can be garnered from a review of Chapters 5 and 6 as well as using *CourTools*. *CourTools*, developed by Ostrom et al. (2005) at the National Center for State Courts, consists of ten measures of performance, supplemented with an implementation guide, which the two leaders can use to suggest how performance can be linked to culture.[2]

To facilitate the measurement of what constitutes a well-performing court, performance is defined in terms of service delivery, a concept associated with the outcomes of public institutions. For courts specifically, key services include how individuals are treated, the manner in which cases are handled, and the integrity of how a court controls its operations. Courts exist to provide the services of a controlled, efficient, and orderly legal process. By introducing the conceptual connection between culture and performance with illustrative measures and their interpretation, the two administrative leaders lay the groundwork for more intensive analysis of the organizational structure needed to continue the move to a new culture.

Organizing to Direct Cultural Change

The substantial range and depth of work areas affected by culture make the undertaking labor intensive even if consensus reigns. Because translating preferences into action is a challenge, what actions might a court take to facilitate establishing and maintaining a preferred cultural mosaic?

A review of the private sector management literature on successful culture change makes clear the difficulty of the task. Companies, like courts, can resist change with great intensity. Kotter and Heskett (1992) stress that overcoming this reluctance to change requires a special combination of action and leadership that focuses on the needs of the customer. As they summarize their findings, they also provide a blueprint for creating a performance-enhancing culture:

> In the cases of successful change that we have studied, we have always found one or two unusually capable leaders on top . . . These leaders began by establishing a sense of crisis or need for change, and then by creating a new direction for their firms based on a customers-are-king philosophy and contextually appropriate business strategies. They challenged the status quo with very basic questions: Is this what the customers really need and want? Is this the most effective or productive way to deliver those products and services? They gathered all the information necessary to answer those questions. They were decisive—making choices about direction and acting on those choices. (p. 144)

What these observations make clear is the absolute necessity of committed and decisive leadership to deliver what the customer needs and wants. For courts, the effective provision of justice requires explicitly incorporating the delivery of high quality service and value to court customers, including litigants, attorneys, witnesses, jurors, the public, and funding authorities. Therefore, to successfully implement cultural change in courts, the onus is on a court's executive management team.

Shaping the duties and responsibilities of judges and court administrators in concrete ways will support the process of cultural change. Five essential aspects of an administrative leadership team's charge warrant attention by judicial bodies.

First, the length of terms of presiding judges should be aligned with the duration of the cultural change process. Specifically, the tenure of a court's chief administrative leader should track the expected amount of time to move toward and, at least initially, monitor the effects of modifications in work orientations. The time-frame for accomplishing the planned change likely involves a more extended period than the one- and two-year terms of office commonly set by court rules in most jurisdictions, especially when the first few months of a presiding judge's service are a learning experience and the last several months are absorbed in contemplating a return to normal caseload chores.

Second, a presiding judge should delegate authority to other members of the court in overseeing the pace and degree of progress and monitoring expected improvements in institutional performance. Culture manifests itself in intricate decision-making situations surrounding the handling and treatment of individual cases, litigants, attorneys, witnesses, jurors, courtroom staff, and observers, and not just the broad outlines of what a court does. Consequently, it is not humanly possible for a single presiding judge to check and correct every effort directed to improving how work is done in multiple areas ranging from *case management* to *judge–staff relations* to *courthouse leadership*.

Developing an administrative leadership team, including existing or newly created associate presiding judge positions as well as court administrators and senior court managers, with a coordinated division of responsibilities across work areas, is highly desirable. The team determines and reports on how well both the changes from one culture to another and the consequences of those changes are occurring. Associate presiding judges might chair committees, including other judges and staff, to supervise planned activities in particular areas and the progress made in cultural change and performance. The presence of these additional administrative leaders also contributes to the desired continuity in the direction of the implementation process. Consequently, planning for maximum feasible participation is a valuable preparatory task.

Third, standard statistical and operational reporting should be amended as necessary to ensure an orderly flow of information on how well both intended changes in work orientations and the consequences of those changes are occurring. Information should be gathered and processed according to a planned schedule with systematic types of assessments, rather than casually and anecdotally. Moreover, a court administrator should be authorized to synthesize the information gathered by other members (or committees) of the leadership team for subsequent review by the presiding judge. Throughout the process, the presiding judge should highlight success stories for dissemination, as appropriate, to all court personnel and other organizations in the justice system.

Fourth, the authority of the presiding judge in determining how closely the court is approximating desired cultural changes and higher performance should be established. The authority should extend to specifying what policies, procedures, and practices warrant modification to bring them into conformity with agreed-upon changes. For example, if in the area of case management, elapsed times on resolving cases are to be assembled from all chambers in a particular format in terms of meeting timeliness criteria, and some chambers fail to comply with agreed upon reporting schemes, the presiding judge shall consult with those chambers to gain desired compliance. Similar approaches are appropriate to respond to parallel situations in other work areas (e.g., failure by some chambers to submit staff performance reviews and employee satisfaction surveys by court personnel as expected in the area of *judge–staff relations*). Finally, if planned performance gains (e.g., relatively more litigants are satisfied with the clarity of court orders) are not realized, the presiding judge has the responsibility of inquiring why the results are falling short. The presiding judge should seek an explanation for why a particular chamber, division, unit, or program is not meeting desired goals by consulting individuals in the appropriate organizational group to determine what corrective action is required.

Fifth, the presiding judge should foster effective governance of the court in regard to the initiative on culture and performance by holding and chairing regular, periodic meetings of the entire bench, as well as court administrators and senior managers, where appropriate, to review work in progress. These sessions might coincide or expand upon existing monthly meetings of the judges. A planned agenda based on input and advice solicited from all of the judges ensures that serious problems or difficulties are not overlooked or ignored. The purpose of the meetings is to enable all judges to hear what the presiding judge, the administrative team, designated committees, and individual judges have to say about problems of and prospects for meeting intended objectives and for the group to share ideas on developing strategies for future implementation activities.

Thus, courts seeking cultural change and higher performance can take identifiable steps to organize themselves in ways conducive to the implementation process. Refinements in the duties and responsibilities of administrative leaders should be effective across a broad spectrum of desired cultural configurations and intended performance improvements.

Connections to Larger Questions

Enlarging the study of culture, work, and institutional performance in public sector organizations is a dominant theme in contemporary literature. A primary goal of the current research is to elevate awareness of courts as organizations. Largely overlooked by organizational scholars, courts are deserving of greater study as important public institutions parallel to legislative and executive bodies. Not only are courts charged with providing due process and equal protection to individual litigants, judges have been given the responsibility of ensuring all components of society operate according to the law. Thurman Arnold (1962, p. 128) has argued that the criminal trial "overshadows all other ceremonies as a dramatization of the values of our spiritual government, representing the dignity of the State as an enforcer of law, and, at the same time, the dignity of the individual when he is an avowed opponent of the State, a dissenter, a radical, or even a criminal." Given the critical role of America's trial courts, attention to issues of court organizational effectiveness seem long overdue. In addition, as the culture of courts has been explored, several analysis strategies have emerged that may be relevant to future studies of other public sector organizations.

To begin, researchers should consider investigating public sector culture in other settings with similar tools of analysis. The techniques employed in the current research borrow from the work of Quinn and his colleagues (1983, 1988, 1991) in their studies of private sector effectiveness. Because the methodology of Cameron and Quinn (1999) proves adaptable in the study of court culture, other public institutions should be amenable to parallel applications. The content of the values, dimensions, and work areas undoubtedly will vary from institution to institution, but the methodology seemingly is sufficiently flexible to permit necessary substantive modifications.

In particular, closer attention should be paid to identifying relevant values for other public organizations and determining how these individual values shape how work is done. This agenda comports with the stress placed on how clusters of values form and affect the extent that goals are achieved, according to the literature on organizational culture. Taking up the mantle of Wilson's suggestion that an organization's culture is akin to an individual's personality, a set of salient values can be isolated and analyzed employing the Quinn and Rohrbaugh methodology. In the current study, the result is a characterization of four cultural archetypes pertaining to trial courts. Once a researcher isolates the important values for a given public organization, it opens the possibility of identifying pertinent cultural archetypes.

This research shows that it should be no surprise to find multiple cultures at play in other public sector organizations. Once the relevant work areas or content dimensions are identified, it is possible to isolate and explore in a systematic way how different cultures affect the fundamental way work is done. The existence of multiple cultures raises new questions. Do leaders need to encourage greater dominance in current cultures? How are leaders supposed to lead when the organization prefers quite different cultures for different areas of work? The complexities seen among the twelve courts call for more advanced thinking by organizational theorists on how such realities are to be accommodated.

Taking our own recommendations to heart, we conclude by speculating on the applicability of extending the current framework to trial courts concerned with different types of disputes, such as civil, family, juvenile, and probate. Broadening the scope of analysis is possible because despite the unique set of substantive laws governing other types of disputes, they all share an essential characteristic. In every court, cases move from one key procedural event to another. To execute this common process, the activities represented by the five areas of the court culture framework occur in every type of case. As a result, *case management style* happens in civil cases just as in criminal cases. *Judge–staff relations* exist in probate cases just as in criminal cases. *Courthouse leadership* is exercised in juvenile cases just as in criminal cases.

Furthermore, how the work is to be done in each area is more likely to be shaped by cultural values such as independence, discretion, inclusiveness, and efficiency than by differences in evidentiary standards, rights of the parties, and severity and type of possible sanctions imposed on a losing party among courts. Legal criteria indicate more what goals must be reached than how to achieve the goals. In fact, appellate courts are likely to be amenable to cultural examination because the key procedural events are more definable and similar across appellate courts than trial courts (Chapper and Hanson, 1990). Hence, it is reasonable to expect that a common value matrix is applicable to all types of courts.

Experts and practitioners are likely to have multiple hunches and notions to explain anticipated cultural variation. What judges and court administrators think are appropriate work orientations will likely vary by case type and differ from what was found for criminal courts. For example, in the area of *case management style*, judges with a civil docket may prefer to give greater deference to the bar; in the area of *judge–staff relations*, probate judges may want to grant greater independence to legally-trained staff; and, in the area of *courthouse leadership*, judges handling juvenile dependency cases may seek to develop strong connections with social welfare agencies. Therefore, despite variation in work orientations across areas of law, the court culture framework opens up a valuable vista to future court studies.

The ability to measure culture by borrowing the tools available in the organizational culture literature highlights the relevance of the methodologies to the fields of public administration, public policy, and public management. Without claiming that the use of those tools answers all questions, court scholars and other public sector experts would benefit by adapting ideas from outside the perimeter of their own fields. Recognition and acceptance of broader perspectives are central to advancing research frontiers.

Appendices

APPENDIX 2-1: COURT CULTURE ATTRIBUTES

1. **Case Differentiation**—Judges and court staff use established guidelines and timely information to determine the most appropriate track for each case in terms of attention and resources.
2. **Chain of Command**—Explicit lines of authority between judges and court staff create a clear division of labor and formalize expectations that judges and court staff will do the jobs that they are assigned.
3. **Collaborative Problem Solving**—Judges and court managers seek participation from a diverse set of individuals (e.g., judges, court staff members, and attorneys) and often measure court user preferences when designing and introducing policy changes.
4. **Collegiality**—Information is often shared through informal channels that reflect personal relations among judges and court staff. When collective or group decisions are made on administrative matters, judges and court staff strive for consensus and to reconcile differences.
5. **Constrained Change**—Court-wide changes are inhibited because each judge exercises a wide scope of latitude and creativity in the choice of case-processing practices, and judges are perceived to resist court-wide monitoring.
6. **Continuity with the Past**—Court policies, procedures, and practices unfold gradually so they tend to be absorbed and internalized over long periods. Therefore, accepted practices are slow to change, stability and predictability are emphasized, and confrontation minimized.

7. **Decentralization**—The application of established court rules and procedures in practice are open to interpretation by semi-autonomous work teams of individual judges and corresponding court staff.
8. **Discretion**—There are few limitations on the ability of judges and court staff to interpret court policies governing individual case-related and administrative decisions.
9. **Efficiency**—The court seeks cutting edge technology and modern administrative methods to support administrative procedures that reduce errors and enhance the timeliness of case processing and the accuracy of record keeping.
10. **Flexibility**—There are many acceptable ways to administer court rules and procedures in line with meeting established court-wide performance goals. Centralized leadership is downplayed.
11. **Innovation**—Judges and court staff monitor overall court performance and are encouraged to discuss explicit ways to better organize and use resources.
12. **Judicial Consensus**—Judicial expectations concerning key procedural events come from a working policy built on the deliberate involvement and planning of the entire bench. Follow through is championed and encouraged by a presiding (administrative) judge.
13. **Rule-oriented**—Written court procedures and policies developed by the court's administrative leadership are applied uniformly. The court is committed to the use of case flow management (e.g., early case control, case coordination, and firm trial dates) with the support of court staff.
14. **Self-managing**—Individual judges have considerable control over their own dockets and are relatively free to make their own determinations on when key procedural events are to be completed.
15. **Sovereignty**—Each judge and corresponding court staff members are concerned with their own daily responsibilities and have little interest in planning efforts aimed at improving court-wide performance.
16. **Teamwork**—Appropriate staff members, drawing from different departments and divisions if necessary, work collaboratively to perform specific case processing and administrative tasks.

APPENDIX 2-2: PAIRED COMPARISON EXERCISE

Table 2-2.1 presents part of the overall questionnaire used to formulate the similarities and dissimilarities among our 53 respondents.

Each respondent was asked the extent to which sixteen possible values, concerning the organization of criminal courts, are related one to the other. The exercise asks how does each of the sixteen values either complement or compete with the other fifteen values. In this

TABLE 2-2.1. PAIRED COMPARISON EXERCISE

Discretion – There are few limitations on the ability of judges and court staff to interpret court policies

Compared to:

Item	Attribute	Short Description	Dissimilar ⟵						⟶ Similar
1	**Rule-Oriented**	Written court procedures and policies are developed by judicial leaders and are applied uniformly	1	2	3	4	5	6	7
2	**Innovation**	Judges and court staff monitor overall court performance and are encouraged to discuss explicit ways to better organize and use resources	1	2	3	4	5	6	7
3	**Flexibility**	There are many acceptable ways to administer court rules and procedures; centralized judicial leadership is downplayed	1	2	3	4	5	6	7
4	**Collaboration**	Judges and court administrators collaborate to achieve results; all are committed to team-oriented behavior; barriers are broken down to ensure team effectiveness	1	2	3	4	5	6	7
5	**Continuity with Past**	Accepted practices are slow to change; stability and predictability are emphasized	1	2	3	4	5	6	7
6	**Case Differentiation**	Judges and court administrators use established guidelines and timely information to determine the most appropriate track for each case in terms of attention and resources	1	2	3	4	5	6	7
7	**Constrained Change**	Court-wide changes are inhibited because each judge exercises wide latitude in the choice of case-processing practices	1	2	3	4	5	6	7
8	**Chain of Command**	Explicit lines of authority among judges and court staff create clear divisions of labor and formalize the expectation that all will do the jobs that they are assigned	1	2	3	4	5	6	7
9	**Teamwork**	Appropriate court staff members, drawing from different departments and divisions, work collaboratively to perform specific case-processing and administrative tasks	1	2	3	4	5	6	7
10	**Self-Managing**	Individual judges have considerable control over their own dockets and are relatively free to make their own determination concerning the timing of key procedural events	1	2	3	4	5	6	7
11	**Sovereignty**	Judges and court staff members are concerned with their own daily responsibilities and have little interest in planning efforts aimed at improving court-wide performance	1	2	3	4	5	6	7
12	**Decentralization**	The application of established court rules and practices is open to interpretation by semi-autonomous work teams of individual judges and courtroom staff	1	2	3	4	5	6	7
13	**Efficiency**	Court seeks cutting edge technology and modern administrative methods to support court administration	1	2	3	4	5	6	7
14	**Collegiality**	Information flows through informal channels reflecting personal relations among judges and court staff	1	2	3	4	5	6	7
15	**Judicial Consensus**	The timing of key procedural events comes from working consensus among the judges built upon the deliberate involvement and planning of the entire bench	1	2	3	4	5	6	7

context, each respondent made the 120 pair-wise comparisons. As can be seen in Table 2-2.1, the survey instrument provides short definitions for each of the 16 values. For this exercise, the respondents were asked to accept these definitions.

It is recognized that a criminal trial court might very well pursue many of these goals. In fact, it is likely that the sixteen values are present in some way or form in most courts. However, it is important to know what court experts see as the conceptual linkages among the values. How are these values, which are the building blocks of the study of court culture, related in the minds of practitioners and observers of courts? Each respondent was asked to view each value in general as a goal or value a court might pursue. Given the meaning of the values as defined in the questionnaire, they were asked to identify the degree to which a value is or is not related to each of the others. In other words, what are the linkages among the values at a theoretical level relating to courts (not for any one certain court)?

With respect to the mechanics of the exercise, on each page the respondents were asked to circle the number corresponding to the degree of relatedness (i.e., 1 = unrelated/dissimilar, 7 = very related/very similar) between the values listed in **bold** at the top of the column and the values listed directly below. For example, on the first page of the paired comparisons survey, each respondent was asked to compare and contrast *discretion* with fifteen other values listed directly below. From their perspective, how similar or dissimilar is *discretion* with the value of *rule-oriented*, the value of *innovation*, and so forth? In making their comparisons and contrasts, the respondents were asked to conduct their own "thought experiment." The goal is to gain their assessment of the degree to which different values would likely occur together in the same setting, although courts in the real world might vary in the degree to which they pursue each of two similar values. In addition, each respondent was asked to not limit their sense of how closely different values complement one another in terms of the values maintained by the court that they know best. Finally, the following definitions of *dissimilar* and *similar* were offered when comparing each pair of cultural values in the exercise: Are the two values *similar* in the sense that (a) the presence of one does not preclude the presence of the other and (b) the two values often co-occur in the same court? Are the two values *dissimilar* in the sense that (a) the presence of one decreases the likelihood of the other and (b) the two values rarely co-occur in the same court?

APPENDIX 2-3: THE MULTIDIMENSIONAL SCALING RESULTS

The SPSS ALSCAL multidimensional scaling algorithm was used to analyze the paired comparison data highlighted in Appendix 2-2.[1] Both two and three-dimensional solutions were computed. The two dimensional solution was ultimately selected: the squared correlation coefficient between the scaled distances and the input dissimilarities is .82 and the Kruskal Stress measure is .19.[2] In addition, the weights of all participants with regard to each dimension were positive,[3] and the individual correlations of the distances with the original similarities were quite high.[4] Not only is the fit for the two-dimensional solution quite good, less than 15% of the individual judge weights on the three-dimensional solution are greater than the corresponding weights for the first two dimensions.[5] When coupled with the ease of interpretation of the two dimensional solution, it is likely that the judicial proximities can be represented quite accurately in two dimensions.[6]

When WMDS yields useful insights, these generally come from an examination and interpretation of the resulting configuration. As Young (1987) notes, the WMDS approach is based on the premise "a picture is worth a thousand numbers." Table 2-3.1 presents configuration coefficients for the sixteen attributes for each of the two dimensions.

TABLE 2-3.1. CONFIGURATION COEFFICIENTS

Cultural Attribute	Dimension #1	Dimension #2
Case Differentiation	1.093	–0.355
Chain of Command	0.604	–1.560
Collaboration	0.956	1.032
Collegiality	–0.371	1.058
Constrained Change	–1.341	–0.897
Continuity	–0.150	–1.774
Decentralization	–1.317	0.187
Discretion	–0.873	0.895
Efficiency	0.954	0.613
Flexibility	–0.863	1.120
Innovation	0.307	1.355
Judicial Consensus	1.326	0.140
Rule-Oriented	1.044	–1.264
Self-Managing	–1.303	–0.250
Sovereignty	–1.306	–1.250
Teamwork	1.045	0.800

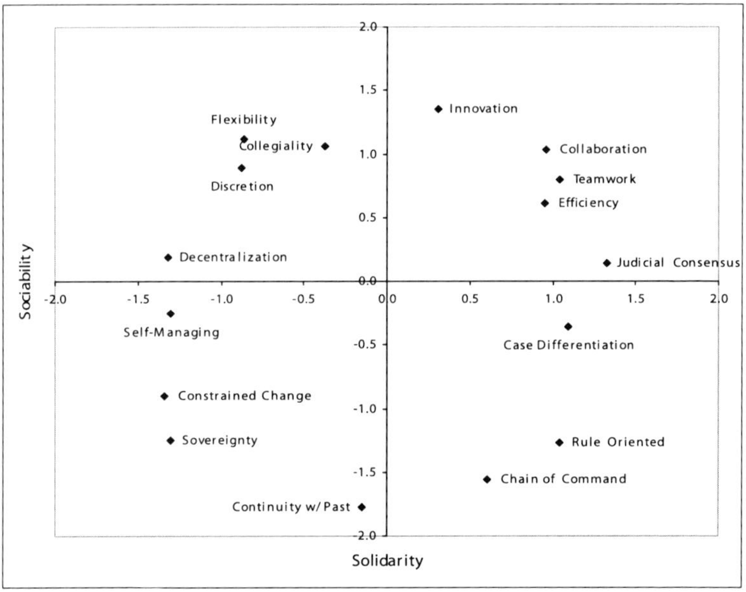

Fig 2-3.1 Configuration Plot

As can be seen in Table 2-3.1, the first dimension is anchored at the positive end by Judicial Consensus, Efficiency, Rule-Oriented, Collaboration, Teamwork, and Case Differentiation at one end and Self-Managing, Sovereignty, Decentralization, Constrained Change, Discretion, and Flexibility at the other. This dimension appears to be tapping the extent to which a court has clearly understood and shared goals, common tasks, and agreed upon procedures for reaching the goals. At the one end, a court with these values would pursue shared goals/tasks, have agreed upon procedures for reaching the goals, and value communication within the court. At the other end, a court with these values would value independence, autonomy, and individuality. This dimension appears similar in content to the Control/Flexibility dimension of Quinn and the Solidarity dimension of Goffee and Jones. Although not identical, this dimension is also similar to the one concerned with discretion in Nardulli, Eisenstein, and Flemming (1988).

Turning to the second dimension, Table 2-3.1 shows that it is anchored by Innovation, Collegiality, Collaboration, Flexibility, Teamwork, and Discretion at one end and by Sovereignty, Constrained

Change, Rule-Oriented, Chain of Command, and Continuity at the other. This dimension appears to align with how individuals within the courthouse community relate to one another. As such, it is similar to the dimension of Sociability as well as the personnel matters dimension suggested by Nardulli, Eisenstein, and Flemming (1988). At one end of the dimension, the court is connected in a communal/clan way while at the other there is little need for social interaction as the rules and structure determine what is to be done.

To see how the two dimensions work together, Figure 2-3.1 presents a configuration where each point is labeled to indicate the cultural attribute it represents. Using the two dimensions in tandem, it is possible to provide a map of the social architecture inherent in each of the culture types that were identified.

APPENDIX 3-1: COURT CULTURE ASSESSMENT INSTRUMENT

Court Culture and Performance Project
National Center for State Courts

Court Culture Assessment Instrument

Thank you very much for participating in our project. We would like all judges and court administration staff to complete this survey.

The Court Culture Assessment Instrument (CCAI) is designed to assess five key dimensions of court culture—Dominant Case Management Style, Judicial and Court Staff Relations, Change Management, Courthouse Leadership, and Internal Organization. In completing the questionnaire, you will be providing a picture both of how your court currently operates in terms of key culture-related values and how you would prefer the court to operate. There are no right or wrong answers for these questions.

Following are five tables each consisting of four sets of statements. The statements in each table are expressions of values that might be more or less emphasized in the local legal culture of your court. For each set of four statements, please identify the *relative* degree of emphasis that you think is placed on the value by your court. Divide 100 points among these four alternatives depending on the degree to which you believe each alternative is emphasized by your court. Give a higher number of points to the alternative that is most often emphasized.

For example, in Dominant Case Management Style, if you think alternative III is most descriptive of the CURRENT emphasis in your court, alternative I is somewhat descriptive, and alternatives II and IV are seldom descriptive, you might give 70 points to III, 20 points to I, and 5 each to II and IV. Please remember that the points allocated to responses I, II, III, and IV should total 100.

Turning to your PREFERRED emphasis, you might feel that alternatives I and IV should be emphasized in your court while alternatives II and III should receive much less emphasis. To reflect these preferences, you might give 40 points to I and IV and 10 points each to II and III.

Dominant Case Management Style		**Current**	**Preferred**
I	There is general agreement on performance goals, but centralized judicial and administrative staff leadership is downplayed and creativity is encouraged. As a result, there are alternative acceptable ways for individual judges to apply court rules, policies, and procedures.	20	40
II	Judicial expectations concerning the timing of key procedural events come from a working policy built on the deliberate involvement and planning of the entire bench. Follow through on established goals is championed and encouraged by a presiding (administrative) judge.	5	10
III	There is limited discussion and agreement on the importance of court-wide performance goals. Individual judges are relatively free to make their own determinations on when key procedural events are to be completed.	70	10

Dominant Case Management Style (continued)		Current	Preferred
IV	Judges are committed to the use of case flow management (e.g., early case control, case coordination, and firm trial dates) with the support of administrative and courtroom staff. Written court rules and procedures are applied uniformly by judges.	5	40
	Total	100	100

The five sets of four statements about CURRENT and PREFERRED emphasis are listed on the next three pages.

Dominant Case Management Style		Current	Preferred
I	There is general agreement on performance goals, but centralized judicial and administrative staff leadership is downplayed and creativity is encouraged. As a result, there are alternative acceptable ways for individual judges to apply court rules, policies, and procedures.		
II	Judicial expectations concerning the timing of key procedural events come from a working policy built on the deliberate involvement and planning of the entire bench. Follow through on established goals is championed and encouraged by a presiding (administrative) judge.		
III	There is limited discussion and agreement on the importance of court-wide performance goals. Individual judges are relatively free to make their own determinations on when key procedural events are to be completed.		
IV	Judges are committed to the use of case flow management (e.g., early case control, case coordination, and firm trial dates) with the support of administrative and courtroom staff. Written court rules and procedures are applied uniformly by judges.		
	Total	100	100

Judicial and Court Staff Relations		Current	Preferred
I	An effort is made by judges to limit the psychological distance between them and administrative courtroom staff. Hierarchy and formal processes exist, but court staff members go outside normal channels when it seems appropriate to "do the right thing."		
II	Judges value and promote a diverse workforce and diversity of ideas; act to enhance professional administrative and courtroom staff development; seek to treat all staff with fairness and respect.		
III	Individual judges use their own criteria to monitor, evaluate, and motivate courtroom and other staff. Judges have wide discretion in how they recruit, manage, and organize their courtroom support staff.		
IV	Administrative and courtroom staff members are closely monitored and evaluated through regular and structured performance appraisals. Work related feedback, merit recruitment, and promotion are emphasized.		
	Total	100	100

(continued)

Change Management		Current	Preferred
I	Changes in court policies and procedures occur incrementally through judicial negotiation and agreement. In practice, procedures are seldom rigid, with actual application open to interpretation by semi-autonomous work teams of individual judges and corresponding court staff.		
II	Judges and court managers seek input from a varied set of individuals (e.g., judges, court staff, attorneys, and public) and measure court user preferences concerning policy changes. Individual judges and administrative staff are encouraged to monitor court performance and to recommend necessary adjustments.		
III	Judges resist a rule- and process-bound organizational setting. Centralized change initiatives may be considered unfeasible because each judge exercises a wide scope of latitude in the choice of case processing practices and judges are perceived to resist court wide monitoring.		
IV	Judges and administrative staff seek cutting edge technology and modern administrative methods to support administrative procedures that reduce errors and enhance the timeliness of case processing and the accuracy of record keeping.		
	Total	100	100

Courthouse Leadership		Current	Preferred
I	Judicial and administrative staff leaders seek to build personal relationships and confidence among all judges and court staff members; emphasize mutually agreed upon goals with staff members; attempt to help all obtain satisfaction from work.		
II	Judicial and administrative staff leaders seek to build an integrated justice system community. All judges and court staff are asked to meet organizational performance goals that focus on results that matter to those served by the courts rather than simply those who run them.		
III	Centralized court leadership is inhibited because judges prefer to work with few external controls. Each judge and corresponding courtroom staff members are concerned primarily with their own daily responsibilities and exhibit little interest in efforts aimed at improving court or system-wide performance.		
IV	Judicial and administrative leaders rely on clearly established rules and directives—preferably in writing—to guide court operations. The system may appear impersonal given the emphasis on knowing and using the proper channels to get things done.		
	Total	100	100

Internal Organization		Current	Preferred
I	Information on a wide variety of topics (e.g., caseflow, resources, personnel) is shared through informal channels that reflect personal relations among judges, administrative, and courtroom staff. Judges and court staff strive for consensus and to reconcile differences.		
II	Judges and administrators seek a shared court-wide view of what needs to be accomplished. This knowledge facilitates judges and court staff, drawing from different departments and divisions if necessary, to work collaboratively to perform case processing and administrative tasks.		
III	Courtroom practices reflect the policies and practices employed by individual and autonomous judges. Therefore, accepted practices are slow to change, stability and predictability are emphasized, and confrontation minimized.		
IV	Explicit lines of authority among judges, administrative staff, and courtroom staff create a clear division of labor and formalize expectations that judges and court staff will do the jobs that they are assigned.		
	Total	100	100

County:
Position:

☐ Judge
Years of experience working as judge (circle):
<1 1–5 6–10 11–15 15+

☐ Court Administration
Years of experience working in profession of court administration (circle):
<1 1–5 6–10 11–15 15+

In the Last Year, the Percentage of Time Handling Felony Cases:

☐ Almost never
☐ Occasionally
☐ 50% of the time
☐ Most of the time

Please return completed form to Court Administrator/Court Executive or in the envelope provided.

INDIVIDUAL RESPONSES TO THIS SURVEY WILL BE HELD IN THE STRICTEST CONFIDENCE.

Thank you for your help.

APPENDIX 3-2: ASSESSING VARIATION IN CCAI RESPONSES

California—Current Culture

Content	Culture	Contra Costa					Napa					Ventura				
Dimension	Type	Mean	N	sd	Median	CV	Mean	N	sd	Median	CV	Mean	N	sd	Median	CV
Case Management Style	Communal	14.05	21.00	9.60	10	68%	13.64	11.00	8.09	10	59%	17.21	28.00	15.17	10	88%
	Networked	21.00	21.00	17.92	20	85%	31.36	11.00	10.98	35	35%	26.21	28.00	23.34	15	89%
	Autonomous	31.71	21.00	29.19	15	92%	18.64	11.00	17.48	10	94%	25.18	28.00	24.93	12.5	99%
	Hierarchical	33.24	21.00	21.64	30	65%	36.36	11.00	17.62	35	48%	31.39	28.00	21.72	30	69%
Judge-Staff Relations	Communal	24.76	21.00	17.78	15	72%	21.82	11.00	10.55	25	48%	10.96	28.00	7.39	10	67%
	Networked	26.19	21.00	17.53	20	67%	32.73	11.00	9.84	35	30%	39.68	28.00	22.82	35	58%
	Autonomous	23.33	21.00	19.13	15	82%	10.91	11.00	7.01	10	64%	18.04	28.00	14.55	12.5	81%
	Hierarchical	25.71	21.00	17.41	20	68%	34.55	11.00	14.05	30	41%	31.32	28.00	21.44	26	68%
Change Management	Communal	24.52	21.00	17.67	25	72%	24.55	11.00	16.04	20	65%	17.86	28.00	13.01	17.5	73%
	Networked	22.14	21.00	15.38	20	69%	25.45	11.00	10.11	20	40%	26.43	28.00	14.39	25	54%
	Autonomous	31.67	21.00	21.06	30	66%	11.36	11.00	10.74	10	95%	10.18	28.00	11.42	5	112%
	Hierarchical	21.67	21.00	14.86	20	69%	38.64	11.00	16.45	40	43%	45.54	28.00	23.43	40	51%
Courthouse Leadership	Communal	23.50	22.00	17.15	25	73%	38.75	12.00	19.79	37.5	51%	40.00	28.00	20.41	40	51%
	Networked	17.05	22.00	14.11	12.5	83%	19.17	12.00	7.93	20	41%	29.29	28.00	19.89	30	68%
	Autonomous	35.45	22.00	29.15	27.5	82%	15.83	12.00	10.84	15	68%	16.79	28.00	16.40	10	98%
	Hierarchical	24.00	22.00	19.98	20	83%	26.25	12.00	10.47	25	40%	13.93	28.00	9.06	10	65%
Internal Organization	Communal	19.29	21.00	13.54	20	70%	26.25	12.00	14.94	22.5	57%	23.93	28.00	14.49	20	61%
	Networked	21.90	21.00	15.20	20	69%	31.25	12.00	13.16	27.5	42%	35.71	28.00	25.27	32.5	71%
	Autonomous	26.19	21.00	23.18	20	89%	18.75	12.00	12.08	20	64%	20.18	28.00	19.36	10	96%
	Hierarchical	32.62	21.00	23.43	30	72%	23.75	12.00	11.10	25	47%	20.18	28.00	15.30	12.5	76%

Florida—Current Culture

Content Dimension	Culture Type	Duval Mean	Duval N	Duval sd	Duval Median	Duval CV	Pinellas Mean	Pinellas N	Pinellas sd	Pinellas Median	Pinellas CV
Case Management Style	Communal	27.86	28.00	14.04	27.5	50%	29.38	8.00	12.08	32.5	41%
	Networked	22.50	28.00	17.35	20	77%	15.00	8.00	11.95	15	80%
	Autonomous	34.00	28.00	18.84	32.5	55%	36.88	8.00	24.92	35	68%
	Hierarchical	15.64	28.00	10.15	10	65%	18.75	8.00	12.46	20	66%
Judge-Staff Relations	Communal	27.25	28.00	17.32	20	64%	17.50	8.00	8.86	15	51%
	Networked	30.68	28.00	11.56	30	38%	35.00	8.00	24.93	25	71%
	Autonomous	26.25	28.00	20.12	25	77%	33.13	8.00	30.35	22.5	92%
	Hierarchical	15.82	28.00	14.31	10	90%	14.38	8.00	13.48	10	94%
Change Management	Communal	27.32	28.00	19.22	22.5	70%	32.50	8.00	16.48	30	51%
	Networked	15.71	28.00	9.50	15	60%	17.50	8.00	10.00	17.5	57%
	Autonomous	30.18	28.00	18.03	27.5	60%	22.50	8.00	10.35	30	46%
	Hierarchical	26.79	28.00	17.28	25	65%	27.50	8.00	11.65	25	42%
Courthouse Leadership	Communal	33.39	28.00	18.76	30	56%	18.13	8.00	6.51	20	36%
	Networked	19.64	28.00	14.46	17.5	74%	18.13	8.00	10.67	20	59%
	Autonomous	26.43	28.00	16.88	25	64%	48.75	8.00	19.59	40	40%
	Hierarchical	20.54	28.00	13.83	20	67%	15.00	8.00	7.56	20	50%
Internal Organization	Communal	24.20	28.00	11.53	25	48%	23.75	8.00	7.44	25	31%
	Networked	21.88	28.00	11.15	20	51%	19.38	8.00	8.63	20	45%
	Autonomous	29.46	28.00	19.78	25	67%	33.13	8.00	11.63	32.5	35%
	Hierarchical	24.46	28.00	12.79	25	52%	23.75	8.00	9.16	30	39%

APPENDIX 3-2: ASSESSING VARIATION IN CCAI RESPONSES (Continued)

		Minnesota—Current Culture																			
Content Dimension	Culture type	Dakota					Hennepin					Kandiyohi					Olmsted				
		Mean	N	sd	Md	CV	Mean	N	sd	Md	CV	Mean	N	sd	Md	CV	Mean	N	sd	Md	CV
Case Management Style	Communal	28.46	13.00	20.75	30	73%	20.09	65.00	14.11	20	70%	29.29	7.00	15.92	30	54%	29.50	10.00	18.92	25	64%
	Networked	15.00	13.00	15.41	10	103%	24.62	65.00	18.34	20	75%	24.29	7.00	15.66	15	64%	20.00	10.00	9.43	20	47%
	Autonomous	35.00	13.00	24.07	30	69%	26.91	65.00	19.29	25	72%	21.43	7.00	13.76	20	64%	20.00	10.00	16.67	15	83%
	Hierarchical	21.54	13.00	20.55	15	95%	28.38	65.00	19.23	20	68%	25.00	7.00	14.14	25	57%	30.50	10.00	18.63	25	61%
Judge-Staff Relations	Communal	30.00	13.00	20.51	25	68%	18.66	67.00	11.57	20	62%	14.29	7.00	14.84	10	104%	23.90	10.00	18.79	24.5	79%
	Networked	27.31	13.00	16.78	25	61%	20.07	67.00	11.03	20	55%	36.43	7.00	26.73	25	73%	33.50	10.00	15.99	30	48%
	Autonomous	22.69	13.00	19.54	20	86%	46.72	67.00	19.45	45	42%	18.57	7.00	24.62	10	133%	15.60	10.00	9.08	17.5	58%
	Hierarchical	20.00	13.00	18.03	20	90%	14.55	67.00	8.99	10	62%	30.71	7.00	22.25	40	72%	27.00	10.00	23.94	25	89%
Change Management	Communal	36.92	13.00	18.09	40	49%	25.15	66.00	15.64	25	62%	26.43	7.00	17.01	30	64%	35.00	10.00	11.55	37.5	33%
	Networked	15.00	13.00	7.64	10	51%	23.94	66.00	15.13	20	63%	32.14	7.00	28.26	25	88%	37.40	10.00	11.35	39.5	30%
	Autonomous	28.08	13.00	18.09	20	64%	31.21	66.00	18.00	30	58%	16.43	7.00	10.29	20	63%	10.10	10.00	9.01	10	89%
	Hierarchical	20.00	13.00	14.86	15	74%	19.70	66.00	14.38	17.5	73%	25.00	7.00	12.58	20	50%	17.50	10.00	8.90	20	51%
Courthouse Leadership	Communal	31.54	13.00	21.83	30	69%	20.61	66.00	12.48	20	61%	37.86	7.00	21.96	35	58%	36.50	10.00	15.99	40	44%
	Networked	18.46	13.00	10.68	20	58%	22.12	66.00	12.86	20	58%	26.43	7.00	9.45	30	36%	36.00	10.00	15.95	37.5	44%
	Autonomous	31.54	13.00	18.19	30	58%	36.36	66.00	20.39	32.5	56%	24.29	7.00	20.90	20	86%	11.00	10.00	11.01	10	100%
	Hierarchical	18.46	13.00	8.51	20	46%	20.91	66.00	15.21	20	73%	11.43	7.00	7.48	10	65%	16.50	10.00	13.95	10	85%
Internal Organization	Communal	24.62	13.00	14.21	20	58%	22.27	66.00	11.97	20	54%	30.71	7.00	17.42	20	57%	25.90	10.00	14.07	29.5	54%
	Networked	19.23	13.00	13.05	20	68%	23.48	66.00	14.83	20	63%	33.57	7.00	11.07	35	33%	32.00	10.00	13.37	30	42%
	Autonomous	31.15	13.00	18.05	30	58%	34.09	66.00	19.94	30	58%	15.71	7.00	15.39	10	98%	24.10	10.00	16.48	20	68%
	Hierarchical	25.00	13.00	15.00	20	60%	20.15	66.00	10.67	20	53%	20.00	7.00	15.55	20	78%	18.00	10.00	11.35	17.5	63%

		Minnesota—Current Culture														
		Ramsey					St Louis					Virginia				
Content Dimension	Culture type	Mean	N	sd	Md	CV	Mean	N	sd	Md	CV	Mean	N	sd	Md	CV
Case Management Style	Communal	20.00	10.00	22.85	15	114%	32.00	10.00	22.14	32.5	69%	30.63	8.00	21.12	30	69%
	Networked	26.00	10.00	24.01	20	92%	10.50	10.00	9.85	7.5	94%	14.38	8.00	8.21	10	57%
	Autonomous	19.50	10.00	20.88	10	107%	36.00	10.00	20.11	30	56%	22.50	8.00	16.69	20	74%
	Hierarchical	34.50	10.00	18.77	32.5	54%	21.50	10.00	30.37	10	141%	32.50	8.00	29.15	25	90%
Judge-Staff Relations	Communal	21.00	10.00	15.24	17.5	73%	18.00	10.00	20.03	12.5	111%	21.25	8.00	20.13	15	95%
	Networked	31.50	10.00	24.04	22.5	76%	34.50	10.00	22.04	30	64%	25.63	8.00	16.78	20	65%
	Autonomous	30.50	10.00	20.74	25	68%	22.50	10.00	29.65	10	132%	18.75	8.00	28.00	10	149%
	Hierarchical	17.00	10.00	11.60	12.5	68%	25.00	10.00	17.32	22.5	69%	34.38	8.00	31.56	25	92%
Change Management	Communal	28.00	10.00	11.60	27.5	41%	30.50	10.00	16.74	35	55%	32.14	7.00	24.47	25	76%
	Networked	29.00	10.00	20.92	22.5	72%	23.00	10.00	28.40	12.5	123%	23.57	7.00	13.76	20	58%
	Autonomous	16.50	10.00	17.49	10	106%	33.50	10.00	18.11	30	54%	15.00	7.00	18.26	5	122%
	Hierarchical	26.50	10.00	20.42	22.5	77%	13.00	10.00	8.56	12.5	66%	29.29	7.00	19.02	25	65%
Courthouse Leadership	Communal	29.00	10.00	16.96	22.5	58%	30.50	10.00	25.44	20	83%	39.29	7.00	26.05	30	66%
	Networked	28.00	10.00	15.49	27.5	55%	16.50	10.00	10.29	15	62%	19.29	7.00	12.72	15	66%
	Autonomous	29.00	10.00	25.80	20	89%	43.00	10.00	21.11	45	49%	17.14	7.00	17.53	10	102%
	Hierarchical	14.00	10.00	11.25	10	80%	10.00	10.00	7.07	10	71%	24.29	7.00	22.81	20	94%
Internal Organization	Communal	24.50	10.00	13.83	20	56%	20.00	10.00	13.33	20	67%	25.63	8.00	18.79	20	73%
	Networked	25.00	10.00	22.73	20	91%	29.50	10.00	27.13	22.5	92%	26.25	8.00	11.57	27.5	44%
	Autonomous	25.00	10.00	19.15	20	77%	37.50	10.00	22.76	40	61%	24.38	8.00	22.59	15	93%
	Hierarchical	25.50	10.00	17.07	27.5	67%	13.00	10.00	9.49	10	73%	23.75	8.00	20.66	20	87%

APPENDIX 4-1: INTERVIEW LIST

Florida *(February and July 2002)*

Duval (Jacksonville)
- Clerk's Office Technology Officer
- County Court Judge
- Director, Guardian ad litem program
- Administrative Judge for the Felony court
- Director, County Mediation
- Drug Court Administrator
- Chief Assistant Public Defender
- Felony Division Public Defender (3)
- Clerk of Court
- Chief Assistant to State Attorney
- Presiding Judge
- Trial Court Administrator

Pinellas (St. Petersburg)
- Trial Court Administrator
- Presiding Judge
- Chief Public Defender
- Clerk of Court
- Chief Deputy Public Defender
- Felony division Public Defender's (2)
- Circuit Court Judge Felony Division (3)
- Deputy Court Administrator
- Criminal Justice Information Coordinator
- Chief Deputy State Attorneys Office
- Felony Prosecutor (Assistant State Attorney) (2)

California

Contra Costa *(March 2002)*
- Chief District Attorney
- Chief Deputy District Attorney
- Presiding Judge
- Chief Public Defender
- Assistant Executive Officer
- District Attorney

Napa— *Visit 1 (March 2002)*
- Chief Public Defender
- Deputy Public Defender
- District Attorney
- Presiding Judge

Napa— *Visit 2 (June 2002)*
- Court Executive Officer
- Assistant CEO
- Deputy District Attorney
- Chief Deputy PD
- Deputy PD (2)
- Chief Deputy District Attorney (2)
- Judge (2)

Ventura— *Visit 1 (March 2002)*
- Presiding Judge
- Court Executive Officer
- Court Executive Assistant
- Deputy District Attorney
- Chief Public Defender
- Court Program Manager
- Judge

Ventura— *Visit 2 (June 2002)*
- Court Executive Office
- Chief Deputy District Attorney
- Senior Deputy PD
- Felony Prosecutor
- Assistant PD
- Felony Prosecutor
- Felony Trial Lawyer

Minnesota

Dakota— *Visit 1 (May 2002)*
- District Court Administrator
- Court Administrator
- Administrator
- Presiding Judge
- Chief County Attorney
- Chief Public Defender

Dakota— *Visit 2 (Aug 2002)*
- Judge (2)
- Chief PD
- Assistant Public Defender Felony Division (3)
- Presiding Judge
- District Court Administrator
- District Attorney

Hennepin— *Visit 1 (May 2002)*
- Chief Public Defender
- Chief Deputy County Attorney
- Presiding Judge
- District Court Administrator
- City Attorney

Hennepin— *Visit 2 (Aug 2002)*
- Group Presentation
- Judge
- Criminal Presiding Judge
- Deputy County Attorney (3)
- Public Defender (3)
- Assistant Presiding Judge
- District Court Administrator

Kandiyohi— *Visit 1 (May 2002)*
- Judge (3)
- Court Administrator
- County Attorney
- Public Defender

Kandiyohi— *Visit 2 (Aug 2002)*
- Judge (2)
- Court Administrator
- City Prosecutor
- County Attorney
- Assistant Public Defender

Olmsted— *Visit 1 (May 2002)*
- Presiding Criminal Division Judge
- Court Administrator
- Judge
- District Court Administrator
- County Attorney
- City Attorney
- Assistant Public Defender

Olmsted— *Visit 2 (Aug 2002)*
- Presiding Criminal Division Judge
- County Attorney
- City Attorney
- Assistant Public Defender
- District Court Administrator
- Felony Trial Judge

Ramsey— *Visit 1 (May 2002)*
- Presiding Judge
- Judge
- District Court Administrator
- Criminal Division Administrator
- County Attorney
- City Attorney
- Chief Public Defender

Ramsey— *Visit 2 (Aug 2002)*
- Presiding Judge
- Assistant Presiding Judge
- Criminal Division Judge
- District Court Administrator
- Criminal Division Administrator
- County Attorney
- County Attorney (DA) (2)
- Public Defender (2)

St. Louis—Duluth— *Visit 1 (May 2002)*
- Assistant Presiding Judge
- Court Administrator
- Assistant County Attorney
- Chief Public Defender

St. Louis—Duluth— *Visit 2 (Aug 2002)*
- Presiding Judge
- Judge (3)
- Prosecutors (2)
- Chief Public Defender
- Public Defender

St. Louis—Virginia— *Visit 1 (May 2002)*
- Presiding Judge
- Deputy Court Administrator
- County Attorney
- Public Defender

St. Louis—Virginia— *Visit 2 (Aug 2002)*
- District Court Administrator
- Prosecutor (2)
- Public Defender (2)
- Judge

APPENDIX 4-2: INTERVIEW PROTOCOL

Background Information

1. How long have you been an attorney (judge, worked for the court)?
2. How long have you been with this office (court)?
3. How long have you handled felony cases?

Case Management

All Respondents

4. Explain what happens operationally after ARREST?
5. What is the next stage in the case?
6. What happens at this next stage in the case?
7. How effective is this step?
8. What is the time interval between stages? *(Repeat questions through sentencing)*

Public Defenders

9. When does the assignment of defense counsel occur?
10. Are there any problems at this step?
11. When does the PD usually meet the client?

Prosecutors:

12. At what stage of the criminal proceedings are felony cases assigned to prosecutors?

13. What is the assignment system? (One attorney handles the entire felony case? Or different attorneys handle different stages?)

All Attorneys

14. When does the exchange of discovery package occur?
15. Does exchange of discovery usually occur when scheduled?
16. When do prosecutors make a plea offer in most cases?
17. When do prosecutors make their best offer?

All Respondents

18. Does the court hold management conferences (pretrial, status) to ensure counsel are prepared, to help the judge prepare for trial, and to increase the prospects for settling some or all issues in the case?
19. What happens at these conferences? Are these management conferences effective?
20. When do pretrial motions take place?
21. Are trial continuances a problem? How often do they occur?
22. Do you believe that the court should provide reasonably firm and predictable trial dates so that almost all trials actually begin on or shortly after the first scheduled trial date?
23. Is delay a problem in felony adjudication in your court?
24. What are the most significant causes of pretrial delay that exist in felony cases?

Interagency Communication and Cooperation

25. Has the court been able to create and maintain an effective presiding judge/court manager executive team?
26. Does the court strive to build consensus within the court and across the justice community about the need for effective case-flow management?
27. Does the court seek consensus among bench, staff, and justice system partners, when appropriate, of the need to make changes and the feasibility of proposed solutions?
28. Does the court act decisively and exert leadership with respect to case-flow management?
29. Are there any formal or informal practices or procedures that have been developed to encourage or facilitate dialogue or coordination among the court, prosecutor, and indigent defenders in this jurisdiction?
30. How would you characterize the 'local legal culture' in this jurisdiction?

APPENDIX 5: ATTORNEY SURVEY

Public Defenders and Prosecutors Questions 1–46

Court Culture and Performance Project
National Center for State Courts

Trial Court Process Survey

Thank you very much for participating in our project. We would like all prosecuting attorneys and public defenders to complete this survey.

	How Strongly Agree or Disagree					
From My Point of View:	**Strongly Disagree**	**Disagree**	**Neither Agree or Disagree**	**Agree**	**Strongly Agree**	**Not Applicable**
1 Delay in felony case adjudication is a problem in this jurisdiction.	**1**	**2**	**3**	**4**	**5**	**NA**
2 There are clear goals in this jurisdiction for how long it should take to dispose of felony cases.	**1**	**2**	**3**	**4**	**5**	**NA**
3 Our system should be able to dispose 100% of all felony cases within 1 year after first arrest.	**1**	**2**	**3**	**4**	**5**	**NA**
4 Our court has enough judges to dispose of 100% of felony cases within 1 year after first arrest.	**1**	**2**	**3**	**4**	**5**	**NA**
5 The prosecutor's office has enough attorneys to dispose of 100% of felony cases within 1 year after first arrest.	**1**	**2**	**3**	**4**	**5**	**NA**
6 The system of indigent criminal defense has enough attorneys to dispose 100% of felony cases within 1 year after 1st arrest.	**1**	**2**	**3**	**4**	**5**	**NA**
7 Effective prosecutorial screening and charging procedures minimize the number of felony cases eventually dismissed.	**1**	**2**	**3**	**4**	**5**	**NA**
8 Prosecutor discovery practices do not cause delay in felony adjudication in this jurisdiction.	**1**	**2**	**3**	**4**	**5**	**NA**
9 Public defender discovery practices do not cause delay in felony adjudication in this jurisdiction.	**1**	**2**	**3**	**4**	**5**	**NA**
10 The court adequately monitors the progress of felony cases in this jurisdiction.	**1**	**2**	**3**	**4**	**5**	**NA**

	From My Point of View:	Strongly Disagree	Disagree	Neither Agree or Disagree	Agree	Strongly Agree	Not Applicable
11	There is good communication among the court, prosecutor, and public defender when case management problems arise.	1	2	3	4	5	NA
12	Effective judicial leadership is one of the strengths of the criminal justice system in this jurisdiction.	1	2	3	4	5	NA
13	Effective leadership by the prosecutor is one of the strengths of the criminal justice system in this jurisdiction.	1	2	3	4	5	NA
14	Effective leadership among indigent criminal defense attorneys is a strength of the criminal justice system in this jurisdiction.	1	2	3	4	5	NA
15	The prosecutor's plea bargaining policies contribute to unnecessary delay in felony cases.	1	2	3	4	5	NA
16	Indigent criminal defense attorneys' plea bargaining policies contribute to unnecessary delay in felony cases.	1	2	3	4	5	NA
17	Multiple trial date continuances are routinely granted by judges in felony cases.	1	2	3	4	5	NA
18	The amount of time judges give to cases is proportional to the amount of time the cases merit.	1	2	3	4	5	NA
19	Most juries are representative of the community.	1	2	3	4	5	NA
20	The court protects criminal defendants' constitutional rights.	1	2	3	4	5	NA
21	There is effective legal representation at all critical stages of the legal process for criminal indigent defendants.	1	2	3	4	5	NA
22	Judges give adequate time and attention to the circumstances of individual criminal defendants.	1	2	3	4	5	NA
23	In the past five years, our office budget has kept pace with the increase in our caseload.	1	2	3	4	5	NA
24	Victims of crime are kept informed of all court settings and offender bond status.	1	2	3	4	5	NA
25	The court takes adequate steps to ensure accuracy and availability of court records.	1	2	3	4	5	NA
26	The court works well with other components of the criminal justice system (e.g., DA, PD, Police, Probation).	1	2	3	4	5	NA

(continued)

From My Point of View:	Strongly Disagree	Disagree	Neither Agree or Disagree	Agree	Strongly Agree	Not Applicable
	How Strongly Agree or Disagree					
27 I receive fair compensation for my work as an attorney.	1	2	3	4	5	NA
28 The court has adequate facilities for effective and convenient handling of felony cases.	1	2	3	4	5	NA
29 Criminal defendants understand the court's rulings.	1	2	3	4	5	NA
30 The court is able to process cases efficiently without sacrificing equity and justice.	1	2	3	4	5	NA
31 The court takes appropriate responsibility for enforcement of its orders.	1	2	3	4	5	NA
32 Public areas of the courthouse are safe and accessible.	1	2	3	4	5	NA
33 Information can be obtained on a case quickly and easily.	1	2	3	4	5	NA
34 The court spends its funds wisely.	1	2	3	4	5	NA
35 Court proceedings are easy to understand and follow.	1	2	3	4	5	NA
36 The court is sensitive to the concerns of the average citizen.	1	2	3	4	5	NA
37 Court personnel are helpful and courteous.	1	2	3	4	5	NA

How would You Rate the Following:	Poor		Adequate		Excellent	Don't Know
	How would You Rate the Following					
38 Prosecutors' office experience with felony cases	1	2	3	4	5	NA
39 Prosecutors' preparation for felony hearings and trials	1	2	3	4	5	NA
40 Prosecutors' office felony trial skills	1	2	3	4	5	NA
41 Public Defenders' in your office, experience with felony cases	1	2	3	4	5	NA
42 Public Defenders' in your office, preparation for felony hearings and trials	1	2	3	4	5	NA
43 Public Defenders' in your office, felony trial skills	1	2	3	4	5	NA
44 Privately retained criminal defense attorneys' experience with felony cases	1	2	3	4	5	NA
45 Privately retained criminal defense attorneys' preparation for felony hearings and trials	1	2	3	4	5	NA
46 Privately retained criminal defense attorneys' felony trial skills	1	2	3	4	5	NA

APPENDIX 6: ASSESSING VARIATION IN CCAI RESPONSES

		California—Future Culture														
		Contra Costa					Napa					Ventura				
Content Dimension	Culture Type	Mean	N	sd	Median	CV	Mean	N	sd	Median	CV	Mean	N	sd	Median	CV
Case Management Style	Communal	14.52	21.00	13.12	10	90%	12.55	11.00	12.18	10	97%	21.86	28.00	20.12	17.5	92%
	Networked	32.67	21.00	19.44	30	60%	38.00	11.00	10.86	35	29%	29.46	28.00	20.23	28.5	69%
	Autonomous	9.71	21.00	11.23	5	116%	3.64	11.00	3.93	5	108%	11.07	28.00	11.50	10	104%
	Hierarchical	43.10	21.00	20.70	40	48%	45.82	11.00	13.28	45	29%	37.61	28.00	20.97	40	56%
Judge–Staff Relations	Communal	20.68	22.00	15.83	17.5	77%	10.45	11.00	12.93	5	124%	8.70	27.00	7.92	5	91%
	Networked	40.91	22.00	16.52	40	40%	43.18	11.00	11.02	50	26%	39.07	27.00	20.62	35	53%
	Autonomous	11.14	22.00	7.86	10	71%	3.18	11.00	3.37	5	106%	13.89	27.00	13.89	10	100%
	Hierarchical	27.27	22.00	16.88	25	62%	43.18	11.00	17.50	45	41%	38.33	27.00	21.53	30	56%
Change Management	Communal	19.29	21.00	12.78	20	66%	13.91	11.00	12.09	15	87%	12.41	27.00	14.96	10	121%
	Networked	33.81	21.00	12.84	30	38%	35.73	11.00	12.03	35	34%	30.19	27.00	17.95	30	59%
	Autonomous	10.71	21.00	8.56	10	80%	3.18	11.00	3.37	5	106%	5.37	27.00	7.59	0	141%
	Hierarchical	36.19	21.00	12.14	40	34%	47.18	11.00	9.45	50	20%	52.04	27.00	23.13	40	44%
Courthouse Leadership	Communal	41.14	22.00	14.39	37.5	35%	41.50	12.00	9.52	40	23%	47.41	27.00	21.85	40	46%
	Networked	34.32	22.00	15.91	30	46%	28.58	12.00	12.56	31.5	44%	31.85	27.00	20.15	30	63%
	Autonomous	6.59	22.00	6.62	5	100%	4.17	12.00	5.15	2.5	124%	7.96	27.00	12.35	5	155%
	Hierarchical	17.95	22.00	14.77	17.5	82%	25.75	12.00	8.92	22.5	35%	12.78	27.00	10.59	10	83%
Internal Organization	Communal	27.86	21.00	12.31	30	44%	17.75	12.00	12.28	17.5	69%	23.52	27.00	15.80	20	67%
	Networked	43.81	21.00	14.91	45	34%	53.58	12.00	17.54	50	33%	48.89	27.00	21.54	40	44%
	Autonomous	11.19	21.00	14.99	5	134%	5.42	12.00	4.98	5	92%	9.26	27.00	9.78	10	106%
	Hierarchical	17.14	21.00	10.91	15	64%	23.25	12.00	14.60	20	63%	18.33	27.00	14.21	20	78%

(continued)

APPENDIX 6: ASSESSING VARIATION IN CCAI RESPONSES (Continued)

		Florida—Future Culture									
		Duval					Pinellas				
Content Dimension	Culture Type	Mean	N	sd	Median	CV	Mean	N	sd	Median	CV
Dominant Case Management Style	Communal	26.00	25.00	15.14	25	58%	26.88	8.00	12.80	27.5	48%
	Networked	29.40	25.00	19.22	25	65%	15.00	8.00	14.14	10	94%
	Autonomous	22.00	25.00	14.79	20	67%	21.88	8.00	26.18	15	120%
	Hierarchical	22.60	25.00	15.82	20	70%	36.25	8.00	21.34	35	59%
Judicial and Court Staff Relations	Communal	23.92	25.00	15.49	25	65%	17.50	8.00	8.86	15	51%
	Networked	32.36	25.00	17.72	30	55%	33.13	8.00	17.92	27.5	54%
	Autonomous	24.20	25.00	15.39	25	64%	33.13	8.00	21.54	22.5	65%
	Hierarchical	19.52	25.00	13.37	20	68%	16.25	8.00	13.02	20	80%
Change Management	Communal	17.60	25.00	15.89	10	90%	26.25	8.00	20.66	15	79%
	Networked	24.40	25.00	18.10	20	74%	23.75	8.00	11.88	20	50%
	Autonomous	27.40	25.00	19.16	25	70%	12.50	8.00	8.86	10	71%
	Hierarchical	30.60	25.00	17.46	25	57%	37.50	8.00	15.81	40	42%
Courthouse Leadership	Communal	34.12	25.00	19.35	30	57%	32.50	8.00	15.81	30	49%
	Networked	25.32	25.00	13.79	20	54%	30.00	8.00	9.26	30	31%
	Autonomous	19.40	25.00	19.49	20	100%	23.75	8.00	21.34	20	90%
	Hierarchical	21.16	25.00	13.90	20	66%	13.75	8.00	11.88	10	86%
Internal Organization	Communal	25.52	25.00	11.51	25	45%	32.50	8.00	15.81	35	49%
	Networked	26.32	25.00	9.56	25	36%	32.50	8.00	18.32	30	56%
	Autonomous	26.20	25.00	19.54	25	75%	16.88	8.00	12.23	10	72%
	Hierarchical	21.96	25.00	10.46	25	48%	18.13	8.00	13.08	10	72%

Content Dimension	Culture Type	Dakota					Hennepin					Kandiyohi					Olmsted				
		Mean	N	sd	Md	CV	Mean	N	sd	Md	CV	Mean	N	sd	Md	CV	Mean	N	sd	Md	CV
Dominant Case Management Style	Communal	20.00	13.00	19.90	10	99%	17.28	65.00	12.84	15	74%	14.71	7.00	8.79	15	60%	15.25	10.00	13.67	12.5	90%
	Networked	22.31	13.00	12.18	20	55%	32.72	65.00	20.83	30	64%	36.14	7.00	22.34	35	62%	30.50	10.00	14.62	32.5	48%
	Autonomous	15.77	13.00	18.47	10	117%	11.57	65.00	10.50	10	91%	15.57	7.00	18.46	10	119%	7.75	10.00	11.93	5	154%
	Hierarchical	41.92	13.00	23.85	40	57%	38.43	65.00	21.87	40	57%	33.57	7.00	15.74	30	47%	46.50	10.00	17.80	47.5	38%
Judge–Staff Relations	Communal	26.92	13.00	17.50	20	65%	19.18	67.00	12.66	20	66%	17.86	7.00	17.29	20	97%	20.50	10.00	15.17	25	74%
	Networked	39.62	13.00	17.50	40	44%	36.72	67.00	15.80	30	43%	45.00	7.00	29.86	30	66%	38.50	10.00	11.56	35	30%
	Autonomous	13.46	13.00	11.07	10	82%	20.30	67.00	16.90	10	83%	7.86	7.00	6.99	10	89%	16.00	10.00	14.10	15	88%
	Hierarchical	20.00	13.00	15.55	20	78%	23.81	67.00	15.96	20	67%	29.29	7.00	20.09	40	69%	25.00	10.00	23.92	20	96%
Change Management	Communal	20.38	13.00	13.46	20	66%	18.74	65.00	12.66	20	68%	21.43	7.00	16.51	25	77%	25.00	10.00	12.47	25	50%
	Networked	30.38	13.00	15.61	30	51%	35.35	65.00	15.04	35	43%	38.57	7.00	28.68	30	74%	37.00	10.00	9.78	40	26%
	Autonomous	11.92	13.00	13.47	10	113%	12.38	65.00	11.49	10	93%	7.14	7.00	9.06	5	127%	6.00	10.00	8.10	2.5	135%
	Hierarchical	37.31	13.00	20.48	30	55%	33.52	65.00	15.48	30	46%	32.86	7.00	15.24	30	46%	32.00	10.00	13.78	32.5	43%
Courthouse Leadership	Communal	50.00	13.00	18.93	45	38%	36.19	67.00	15.18	40	42%	55.71	7.00	19.67	50	35%	38.50	10.00	12.70	37.5	33%
	Networked	25.23	13.00	13.60	30	54%	38.58	67.00	18.00	40	47%	30.00	7.00	11.90	30	40%	42.50	10.00	12.96	40	31%
	Autonomous	8.46	13.00	10.28	5	122%	10.60	67.00	10.57	10	100%	6.43	7.00	11.07	0	172%	4.00	10.00	4.59	2.5	115%
	Hierarchical	16.31	13.00	14.68	10	90%	14.63	67.00	10.71	10	73%	7.86	7.00	7.56	5	96%	15.00	10.00	13.33	10	89%
Internal Organization	Communal	31.15	13.00	16.35	40	52%	23.86	66.00	13.24	20	55%	30.00	7.00	18.93	20	63%	27.00	10.00	16.36	30	61%
	Networked	35.00	13.00	14.86	35	42%	48.11	66.00	18.81	42.5	39%	40.00	7.00	7.64	40	19%	44.00	10.00	16.96	42.5	39%
	Autonomous	18.08	13.00	20.57	10	114%	12.27	66.00	11.54	10	94%	10.71	7.00	13.36	5	125%	11.50	10.00	12.26	10	107%
	Hierarchical	15.77	13.00	9.76	15	62%	15.76	66.00	10.05	15	64%	19.29	7.00	17.42	15	90%	17.50	10.00	14.19	10	81%

Minnesota—Future Culture (table title)

(continued)

APPENDIX 6: ASSESSING VARIATION IN CCAI RESPONSES (Continued)

		Minnesota—Future Culture														
		Ramsey					Duluth					Virginia				
Content Dimension	Culture Type	Mean	N	sd	Md	CV	Mean	N	sd	Md	CV	Mean	N	sd	Md	CV
Dominant Case Management Style	Communal	20.00	10.00	21.08	12.5	105%	19.50	10.00	20.74	17.5	106%	20.00	8.00	18.52	15	93%
	Networked	29.00	10.00	22.09	25	76%	23.00	10.00	18.29	25	80%	25.63	8.00	16.78	25	65%
	Autonomous	11.50	10.00	12.48	10	109%	9.50	10.00	9.85	7.5	104%	15.63	8.00	13.48	10	86%
	Hierarchical	39.50	10.00	18.48	35	47%	48.00	10.00	32.68	37.5	68%	38.75	8.00	30.91	35	80%
Judge–Staff Relations	Communal	12.50	10.00	12.30	7.5	98%	21.00	10.00	21.71	15	103%	18.75	8.00	20.13	15	107%
	Networked	39.00	10.00	25.69	32.5	66%	39.50	10.00	28.52	35	72%	31.88	8.00	30.23	27.5	95%
	Autonomous	27.50	10.00	22.64	17.5	82%	21.00	10.00	31.25	7.5	149%	8.75	8.00	11.26	5	129%
	Hierarchical	21.00	10.00	16.96	20	81%	18.50	10.00	12.70	20	69%	40.63	8.00	29.81	40	73%
Change Management	Communal	17.00	10.00	14.57	15	86%	13.00	10.00	10.59	15	81%	27.86	7.00	21.96	20	79%
	Networked	40.00	10.00	20.68	37.5	52%	53.50	10.00	21.35	50	40%	30.00	7.00	14.43	30	48%
	Autonomous	7.50	10.00	9.20	5	123%	6.00	10.00	7.75	5	129%	11.43	7.00	13.14	5	115%
	Hierarchical	35.50	10.00	25.22	27.5	71%	27.50	10.00	16.20	27.5	59%	30.71	7.00	18.58	25	60%
Courthouse Leadership	Communal	31.50	10.00	13.13	30	42%	41.50	10.00	24.73	37.5	60%	43.57	7.00	23.93	30	55%
	Networked	42.00	10.00	16.19	40	39%	37.00	10.00	21.24	42.5	57%	27.86	7.00	12.20	25	44%
	Autonomous	8.50	10.00	9.73	5	115%	4.00	10.00	9.37	0	234%	10.71	7.00	13.67	5	128%
	Hierarchical	18.00	10.00	19.03	10	106%	17.50	10.00	25.08	7.5	143%	17.86	7.00	17.29	20	97%
Internal Organization	Communal	23.50	10.00	13.34	25	57%	25.50	10.00	14.62	30	57%	26.25	8.00	17.88	22.5	68%
	Networked	35.50	10.00	22.79	25	64%	51.00	10.00	19.83	47.5	39%	34.38	8.00	12.37	40	36%
	Autonomous	12.00	10.00	9.49	10	79%	5.50	10.00	6.43	5	117%	10.63	8.00	9.80	7.5	92%
	Hierarchical	29.00	10.00	19.69	27.5	68%	18.00	10.00	14.18	20	79%	28.75	8.00	20.13	27.5	70%

Notes

Chapter 1

1. This conventional wisdom, with its emphasis on structure and process over results and outcomes, is exemplified by the American Bar Association's *Standards Relating to Court Organization* (revised in 1990) and *Standards Relating to Trial Courts* (revised in 1992).

2. For example, Ostrom and Hanson (1999, p. 84) describe a generic set of prescribed steps to reduce case processing delay: The field of court management has developed the ingredients for success in reducing court delay. The prescribed way to achieve timeliness consists of a series of specific actions that the court needs to take the lead in implementing. They include establishing time goals, promoting formal and informal communications among judges and attorneys, and creating opportunities for attorneys to provide input and advice on procedural changes. Despite the intuitive appeal of these steps, many delay reduction efforts are unsuccessful. In addition, the transfer of procedures found to work in one court to another court is often hindered because of differences in underlying cultural values and norms.

3. For example, Mohr (1976, p. 840) observes: "As an organization theorist I feel that although the fit between courts and organizations is not an altogether comfortable one, there are some themes in organization theory that may be helpful in the study of the courts." Although Mohr's focus is different than ours and in spite of the fact that he thinks the contribution of organization theory will be small, his article is the primary acknowledgement in the court field that trial courts—as institutions—are public organizations.

4. Assigned counsel or contract attorneys handle only conflict cases when a public defender must decline an appointment and private counsel are retained in only a small proportion of cases.

5. The electoral process in Florida affects both the court and the system in which the judiciary is expected to exert a leadership role. Florida's judges emphasize their independence from each other and from the court's presiding judge and presiding judges of the court's divisions in deciding how to handle their cases purposefully and deliberatively. Moreover, the primacy of elections in Florida accentuates the respective missions of prosecutors and defense attorneys in protecting society versus protecting constitutional rights of defendants. They truly see themselves representing different institutions because of their elected constitutional officer status. As a result, Florida's judges confront the particularly challenging role of identifying and promoting mutually beneficial ways for the contending attorneys to cooperate in resolving cases timely and fairly.

6. Hybrid calendars combine elements of individual and master calendar systems.

7. One of this study's assumptions is that the similarities in courts' caseload compositions are more striking than their differences. Workload responsibilities might vary because some courts have a higher percentage of very serious, high stakes contested cases (e.g., homicide cases that go to trial) than other courts. However, it is not likely that any trial court is confronted with a caseload where the percentage of homicide cases exceed the percentage of the less serious, more routine burglary or illegal drug possession cases. It is possible, and even probable, that some trial courts have dockets where the percentage of crimes against the person are greater than burglary or drug possession violations. Such situations, which run counter to the sense of what cases look like, might occur because of vigorous law enforcement and prosecutorial action to deter, apprehend, and convict sexual or child abuse offenders.

8. For example, Church et al. found among criminal courts the median number of days from the date of arraignment to resolution ranged from 33 days in Wayne County, Michigan to 328 days in Bronx County, New York (1978). Ostrom and Hanson found the median number of days from date of arrest to resolution ranged from 81 days in Cincinnati, Ohio to 336 days in Hackensack, New Jersey (1999).

Chapter 2

1. The importance and difficulty of management in public sector organizations is reinforced by Rainey's observations (2003):

> Although virtually everyone accepts the premise that all executives and managers face very similar tasks and challenges, a strong and growing body of evidence suggests that public managers operate within contexts that require rather distinctive skills and knowledge.

An important question is whether the distinctive skills and knowledge from the private sector studies of organizations can be transferred to the public domain.

2. This list was culled from a comprehensive list of thirty-nine indicators of possible measures of organizational effectiveness identified in the literature previously by Campbell and his colleagues (1974).

3. Quinn and Rohrbaugh (1983, p. 368) invited 76 organizational theorists to participate; 48 agreed to participate, and 40 actually completed the 136-paired comparisons. An illustration of paired comparison in the current study is presented in Appendix 2-1.

4. The technique used by Quinn and Rohrbaugh was multidimensional scaling, which is discussed by Carroll and Chang (1970).

5. Goffee and Jones (1998, p. 22) argue: "Despite their lack of frequent mention in the popular business press, sociability and solidarity actually have a long, well-established, and respected pedigree; indeed, they are constants of the sociological tradition as it emerged from the philosophical legacy of the French Revolution with its ardent calls for Liberty, Equality, and Fraternity. What creates the last of these three—fraternity, or more colloquially, community—has been a central focus of sociology ever since. Consequently, using these two dimensions is a return to the historical roots of the discipline of sociology."

6. The individuals were chosen purposively to include a range of judges, administrators, attorneys, and scholars who were thoughtful and experienced. The sample is geographically diverse. The important factor for the research—just as it was for Quinn and Rohrbaugh (1983)—is that the evaluators are knowledgeable and thoughtful.

7. The individuals included twenty-six judges, one prosecutor, one criminal defense attorney, twenty-three court administrators, and two court scholars.

8. Quinn moved from the initial seventeen values to twenty-four in his subsequent analyses. The development of the implicit value matrix required altering some of the original concepts to better fit the organizational typology.

Chapter 3

1. The format of OCAI has been used numerous times, and its validity and reliability have been established (Quinn and Spreitzer 1991; Kalliath 1999).

2. To prevent respondents from being affected by the connotation of the names given to the four cultures, the cultural orientations are represented in a neutral fashion by Roman Numerals: I stands for Communal, II for Networked, III for Autonomous, and IV for Hierarchical.

3. Cameron and Quinn (1999) indicate the type of scale used in the current research's questionnaire is an ipsative rating scale. Compared to the frequently-used alternative Likert scale, the ipsative scale provides an ideal way to differentiate between courts of different culture types. A disadvantage is that it does not produce independent responses—the response to alternative A in question 1 is related to the response to alternative B and so on.

Consequently, normal correlational analyses are not usually appropriate. There are several sources that provide alternative statistical techniques for use with this kind of data (Cameron and Freeman 1991; Zammuto and Krakower 1991). In the policy field, McIver and Ostrom (1976) use a similar type of ipsative scale in their analysis of police services. They provide appropriate ways of using correlation between ipsative scale ratings and an independent variable. The decision to use the ipsative ratings from the CCAI does not pose a problem for the current research. Highlighting cultural differences between courts is a chief interest. Additionally, because of resource constraints, courts must make trade-offs about which performance measures are most important. The CCAI accommodates this reality.

4. The response rate varied across the sites. In all, we had 210 respondents including 133 judges and 77 senior court administrators specializing in criminal dockets. Due to the small number of responses by administrators in some of the courts, the responses for judges and senior administrators were combined.

5. Cameron and Quinn (1999, pp. 31–32) note that the diagonally opposite culture types represent competing values. "The competing or opposite values in each quadrant give rise to the name ... Competing Values Framework."

6. It is important to realize the gains in insight and understanding from creating the pictures comes at the cost of not having any mechanical way (e.g., statistical significance) of interpreting them.

7. To calculate the emphasis on *solidarity*, add the scores for *networked* and *hierarchical*—in this case 61 of the 100 points are in the culture types emphasizing *solidarity*. To calculate the emphasis on *sociability*, add the scores for *networked* and *communal*—in this case only 46 of the 100 points are in culture types emphasizing *sociability*.

8. In this regard, Cameron and Quinn (1999, p. 71) observe: "Paradoxes often exist in cultural profiles. It is not unusual to see cigar shaped profiles, for example. It need not be the case that an organization must be dominated by one side of the Organization Profile form or the other, or that it emphasizes the top or the bottom of the profile. ... This may be a sign of strength as much as a sign of weakness... We concluded that effective organizations are able to behave in flexible and sometimes contradictory ways."

9. Geometrical shapes are used in a metaphoric manner. Strictly speaking, the four-sided shapes in the kite diagrams are quadrilaterals. The square, rectangle, rhombus, trapezoid, kite, and parallelogram are quadrilaterals. In geometry, a kite is a four-sided figure in which the two pairs of adjacent sides have the same length; a parallelogram is a four-sided figure whose opposite sides are parallel; a square has four, equally long sides which are at right angles to each other; and a trapezoid is a four-sided figure with two parallel sides.

10. Correlations can range in numerical value from + 1.0 to –1.0. The closer responses are to one another, the higher the positive correlation. Negative correlations indicate responses from one court are opposite that of another

court. For example, the negative correlation between Contra Costa and Kandiyohi (–0.31) reflect Kandiyohi's greater emphasis on *communal* and *networked* cultures and Contra Costa's greater emphasis on *autonomous* and *hierarchical* cultures.

11. To turn the similarity scores represented by the product moment correlations into a measure of dissimilarity, the following transformation suggested by Trosset (2000) is employed:

$$\sqrt{2^*(1 - r_{kr})}$$

To analyze the paired comparison data, the SPSS ALSCAL multidimensional scaling algorithm is used. A two-dimensional solution was computed and found to be quite good: The squared correlation coefficient between the scaled distances and the input dissimilarities is 0.91, and the Kruskal Stress_1 measure is 0.13.

12. The lack of a preponderance of *autonomous* court cultures counters both conventional wisdom and scholarly literature by Lipsky and others that courts are essentially *autonomous* institutions because of the need for discretion to allow judges to make decisions on an individual case basis. Lipsky and others consider courts to be an example of what he calls a "street-level bureaucracy" along with jails, schools, public hospitals, and so forth. See Lipsky (1976); Weatherly and Lipsky (1977); and Prottas (1978).

Chapter 4

1. The interviewers took careful notes; general observations along with quotes were transcribed and fit into an overall matrix that highlights the range of responses in each court. The interview notes were not verbatim; hence, there is no transcript.

2. As an example, one *networked* court in our sample uses a motor home to conduct court proceedings directly in the communities. This vehicle also provides a way to reach out to homeless populations.

3. Vertical representation refers to the practice of an attorney maintaining responsibility for the case through all proceedings from filing through resolution.

Chapter 5

1. Timeliness has been a centerpiece of the court management and performance literature. Judges are seen as having primary responsibility for determining how long cases take to be resolved, but attorneys are seen as important collaborators. A leading management expert, along with several colleagues, notes the "... centrality of the local culture to the pace of trial court litigation" (Mahoney et al. 1988, p. 200). The implication is court culture will have a significant impact on delay reduction. See, for example, Zeisel

et al. (1959); Church et al. (1978); Friesen et al. (1978); Neubauer et al. (1981); Fleming et al. (1987); Luskin and Luskin (1986, 1987); Hewitt et al. (1990); Goerdt et al. (1991); and Ostrom and Hanson (1999).

2. The combination of timeliness, access and fairness, and managerial effectiveness emerged after completion of the current research as a performance framework developed by Ostrom et al (2005) for use by courts. Called *CourTools*, the framework consists of ten measures of timeliness, access and fairness, and managerial effectiveness for courts to apply themselves on an ongoing basis. See: www.courtools.org.

3. See, for example, Hanson et al. (1984); Chapper et al. (1984); Chapper and Hanson (1983); Boersema et al. (1991); and Ostrom and Hanson (1999).

4. According to the ABA, 90 percent of all felony cases should be resolved within 120 days or fewer after arrest. Whereas no court under study achieves this goal, Hennepin manages to resolve a higher percentage (74%) than any other court.

5. According to the ABA, 100 percent of all felony cases should be resolved within 365 days or fewer after arrest. Ramsey manages to resolve 96 percent of its cases within this time-frame.

6. A median is a half-way-point in a set of cases. Timeliness as measured by the use of a median figure means that 50% of the cases are resolved in fewer than the median number and 50% take more than the median number. In Hennepin, for example, half of the felony cases are resolved in fewer than 64 days and 50% take more than 64 days to resolve. In contrast, in Olmsted, 50% of the cases are resolved in fewer than 96 days and 50% take more than 96 days to resolve.

7. Case weights are estimates of how much work time, in minutes, judges actually spend, on average, in resolving different types of criminal cases. In other words, it presents the sum of minutes of judge time spread over the life of the case. The larger the case weight, the greater the average amount of work time required to move a case from filing to disposition. For more detail, see *Minnesota Judicial Workload Assessment, 2002* (2003).

8. The principle of proportionality states every case should receive individual attention, but the amount of attention should be proportional to the attention the case warrants. More complicated, difficult, and serious cases should receive more attention than routine, relatively uncomplicated and less serious cases. This principle is intended to maintain equality and due process in the treatment of cases, but it is also intended to achieve those values in light of limited resources (Woolf [1996]; Ostrom and Hanson [1999]). The information on case weights shows that Hennepin does not achieve timeliness by a disregard for the seriousness of the offenses. Judicial attention in Hennepin is in proportion to case seriousness. However, Hennepin's *hierarchical* culture contributes to resolving cases within a tighter time-frame than the other courts in the state.

9. Despite the essential validity of attorneys' perspectives on how well courts achieve access, fairness, and managerial effectiveness, questions on how

well courts do generally rather than in particular, specific cases might prompt somewhat overly critical views because isolated negative incidents might be remembered more clearly than the general pattern. However, this possible limitation does not negatively influence the current research because such selective remembrances should not vary by culture.

10. The actual scale score is determined by simply adding the values of the six variables included in the scale. Only those attorneys that answer all of the applicable questions are included in the analysis.

11. Cronbach alpha assesses the reliability of a rating composed from a group of survey items that are thought to measure some underlying factor (e.g., performance measure). An overall scale score is computed by summing the values for each of the items in the scale. Typically, the cut-off value for scale reliability is 0.50.

12. The three scales are standardized separately for prosecutors and defense attorneys so that each has a mean of zero and a standard deviation of 1.00.

13. This criticism goes beyond the critiques of case-flow management. The academic critics assert that judicial administration has shifted from traditional concerns about the individual to managing aggregates. This criticism was initially aimed at corrections, hence the name of "the new penology," and used to describe the shift from punishing individuals to managing aggregates of dangerous groups of prisoners. However, as the scholars developed their ideas, courts became targets of criticism for their alleged focus on managing aggregate caseloads and backlogs rather than doing justice in individual cases. See, for example, Feeley and Simon (1992, 1995, 2002).

Chapter 6

1. The courts' preferred *hierarchical* culture in case management does not doom courts to receiving low grades in achieving access, fairness, or managerial effectiveness. To avert that possibility, however, courts need to improve their communication and actions concerning timeliness, access, fairness, and managerial effectiveness. Needed improvements are described in Chapter 7.

2. All other culture kites are available online at: www.ncsconline.org/courtculture/.

3. Cameron and Quinn (1999, p. 65), when discussing the absence of congruence, suggest that discrepancies (across content dimensions) "may indicate a lack of focus, it may indicate that the culture is unclear to the respondents, or it may indicate that the complexity of the environment requires multiple emphases in different elements of the organization."

Chapter 7

1. The concept of proportionality is discussed in more detail in Ostrom and Hanson, *Efficiency, Timeliness and Quality* (1999).

2. See: www.courtools.org.

Appendices

1. A square asymmetric matrix was chosen (since the upper half of the matrix is missing). The Individual Differences Euclidean Distance was used with an ordinal level of measure with instructions to untie tied observations, with matrix conditionality.

2. In interpreting the square correlation measure, Jacoby (1998) observes: "... the R^2 between the distances and the data values is actually a conservative measure of model fit. Since the input data are assumed to be ordinal-level, the appropriate comparison is between the rank-orders of the data values and the scaled-distances. An alternative measure, Kruskal's $Stress_1$, does measure the degree of monotonic fit.... However this coefficient is a badness of fit statistic (increasing values correspond to worse scaling solutions), so it is difficult to interpret."

3. The examination of the dimension weights, which provide an indication of which of the two dimensions is viewed as most important for each of the respondents, reveal a number of interesting features. First, the preponderance of the judges emphasizes the Solidarity dimension over the Sociability dimension. Second, the vast majority of the court administrators emphasize the Sociability dimension over the Solidarity dimension. This suggests that the emphasis of one dimension over another may be related to one's role in the trial court. Third, the two academics place equal emphasis on each of the dimensions. Finally, the defense attorney places heavy emphasis on the Sociability dimension while the prosecutor emphasizes the Solidarity dimension. The plausibility of the dimension weights provides another indication of the validity of the results.

4. The results of this study compare quite favorably with the results of the original Quinn and Rohrbaugh study. In that study they report an overall correlation of .63 of the distances in their three-dimensional solution and the original similarity judgments. They also note that the weights of all the participants with regard to each dimension were positive, and the individual correlations of the distances with the original similarities was generally quite high (an average of .62).

5. The fit measures for the three dimensional solution are .14 and .86. The first two dimensions of the three dimensional solution are almost identical to the two dimensions reported below. The interpretation of the third dimension is somewhat problematic—it is very similar to the first dimension. Interestingly, the third dimension appears to be similar to the third dimension in Quinn and Rohrbaugh's original work—means versus ends. After presenting it in the research article, subsequent treatments of their model utilize the two dimensional version.

6. The WMDS solution was compared to the straightforward MDS solution (i.e., not allowing individual judge weights). The WMDS solution is preferable on both statistical and substantive grounds.

References

Allison, Graham T. 1988. "Public and Private Management." In Richard J. Stillman, *Public Administration: Concepts and Cases*, 4th ed. New York: Houghton Mifflin, 283–298.

American Bar Association. 1987. *Standards Relating to Trial Courts, As Amended.* Chicago: American Bar Association.

———. 1990. *Standards Relating to Court Organization.* Chicago: American Bar Association.

Arnold, Thurman. 1962. *The Symbols of Government.* New York: Harcourt, Brace and World.

Blumberg, Abraham. 1967. "The Practice of Law as a Confidence Game: Organizational Cooptation of the Profession." *Law & Society Review* 1: 15–39.

Boersema, Craig, Roger A. Hanson and Susan Keilitz. 1991. "State Court-annexed Arbitration: What do Attorneys Think?" *Judicature* 75: 28.

Bohlman, Bruce E. and Erick J. Bohlman. 1994. "Wandering in the Wilderness of Dispute Resolution: When Do We Arrive at the Promised Land of Justice." *North Dakota Law Review*, 70: 235.

Boyum, Keith O. 1979. "A Perspective on Civil Delay in Trial Courts." *Justice System Journal* 5: 170–186.

Buckingham, Marcus and Curt Coffman. 1999. *First, Break All The Rules: What The World's Greatest Managers Do Differently.* New York: Simon and Schuster.

Butler, Byron W. 1977. "Presiding Judges' Role Perceptions of Trial Court Administrators." *Justice System Journal* 3: 181.

Caldeira, Greg A. 1977. "The Incentives of Trial Judges and the Administration of Justice." *Justice System Journal* 3: 163.

Cameron, Kim S. and Robert E. Quinn. 1999. *Diagnosing and Changing Organizational Culture: Based Upon the Competing Values Framework*. Reading, MA: Addison-Wesley.

Cameron, Kim S. and Sarah J. Freeman. 1991. "Cultural Congruence, Strength, and Type: Relationships to Effectiveness." *Research in Organizational Change and Development* 5: 23–58.

Carroll, J. D. and J.-J. Chang. 1970. "Analysis of Individual Differences in Multidimensional scaling via an N-way generalization of 'Eckart-Young' Decomposition." *Psychometrika* 35: 283–319.

Chapper, Joy A. and Roger A. Hanson. 1983. "The Attorney Time Savings/Litigant Cost Savings Hypothesis: Does Time Equal Money?" *Justice System Journal* 8: 258.

———. 1990. *Intermediate Appellate Courts: Improving Case Processing.* Williamsburg, Va.: National Center for State Courts.

Chapper, Joy A., Kathy L. Shuart, Lynae K. E. Olson, Michael D. Planet, Paul R. J. Connolly and Saundra L. S. Smith. 1984. *Attacking Litigation Costs and Delay*. Chicago: American Bar Association.

Church, Thomas W., Jr. 1982. "The 'Old' and the 'New' Conventional Wisdom." *Justice System Journal* 8: 712.

Church, Thomas W., Jr., Alan Carlson, Jo-Lynne Q. Lee and Teresa Tan. 1978. *Justice Delayed: The Pace of Litigation in Urban Trial Courts*. Williamsburg, Va.: National Center for State Courts.

Church, Thomas W., Jr., Jo-Lynne Q. Lee, Teresa Tan, Alan Carlson and Virginia McConnell. 1978. *Pretrial Delay: A Review and Bibliography.* Williamsburg, Va.: National Center for State Courts.

Commission on Trial Court Performance Standards. 1990. *Trial Court Performance Standards, With Commentary*. Williamsburg, Va.: National Center for State Courts.

Conference of State Court Administrators. 1983. *National Time Standards for Case Processing.* Adopted by resolution July 27, 1983.

Deal, Terrence E. and Allan A. Kennedy. 1982. *Corporate Cultures: The Rites and Rituals of Corporate Life.* Reading, Mass: Addison-Wesley.

Diamond, Jared. 1997. *Germs, Guns, and Steel: The Fates of Human Societies.* New York: W.W. Norton & Co.

DiIulio, John J. Jr. 1989. "Recovering the public management variable: Lessons from schools, prisons, and armies." *Public Administration Review* 49 (2): 127–133.

———. 1993. "Measuring Performance When There Is No Bottom Line. In *Performance Measures for the Criminal Justice System.* U.S. Department of Justice, Bureau of Justice Statistics, 143–156.

———. 1994. "Principled Agents." *Journal of Public Administration Research and Theory* 4: 277–320.

Dubois, Philip L., ed. 1982. *The Analysis of Judicial Reform.* Lexington, Mass: D.C. Heath and Company.

Eisenstein, James and Herbert Jacob. 1977. *Felony Justice: An Organizational Analysis of Criminal Courts*. Boston: Little Brown.

Eisenstein, James, Roy Fleming and Peter Nardulli. 1987. *The Contours of Justice: Communities and Their Courts.* Boston: Little and Brown.

Feeley, Malcolm. 1983. *Court Reform on Trial: Why Simple Solutions Fail.* New York: Basic Books.

———. 1979. *The Process Is the Punishment: Handling Cases in a Lower Criminal Court.* New York: Russell Sage Foundation.

Feeley, Malcolm and Jonathan Simon. 1992. "The New Penology: Notes on the Emerging Strategy of Corrections and its Implications." *Criminology* 30: 449–474.

———. 1995. "True Crime: The New Penology and Public Discourse on Crime." In Thomas G. Blomberg and Stanley Cohen, eds. *Punishment And Social Control: Essays In Honor Of Sheldon Messinger*. New York: Aldine-de-Gruyter.

———. 2002. "The Forms and Limits of the New Penology." In Tom Baker and Jonathan Simon, eds. *Embracing Risk: The Changing Culture Of Insurance And Responsibility*. Chicago: University of Chicago Press, 177–208.

Fleming, Roy, Peter Nardulli and James Eisenstein. 1987. "The Timing of Justice in Felony Trial Courts." *Law and Policy* 9: 179.

———. 1992. *The Craft of Justice.* Philadelphia, PA: University of Pennsylvania Press.

Friesen, Ernest C., Edward C. Gallas and Nesta M. Gallas. 1971. *Managing the Courts*. Indianapolis: Bobbs-Merrill.

Friesen, Ernest C., Jr., Joseph Jordan and Alfred Sulmonetti. 1978. *Arrest to Trial in Forty-Five Days.* Los Angeles, CA: Whittier College School of Law.

Gallas, Geoff. 1976. "The Conventional Wisdom of State Court Administration: A Critical Assessment and an Alternative Approach." *Justice System Journal*, 2: 35.

———. 1987. "Judicial Leadership Excellence: A Research Prospectus." *Justice System Journal*, 12: 39.

Goerdt, John, Christopher Lomvardias, Geoff Gallas and Barry Mahoney. 1991. *Reexamining the Pace of Litigation in 39 Large Urban Courts.* Williamsburg, Va.: National Center for State Courts.

Goffee, Rob and Gareth Jones. 1998. *The Character of a Corporation.* New York: Harper Business.

Hanson, Roger A., Lynae K. E. Olson, Kathy L. Shuart and Marlene Thornton. 1984. "Telephone Conferencing in Criminal Court Cases." *University of Miami Law Review*, 38: 611.

Hanson, Roger, Brian Ostrom and Ann Jones. 2002. "Effective Adversaries for the Poor." In Malcolm Feeley and Setsuo Miyazawa, eds. *The Japanese Adversary System in Context.* New York: Palgrave MacMillan.

Hanson, Roger, Brian Ostrom, William Hewitt and Christopher Lomvardias. 1992. *Indigent Defenders: Get the Job Done and Done Well.* Williamsburg, Va.: National Center for State Courts.

Henderson, Thomas A. and Cornelius M. Kerwin. 1982. "The Changing Character of Court Organization." *Justice System Journal* 7/3: 449–469.

Heumann, Milton. 1975. *Plea Bargaining: The Experiences of Prosecutors, Judges, and Defense Attorneys.* Chicago: University of Chicago Press.

Hewitt, William, Geoff Gallas and Barry Mahoney. 1990. *Courts That Succeed.* Williamsburg, Va.: National Center for State Courts.

Jacoby, William G. 1998. "Presidential Campaign Effects on Citizens' Candidate Preferences." Paper prepared for delivery at the 1998 Annual Meeting of the American Political Science Association, Boston, MA, September 3–6.

Kalliath, Thomas J. 1999. "A Confirmatory Factor Analysis of the Competing Values Instrument." *Educational and Psychological Measurement.* 59 (February): 143–158.

Kotter, John P. and James L. Heskett. 1992. *Corporate Culture and Performance.* New York: Free Press.

Lipsky, Michael. 1976. *Street Level Bureaucracy.* New York: Russell Sage Foundation.

Luskin, Mary Lee and Robert C. Luskin. 1986. "Why So Fast, Why So Slow: Explaining Case Processing Time." *The Journal of Criminal Law and Criminology* 72: 190.

———. 1987. "Case Processing Time in Three Courts." *Law and Policy* 9: 207.

Lynn, Laurence, Jr. 2003. "Public Management." In *Handbook of Public Administration.* London: Sage Publications.

Mahoney, Barry, Alexander Aikman, Pamela Casey, Victor Flango, Geoff Gallas, Thomas Henderson, Jeanne Ito, David Steelman and Steven Weller. 1988. *Changing Times in Urban Trial Courts.* Williamsburg, Va.: National Center for State Courts.

McIver, John P. and Elinor Ostrom. 1976. "Using Budget Pies to Reveal Preferences: Validation of a Survey Instrument." In Terry Nichols Clark, ed. Citizen Preferences and Urban Public Policy. *Policy and Politics*, Vol. 4, No. 4 (June/Special Issue): 87–110.

Mohr, Lawrence B. 1976. "Organizations, Decisions, and Courts." *Law and Society Review.* 10 (Summer): 621–642.

Nardulli, Peter F., James Eisenstein and Roy B. Fleming. 1988. *The Tenor of Justice: Criminal Courts and the Guilty Plea Process.* Urbana, Ill.: University of Illinois Press.

Neubauer, David, Marcia Lipetz, Mary Lee Luskin and John P. Ryan. 1981. *Managing the Pace of Justice: An Evaluation of LEAA's Court Delay Reduction Programs.* Washington: Government Printing Office.

Nimmer, Raymond. 1976. "A Slightly Moveable Object: A Case Study in Judicial Reform in the Criminal Justice Process: The Omnibus Hearing." *Denver Law Journal.* 48: 206

———. 1978. *The Nature of System Change: Reform Impact in Criminal Courts*. Chicago, Ill.: American Bar Foundation.

Ostrom, Brian J. and Roger A. Hanson. 1999. *Efficiency, Timeliness, and Quality.* Williamsburg, Va.: National Center for State Courts.

Ostrom, Brian J., Charles W. Ostrom, Jr., William E. Hewitt, Neal B. Kauder, Robert C. LaFountain and Matthew Kleiman. 2002. *Minnesota Judicial Workload Assessment, 2002.* Williamsburg, Va.: National Center for State Courts.

Ostrom, Brian J., Daniel J. Hall, Richard Y. Schauffler, and Neal Kauder. 2005. *CourTools*. Williamsburg, Va.: National Center for State Courts.

Ouchi, W. 1981. *Theory Z: How American Business Can Meet The Japanese Challenge.* Reading, Mass.: Addison-Wesley.

Ouchi, W. and A. L. Wilkins. 1985. "Organizational Culture." *Annual Review of Sociology* 11: 457.

Pascale, Richard and Anthony Athos. 1981. *The Art of Japanese Management*. New York: Simon and Schuster.

Peters, T. J. and R. H. Waterman 1982. *In Search of Excellence.* New York: Harper Collins.

Pound, Roscoe. 1979. 1906 lecture. "The Cause of Popular Dissatisfaction with the Administration of Justice." Lecture. In A. Leo Levin and Russel R. Wheeler, eds. *The Pound Conference: Perspectives on Justice in the Future*, St. Paul, Minn.: West Publishing.

Prottas, Jeffrey M. 1978. "The Power of the Street Level Bureaucrat in Public Service Bureaucracies." *Urban Affairs Quarterly*, 13: 285.

Quinn, Robert E. 1988. *Beyond Rational Management*. San Francisco, CA: Jossey-Bass.

Quinn, Robert E. and John Rohrbaugh. 1983. "A Spatial Model of Effectiveness Criteria: Towards a Competing Values Approach to Organizational Analysis." *Management Science* 29 (March): 363–377.

Quinn, Robert E. and Gretchen M. Spreitzer. 1991. "The Psychometrics of the Competing Values Culture Instrument and an Analysis of the Impact of Organizational Culture on Quality of Life." In Richard W. Woodman and William A. Passmore eds. *Research in Organizational Change and Development, Volume* 5, pp. 115–142. Greenwich, CT: JAI Press.

Rainey, Hal G. 2003. *Understanding and Managing Public Organizations*, 3rd ed. San Francisco: Jossey-Bass.

Resnick, Judith. 1982. "Managerial Judges." *Harvard Law Review*, 96: 374.

Saari, David A. 1982. *American Court Management: Theories and Practice*, Westport, CT: Quorum Books.

Schein, Edgar. 1999. *The Corporate Culture Survival Guide.* San Francisco, CA: Jossey-Bass.

———. 2004. *Organizational Culture and Leadership*, 3rd ed. San Francisco: Jossey-Bass.

Stott, Keith. 1982 "The Judicial Executive: Toward Greater Congruence in an Emerging Profession." *Justice System Journal* 7: 152.

Tobin, Robert W. 1997. *An Overview of Court Administration in the United States*. Williamsburg, Va.: National Center for State Courts.

———. 1999. *Creating the Judicial Branch: The Unfinished Reform*. Williamsburg, Va.: National Center for State Courts.

Trial Court Performance Standards Commission. 1990. *Trial Court Performance Standards, With Commentary*. Williamsburg, Va.: National Center for State Courts.

Trial Court Performance Standards. 1997. *Trial Court Performance Standards Measurement System Implementation Manual*. Bureau of Justice Assistance. U.S. Department of Justice.

Trosset, Michael W. 2002. "Extensions of Classic Multidimensional Scaling Via Variable Reduction." *Computational Statistics*, 17: 147.

Tufte, Edward R. 1983. *The Visual Display of Quantitative Information*. Cheshire: Graphics Press.

Tukey, John. 1977. *Exploratory Data Analysis*. New York: Wiley.

Tyler, Thomas. 1998. "What is Procedural Justice?: Criteria Used by Citizens to Assess the Fairness of Legal Procedures." *Law and Society Review* 75: 103.

Warren, Roger. 1998. "Reengineering the Court Process." Speech made at the Great Lakes Court Summit, Sept. 24–25 1998, Madison, WI.

Weatherly, Richard and Michael Lipsky. 1977. "Street Level Bureaucrats and Institutional Innovations." *Harvard Education Review*, 47: 171.

Whitaker, Gordon P. and Charles D. Phillips, eds. 1983. *Evaluating Performance of Criminal Justice Agencies*. Beverly Hills: Sage Publications.

Whitaker, Gordon P., Stephen Mastrofski, Elinor Ostrom, Roger B. Parks and Stephen L. Percy. 1989. "Performance Measurement." In William G. Bailey, ed. *The Encyclopedia of Police Science. New York and London: Garland Publishing, Inc.*, 384–390.

Wilson, James Q. 1989. *Bureaucracy*. New York: Basic Books.

Woolf, Henry. 1996. The Right Honourable Lord. "Access to Justice." Report to the Lord Chancellor's Office, London, HMSO.

Yeazell, Stephen C. 1994. "The Misunderstood Consequences of Modern Civil Process." *Wisconsin Law Review*, 631.

Young, Forrest W. and Robert M. Hamer. 1987. *Multidimensional Scaling: History, Theory, and Applications*. Hillsdale, N.J.: Lawrence Erlbaum Assoc.

Zammuto, Raymond F. and Jack Y. Krakower. 1991. "Quantitative and Qualitative Studies of Organizational Culture." In Richard W. Woodman and William A. Passmore, eds. *Research in Organizational Change and Development, Volume 5*, pp. 83–114. Greenwich, CT: JAI Press.

Zeisel, Hans, Harry Kalven and Bernard Buchholtz. 1959. *Delay in the Court*. Boston: Little Brown.

Index